101 All-Time

Fantasy Baseball Teams

Featuring Iconic Characters From Cap Anson to Mike Trout

Jack Sweeney

simply francis publishing company
North Carolina

For information about this title or to order other books and/or electronic media, contact the publisher:

simply francis publishing company

P.O. Box 329

Wrightsville Beach, NC 28480
Website: www.simplyfrancispublishing.com

Email: simplyfrancispublishing@gmail.com

Library of Congress Control Number: 2016935264
Printed in the United States of America
Cover Design: Marie Sweeney
Interior design: Christy King Meares

Publisher's Cataloging-in-Publication

 Sweeney, Jack, 1945- author.
 101 all-time fantasy baseball teams : featuring iconic characters from Cap Anson to Mike Trout / Jack Sweeney.
 pages cm
 Includes bibliographical references and index.
 ISBN-13: 9781630620028
 ISBN-10: 1630620025
 1. Fantasy baseball (Game) I. Title. II. Title: One hundred one all-time fantasy baseball teams. III. Title: One hundred and one all-time fantasy baseball teams.
 GV1202.F33S94 2016   793.93
                  QBI16-600032

Dedication

To my son Michael, with whom I've spent countless hours playing and discussing baseball, my father Gerald, who taught me the game, my daughter Suzanne, who attended my games when she had better things to do, my granddaughter Toni, my traveling partner on our cross-country trips to various ballparks, and to my wife Marie, who provided inspiration, moral support, and was my muse throughout the 13 years I spent writing this book.

Acknowledgements

Many people have helped me to write this book. They have helped by proofreading the text, offering insight and argument with respect to my opinions, and mostly for constructive criticism in general. They are: Marie Sweeney, Toni Wynn, Michael Sweeney, Tim Sweeney, Rich Viglione, Frank Zecha, Richard Weiss, Stryker Warren, Gary Griffis, and Leslie Pearlman.

In particular, I want to thank John Rosenthal for his outstanding editing, Barbara McLaughlin and Christy Meares for their excellent design work, John Horne and the Baseball Hall of Fame Archives Department for providing the photographs, Jerry Cohen and Burns & Levinson for providing legal counsel, and Frank Amoroso and simply francis publishing company for helping to tie it all together.

Table of Contents

First Inning

An Introduction

It was September of 1967, the American League was experiencing the wildest pennant race in its history, and I had just started my first job. I was attending my first department meeting but within 10 minutes I was bored to tears. As I doodled in my notebook, my mind began to wander like it did in high school biology class. I got through that meeting and hundreds of subsequent meetings over the next 45 years by dreaming up my favorite all-time baseball teams in every category imaginable. I created my all-time A-Z teams, my favorite all-left handed teams, ethnic teams, food teams, and dozens of others.

As a kid growing up in New York, I was an avid New York Giants fan. But I followed all the teams in both leagues with a similar passion. I still remember hundreds of pages of baseball lore and box scores that I have read over the years.

All those teams bouncing around in the dark recesses of my mind needed a place to go, as my brain was getting too crowded. Hence this whimsical tour of my 101 all-time teams by various categories, for example; animal names, food names, actual teams, ethnic groups and more. All players represented in this book played in the major leagues at the position in which I have placed them. In some cases like the "B" team, I have Wade Boggs, normally a third baseman, playing first base because a) he can, and b) a gentleman named George Brett is playing third base. Each chapter concludes with a short piece that is related to that team.

1

Most of the players on these teams come from my memory of players and their teams; however I have relied heavily on *The Baseball Encyclopedia* published by Macmillan Publishing Co. I could not have created a crazy nickname team without it. When I first started writing this book in 2002, I discovered that there was already a similar book out there: "The All-Time Baseball Teams Book" by Frank Coffey, St. Martin's Press, 1984. At that time, I had already created 75 teams, and learning that somebody had beaten me into print discouraged me from going further. But upon further reflection, I decided that while indeed there are similarities between the two books, my work is in no way connected with that one.

The guidelines I've tried to follow are: 1) each team consists of the eight position players, a designated hitter, four starting pitchers and one relief pitcher; 2) I use last names in all sections except People, Places, and Things, where I use first or last names. In one case, for my body parts team, I could not find a catcher with either a first or last name to qualify, so I had to come up with a body part nickname: "Schnozz" Lombardi. Nor could I find a shortstop that met my requirements, so I had to pick Larry Kopf. Kopf is German for head; 3) I tried to field the best, or maybe simply my favorite ballplayer, at each position for each team. However, in the People, Places and Things section my priority was to make the reader smile rather than pick the best players, so for instance I have Wildfire Schulte in my crazy first name team outfield instead of Chili Davis, a much better player; 4) I limited my selections to major league players, thus omitting stars that played in the Negro Leagues.

I'm sure many of my readers will disagree with some of my choices. That's exactly the point. This book is meant to start conversations, not end them. Arguing about whether the '27 Yankees could beat the Big Red Machine, or about who's better: Willie, Mickey, or the Duke, is what keeps baseball fans involved in this great game all year round. So plop yourself down in your favorite chair, pour yourself a beer, and enjoy.

Second Inning

People, Places and Things

Animals

1B	Rob Deer	P	Robin Roberts
2B	Nellie Fox	P	Bob Moose
3B	Robin Ventura	P	Joey Jay
SS	Robin Yount	P	Dizzy Trout
OF	Kevin Bass	RP	Ray Lamb
OF	Mike Trout		
OF	Tim Salmon		
C	Johnny Peacock		
DH	Johnny Grubb		

Nellie Fox

"Nellie Fox was my idol."
Joe Morgan

The image of Nellie Fox that sticks in my mind is of him standing around second base with a wad of chewing tobacco that was almost as big as a baseball. Other players I recall that were his equal in tobacco chewing were Harvey Kuenn and Bill Tuttle. And Rocky Bridges may have surpassed them all. The utility infielder played for seven teams in his 11-year career, but the one constant on his baseball card was a giant plug of tobacco bulging out of his right cheek.

When I think of perfection at second base during the 1950s, '60s, and '70s, only Bill Mazeroski measures up to Nellie Fox. Maz also equals Nellie as a tobacco chewer. On his wedding day he exited the church with a wad in his cheek!

At five feet nine inches Fox was the perfect size for a position that demands agility, quickness and a ballerina's sense of balance. Besides having the perfect body for a second baseman, Nellie also had grit. Billy Pierce, his teammate on the Chicago White Sox for 12 years, said that Nellie was the greatest competitor he ever played with. That competitive streak proved to be a valuable asset when he was trying to pivot for the double play with a runner like Mickey Mantle barreling down the line with mayhem on his mind. To my mind no keystone was better at turning the double play than Nellie and his Venezuelan partner at shortstop, Luis Aparicio. Both are in the Hall of Fame due primarily to their defensive prowess.

Born on Christmas Day in 1927 in St. Thomas, Pennsylvania, Nellie started his professional career in the Western League in Nebraska where he played alongside Bobby Shantz, another accomplished diminutive player. Nellie's was truly a fairy tale story. As a youngster all he talked about was playing professional baseball, so in 1944 his parents drove him to a Philadelphia Athletics tryout camp. He was just 16 years old. They were hoping that A's manager Connie Mack would tell him that he was not major league material and that he should stay in school. Their plan backfired, as he was signed to a Minor League contract. He broke into the majors in 1947 with the Philadelphia Athletics, but soon thereafter found a home in Chicago with the White Sox. There he played in almost every game for 13 years before finishing his stellar career with Houston.

In 1959, Fox and his White Sox teammates shocked the baseball world by dethroning the American League champion New York Yankees to win the pennant. The Go-Go Sox were a throwback to the days of Ty Cobb and Eddie Collins, when speed and fundamentals trumped power in winning ballgames. The White Sox lost the World Series to the L.A. Dodgers, but Nellie won an AL MVP Award for his outstanding season. His .306 average, 2 home runs, and 70 RBIs weren't traditional MVP numbers, but his steady defense at second base (he appeared in 156 games) and his leadership made him the clear choice. Aparicio placed second in that year's MVP voting; no other player received a first-place vote.

Nellie's career was indeed memorable. He was first or second in the American League in hits for eight years during the 1950s. He was an All-Star 15 times (12 years)*, and won three Gold Gloves. He was among the best bunters and sacrifice hitters that ever played the game. There's one other statistic that I find to be amazing. He only struck out 216 times in 9,232 at bats, the third best all-time!

Nellie Fox

1. What ballplayer is nicknamed "Kung Fu Panda"?
* From 1959-1962 Major League Baseball played 2 All-Star games per year.

1B	Prince Fielder	P	Herb Score
2B	Neal Ball	P	Chan Ho Park
3B	Clete Boyer	P	Bob Walk
SS	Spike Owen	P	Homer Bailey
OF	Jocko Fields	RP	Bob Locker
OF	Fielder Jones		
OF	Charlie Spikes		
C	Matt Batts		
DH	Cecil Fielder		

Herb Score

"I knew right then that I had seen a man killed by a baseball."
Muddy Ruel after witnessing Ray Chapman being hit by Carl Mays

Baseball is a dangerous game. On August 16, 1920 Ray Chapman, the flashy young shortstop for the Cleveland Indians, was hit in the eye by a Carl Mays spitball. He died 12 hours later. He was 29 years old. His is still the only death directly associated with an on-field injury. As a result, the spitball and scuffed up dirty balls were banned. This is why umpires are obligated to discard balls that get even the slightest mark on them. Batting helmets were recommended after the incident but did not become mandatory until 1971.

Herb Score was born on June 7, 1933 in Rosedale, New York. As a 22-year-old rookie for the Cleveland Indians in 1955 he struck out 245 batters, a rookie record that stood until Dwight Gooden of the New York Mets broke it in 1984. In 1956, Herb was 20-9 and was well on his way to becoming one of the game's elite stars. But the baseball gods would not have it.

On May 7, 1957, Gil McDougal hit Score in the eye with a vicious line drive, breaking numerous bones in his face. McDougal vowed that if Score was blinded by the blast he would immediately retire. The following season, Score regained his 20/20 vision and returned to the mound in late 1958, but he never got his stuff back. The lefty blamed his lackluster performance on a damaged elbow, but many believe it was the hit off McDougal's bat that was the cause. Mickey Mantle said that Score was the toughest pitcher he had ever faced before the injury and Yogi Berra placed him on his all-time team. Would he have been as good as Sandy Koufax or Whitey Ford? One can only speculate.

Herb Score

2. What promising outfielder had his career effectively ended by a Jack Hamilton fastball in 1967?

Body Parts

1B	Harry Cheek	P	Bill Hands
2B	Ollie Beard	P	Mike Beard
3B	Dave Brain	P	Ed Head
SS	Larry Kopf	P	Ricky Bones
OF	Heine Manush	RP	Rollie Fingers
OF	Ted Beard		
OF	George Bone		
C	Schnozz Lombardi		
DH	Barry Foote		

Ernie Lombardi

*"Ernie Lombardi was thrown out at first base
trying to stretch a double into a single."*
Stanley Frank

To win a major league batting title, you need to have multiple assets. It helps to have outstanding hand/eye coordination, rhythm, speed, and luck, among other variables. If you exclude even one of these, the chances of winning a title diminish dramatically. Ernie "Schnozz" Lombardi won the national league batting title in 1938 and 1942, despite being what baseball historian and father of sabermetrics Bill James called "the slowest man to ever play baseball well." A batter usually needs a significant number of leg hits to win. Lombardi never had a leg hit in his career. But he hit line drives so hard he didn't have to run fast. New York Times sportswriter Arthur Daley once said Lombardi's liners were "like a shell leaving a howitzer." He was so slow that an opposing manager quipped that he "ran like he was carrying a piano, and the man that was tuning it." Accordingly, he hit into 261 double plays over his career, and led the league in this category four times, including his batting-title-winning 1938 season.

Lombardi went by many nicknames: Schnozz, Lumbago, Bocci, Cyrano of the iron mask, and Lom. When he came to the plate, three and sometimes all four infielders moved to the outfield. He joked that for three years he thought Pee Wee Reese was an outfielder until he saw him play shortstop. He held the bat with a golf grip, interlocking his hands. Some say this gave him better bat control.

He broke into the majors in 1931 with the Brooklyn Robins but was soon traded to the Cincinnati Reds where he spent most of his career. He was an imposing hulk of a man, standing 6'3" with his weight fluctuating between 230 and 300 pounds. I remember seeing a picture of him holding seven baseballs in his meaty paw. And they talk about Gil Hodges and Johnny Bench having big hands! Ernie's career stats include a .306 batting average, 190 home runs, and 990 RBIs. Besides winning the batting title in 1942 he won the Most Valuable Player Award in 1938, and was elected into the Hall of Fame by the Veterans Committee in 1986.

Ernie Lombardi

3. How many career saves did Rollie Fingers have?

1B	Rudy York	P	Bob Tewksbury
2B	Jeff Kent	P	Reggie Cleveland
3B	Jim Davenport	P	Jose Santiago
SS	John Richmond	P	Rick Austin
OF	Billy Hamilton	P	Max Macon
OF	Fred Lynn		
OF	Daryl Boston		
C	Benito Santiago		
DH	Josh Hamilton		

Fred Lynn

"I'm a Red Sock; I didn't want to leave the Red Sox."
Fred Lynn

Only two players have ever won Rookie of the Year and Most Valuable Player in the same year. One, Ichiro Suzuki, was technically a rookie in 2001 because it was his first year in Major League Baseball. But he was already an established star in Japan long before bringing his talents to the United States. Fred Lynn is the only player in history to legitimately hold that honor. Think about his accomplishment: you come up to the show at the tender age of 22 and win both awards! Mike Trout came within a whisker of duplicating Lynn's feat in 2012, but lost it because Miguel Cabrera decided to be the first player in 45 years to win the Triple Crown.

Fred Lynn was born in Chicago on February 3, 1952. He attended the University of Southern California, and then went straight to the Boston Red Sox in 1974. In Lynn's first full season, 1975, the Red Sox lineup featured another rookie outfielder: Jim Rice. Together, the two were known as the "Gold Dust Twins," and may have been the greatest pair of rookies to ever play in the same outfield.

Rice went to Cooperstown in 2009 and many argue that Lynn belongs there as well. Lynn was elected to the Red Sox Hall of Fame as well as the college baseball Hall of Fame. He probably will not be voted into the Hall, but I think he would have been had he stayed in Boston. He is a borderline Hall-of-Famer as it is, but an entire career at Fenway Park would probably have made him a lock.

Lynn's career batting average at Fenway was a robust .347. His career numbers are: .283 batting average, 306 home runs, 1,111 RBIs, 1,960 hits, 1,063 runs scored and four Gold Gloves in center field. He made the All-Star team nine straight times and in 1983 became the only player to hit a grand slam in the midsummer classic. That home run was one of his favorite personal achievements. Attlee Hammaker, pitching for the National League, intentionally walked Robin Yount to load the bases in order to pitch to Lynn, which made the moment even more thrilling. His four home runs in All-Star competition are second only to Stan Musial.

Fred Lynn

4. Who did Rudy York replace at first base for the Detroit Tigers?

1B	Bill White	P	Three Finger Brown
2B	Frank White	P	Vida Blue
3B	Deacon White	P	Kevin Brown
SS	Larry Brown	P	Doc White
OF	Roy White	RP	Joe Black
OF	Devon White		
OF	Shawn Green		
C	Sammy White		
DH	Ollie Brown		

Vida Blue

*"When I'm throwing good, I don't think
there's a man in the world who can hit me"*
Vida Blue

When Vida Blue made his major league debut in 1970 with the Oakland Athletics, baseball people thought they were seeing the next Sandy Koufax. In his second start he one-hit the Kansas City Royals in a 3-0 shutout. Ten days later he no-hit the Minnesota Twins, missing a perfect game by giving up a walk to Harmon Killebrew. The following year, his first full season, he became the youngest player to win the Most Valuable Player Award at the age of 22. He also won the Cy Young Award. He posted 24 wins, 301 strikeouts, 8 shutouts and a stingy ERA of 1.82. Blue won three straight World Series' with the A's from 1972-74, but he never had another year like that magical 1971 season. What happened?

I don't know. In fact I'm not sure that anything happened that can't be explained by statistical anomaly. After all, Blue played 17 seasons, had a career won-lost record of 209-161, a 3.27 ERA, and 2,175 strikeouts. He was a six-time All-Star and three-time World Series champion. His fastball was clocked at just less than 100 mph, and it was said that he was the hardest throwing lefty of his era. Most pitchers would be thrilled to have this kind of career.

Still, I'm left with the nagging feeling that he could have been better. Two things conspired to diminish his legacy as an all-time great pitcher. The first was that after his phenomenal MVP year he held out for more money. Charley Finley held his ground and Blue missed the first six weeks of the 1972 season (although he did quadruple his salary from $14,750 to $63,000). But the bigger culprit was cocaine. He battled drug addiction for years and in 1983 was found guilty of attempting to buy cocaine. Even so, the San Francisco Giants still thought so highly of him in 1978 that they sent seven players and $300,000 to Oakland to bring Blue across the bay.

One of my pet peeves is to see the media thrust a microphone into a celebrity's face and ask his opinion about the economy, foreign affairs, nuclear proliferation, etc. as if by virtue of their celebrity they were experts in these subjects. Vida Blue shed light on this when he quipped, "It's a weird scene. You win a few baseball games and all of a sudden you're surrounded by reporters and TV men with cameras asking you about Vietnam and race relations." [1] Way to go Vida!

Vida Blue

5. Why do the New York Mets feature blue and orange in their uniforms?

Financials

1B	Norm Cash	P	David Price
2B	Dave Cash	P	Mudcat Grant
3B	Don Money	P	Brad Penny
SS	Ernie Banks	P	Tommy Bond
OF	Barry Bonds	P	Gary Fortune
OF	Walt Bond		
OF	Bobby Bonds		
C	John Buck		
DH	Milt Stock		

Baseball Finances

"Greed is good."
Gordon Gecko

On December 4, 2015, David Price of the Toronto Blue Jays exercised his free agency rights and signed with the Boston Red Sox. His contract calls for him to earn $217,000,000 over 7 years! That's $31,000,000 per year ($2,000,000 per year more than Clayton Kershaw, who was the highest paid pitcher before this deal), making him the highest paid pitcher in major league history. The big 6' 6" lefty won 18 games and lost 5 in 2015, and posted a 2.45 ERA. Price is a 5 time All-Star and won the Cy Young Award in 2012 with a 20-5 record. He is a workhorse who threw 1,300 innings in 2015, 4th most in Major League Baseball. He will be 37 years old when the contract expires. I still can't get my head around these figures without getting a brain cramp.

Ted Williams, arguably the best hitter that ever played the game, became baseball's highest paid player in 1950 when he signed for a $125,000 salary. Adjusting for inflation that comes to about $1,200,000 in today's dollars.

What happened? Television and Marvin Miller happened. Michael J. Haupert of the University of Wisconsin wrote a definitive article on this subject titled "The Economic History of Major League Baseball." He begins the article with a wonderful quote by Jim Bouton: "The reason baseball calls itself a game is because it's too screwed up to be a business." I will throw out some facts and figures gleaned from Mr. Haupert's article and expound at length about the reserve clause and Marvin Miller in a later chapter.

In 1939 the Yankees sold their television rights for $75,000. In 1999 they sold those same rights for $52 million. And in 2014 the Los Angeles Dodgers sold their broadcast rights for $8.3 billion through the 2038 season. That allowed the Dodgers to field a team with a payroll of more than $235 million in 2014. The Houston Astros' payroll of $45 million meanwhile, was barely more than the $30 million the Dodgers paid their ace pitcher, Clayton Kershaw.

I can only wonder what Willie Mays would be worth in today's market.

David Price

6. Who was the first player to earn $1 million in a season?

1B	Klondike Douglas	P	Eppa Rixey
2B	Shooty Babbitt	P	Sloppy Thurston
3B	Offa Neal	P	Wimpy Quinn
SS	She Donahue	P	Crazy Smith
OF	Kiki Cuyler	RP	Mysterious Walker
OF	Wildfire Schulte		
OF	White Wings Tebeau		
C	Yogi Berra		
DH	Yo-Yo Davalillo		

Yogi Berra

" Why has our pitching been so great? Our catcher, that's why. He looks cumbersome, but he's quick as a cat."

Casey Stengel on Yogi Berra

When many casual baseball fans hear the name Yogi Berra the first thought that creeps into their minds is "What a funny guy!" They've heard about his famous quotes and they smile.

Yogi's quotes deserve the attention they get because they are truly hilarious. But for them to overshadow his Hall of Fame career is unfortunate. It's like the awful spectacle some people put their dogs through by dressing them in costumes, as if dogs have no dignity (which I believe they do).

Yogi was born in St. Louis on May 12, 1925. His parents were immigrants from Milan. They say he got the name Yogi because he sat cross-legged like a yogi. He broke into the big leagues in 1946 and retired as a player in 1965. He stood 5'7" and weighed 185 pounds in his prime, the perfect size for a catcher. He won the Most Valuable Player Award three times during the 1950s, including back-to-back trophies in 1954-55. From 1950-56, he never finished lower than fourth place in AL MVP voting. He was an All-Star 18 straight times (15 years), and caught 148 consecutive games without an error.

Perhaps the greatest compliment attributed to Yogi was by his teammates, who said he was the most important player on the powerful Yankee teams of the 1950s.

But it was in the fall classic where Berra really excelled. Yogi holds nine World Series records that I believe will never be broken, 14 World Series appearances, 10 World Series championships, most games (75), most at bats (259), most hits (71), most singles (49), most games caught (63), and most put outs by a catcher (457).

In the early 1940s the St. Louis Cardinals heard about two promising catching prospects right in their backyard, so they sent their scouts to have a look. The two prospects lived across the street from each other in "The Hill" section of St. Louis. Their names were Lawrence Berra and Joe Garagiola.

The Cardinal scouts should have paid closer attention, because they picked Garagiola, making Berra available for the New York Yankees. Garagiola had a better career as a broadcaster than as a player, while Berra went on to become the best catcher ever up to that point (most baseball experts would agree that Johnny Bench subsequently eclipsed him). He showed promise immediately when he knocked in 23 runs in a doubleheader in the Piedmont League.

Yogi was destined to be a catcher. He had the build of a catcher, but he struggled with the nuances of the position when he first came up to the big leagues. Casey Stengel, who became a father figure to Yogi, had Hall of Fame catcher Bill Dickey teach Yogi the finer points of the position, which prompted Yogi to say, "Bill Dickey is learning me his experience." Over time, Berra became an outstanding defensive catcher. He was like a cat behind the plate, and he was also a master at calling pitches.

At the plate, Yogi was a notorious bad ball hitter who always seemed to come through in the clutch. Paul Richards, who managed for many years in the American League, said, "Berra was the toughest man in the league in the last three innings."

Having said all of this, I will nevertheless end this piece by mentioning many of my favorite Yogi-isms. His penchant for pith has resulted in many apocryphal quotes being attributed to him.[2]

When asked what time it was, Berra asked, "You mean now?"

Upon receiving an award, he said, "Thank you for making this day necessary."

When the wife of New York City Mayor John Lindsay said that he looked cool, he replied "Thanks, you don't look so hot yourself."

Talking about the afternoon sun and shadows in left field at Yankee Stadium, Berra said, "It gets late early out here."

When congratulating Johnny Bench for passing his home run record for a catcher: "I always thought the record would stand until it was broken."

On flagging baseball attendance, Berra noted, "If people don't want to come to the ballpark, nobody's going to stop them."

And of course his two most famous pieces of advice are "It ain't over 'til it's over", delivered in 1973, when his Mets team came from behind to beat the Cubs for the National League title, and "You can observe a lot by watching."

Yogi Berra

7. How did "Mysterious" Walker get his nickname?

Food & Drinks

1B	Ham Hyatt	P	Bob Lemon
2B	Chico Salmon	P	David Cone
3B	Pie Traynor	P	Herb Hash
SS	Bobby Wine	P	Peasoup Dumont
OF	Zack Wheat	RP	Larry Sherry
OF	Mike Trout		
OF	Sam Rice		
C	Norm Sherry		
DH	Jim Rice		

Bob Lemon

"I had bad days on the field. But I didn't take them home with me. I left them in a bar on the way home."

Bob Lemon

S tan Musial did it. Smokey Joe Wood did it. Even the Bambino did it. They all switched positions in their careers from pitcher to outfielder. Stan the Man did it early, Ruth did it after compiling some terrific pitching stats, and Smokey Joe later in his career (due to injuries).

But very few players have had a successful big league career— never mind a Hall of Fame one, after switching from outfielder to pitcher. The great Yankee catcher Bill Dickey saw Bob Lemon pitch in the Navy and told the Cleveland Indians skipper, Lou Boudreau, to consider putting him on the mound. In 1946, five years after Lemon became a big leaguer, Boudreau moved him from center field to the mound. As they say, the rest is history.

Lemon began his major league career with Cleveland as a third baseman in 1941, before spending the 1943-45 seasons in the U.S. Navy. He was the Indians' opening day center fielder when he returned in 1946, but midway through the season, Boudreau moved him to the mound. He went on to become one of the most dominating pitchers of the 1950s. In 1948, his first full season as a pitcher, he threw a no-hitter against the Tigers and led the league in complete games with 20. He played his entire 13-year career with the Indians, seven of them as an All-Star.

His career win total of 207 would be considerably higher if he had not lost three full years to the Navy, and if he had started his career as a pitcher. He may well have reached the 300 win plateau. He was also a successful manager, managing the Royals, White Sox, and Yankees.

Lemon's pitching prowess improved significantly when retired Indians great Mel Harder taught him how to throw a slider. Interestingly, Harder also taught teammate Early Wynn how to throw a curveball. The Indians pitching staff of the early 1950s was one of the best ever assembled. Lemon, Wynn, and Bob Feller had Hall of Fame careers and Mike Garcia was a solid fourth starter. One can make a case that Harder was the invisible fifth man in that great rotation.

Lemon won 20 games seven times, and led the American League in complete games five times. He won a World Series as a player in 1948, and as a manager in 1978, with the New York Yankees. He was also second in career home runs (37) for a pitcher.

Bob Lemon was one of the most-liked men in the game. Sportswriter Steve Cady said of him, "The line on Lemon is that the next person to say something bad about him will be the first."

Bob Lemon

8. How did "Pie" Traynor get his nickname?

1B	Davey Crockett	P	Daniel Boone
2B	John Kennedy	P	Kaiser Wilhelm
3B	Howard Johnson	P	Buster Brown
SS	Jack Spratt	P	Van Lingle Mungo
OF	Kit Carson	RP	Wild Bill Donovan
OF	Jack Daniels		
OF	Ethan Allen		
C	Clyde Kluttz		
DH	George Washington		

Wild Bill Donovan

Wild Bill Donovan pitched for a total of 18 seasons in the big leagues between 1898 and 1917. He got his nickname in the minor leagues after walking nine consecutive batters. In 1906 he performed a rare feat even for a position player, never mind a pitcher. After reaching first base, he stole second base, then he stole home on the front end of a double steal.

But 1907 was his signature year. Pitching for a Detroit Tigers team that included Ty Cobb and Sam Crawford, he compiled a 25-4 record and led them into the World Series. That is still the best winning percentage in Tiger history.

An arm injury in 1912 ended Donovan's career as a pitcher, but it did not end his baseball career. In 1915 he became manager of the Yankees, and held that post until 1917. The following year he coached for the Philadelphia Phillies. After bouncing around the major leagues for a few seasons, he managed the Phillies for 44 games in 1921, when he was replaced by Kaiser Wilhelm, his fellow pitcher on the notable names team!

In 1923, Wild Bill swapped compartments on a train bound for Chicago, with George Weiss. The train crashed and Donovan was killed. George Weiss, sitting in Bill's original seat, was unharmed. Donovan was 47 years old.

Van Lingle Mungo

" Van Mungo likes to drink a bit. Anything. Even hair tonic."
Leo Durocher on Van Lingle Mungo

Van Lingle Mungo has perhaps the most lyrical name in baseball history. I used to sing the name to my kid sister, who would follow with "and Bingo was his name-o." Mungo, like Hack Wilson, Pepper Martin and many others, was in many ways the prototypical depression-era ballplayer: a hard drinker and an even harder brawler. Casey Stengel once quipped, "Mungo and I get along fine. I just tell him I won't stand for no nonsense, and then I duck." He was also a very good pitcher, if only for a short time.

Mungo made his major league debut on September 7, 1931 with the Brooklyn Robins, (they officially became the Dodgers in 1933), and spent the next 10 years with the team. His best season was 1936, when he led the National League in strikeouts with 238. Mungo made the All-Star team in 1934, 1936, and 1937. Unfortunately, he hurt his arm at the end of 1937, and even though he played until 1945, he was not the same after his injury.

A famous incident involving Van Mungo reportedly occurred in Cuba, during spring training. He was caught with another man's wife by her husband, who went after him with a machete. Mungo punched the man and got away. Like a scene from "The Godfather", he escaped the country by being smuggled out in a laundry cart to a waiting seaplane.

Van Lingle Mungo

9. What state did frontiersman Davey Crockett represent in Congress?

Countries/Empires

1B	Buck Jordan	P	Mark Portugal
2B	Germany Schaffer	P	Larry French
3B	Germany Smith	P	Al Holland
SS	Woody English	P	Jim Britton
OF	Irish Meusel	RP	Greg Holland
OF	Roman Mejias		
OF	Jimmie Welsh		
C	Jim French		
DH	Brian Jordan		

Baseball Around the World

"Baseball is more than just a game. It has eternal value. Through it one learns the beautiful and noble spirit of Japan."
Suishu Tobitsa

In 1999 I was flying from Hamburg to Frankfurt. I happened to glance at the newspaper the gentleman next to me was reading. He was German, it was a German newspaper, and he was reading baseball box scores! I asked him in my limited German about it and thankfully he asked if I would prefer that we speak English. He said he was a baseball fan and that there were many in Germany who followed American baseball as well as local German teams.

We think of baseball as uniquely *our* national pastime, but indeed it is played on every continent except Antarctica. It was exclusively America's game for decades but even so, we inherited its foundation from other cultures. Some say we refined it from a game played in England, others say it came from Germany. No matter what its origin, in its modern form it is American all the way.

Baseball was introduced to Japan shortly after the Civil War and has been one of its most popular sports ever since. It got a major boost in the 1930s when some of the game's biggest stars, including Babe Ruth, toured there. The American All-Stars outperformed their Japanese counterparts, but in one memorable game, Japan's best pitcher, Eiji Sawamura struck out Charlie Gehringer, Babe Ruth, Lou Gehrig, and Jimmie Foxx in succession.

Baseball is even more popular in Latin America than it is in Japan. Its popularity is rivaled only by futbol (soccer). Indeed the Latin American countries supply a great deal of talent to the major leagues and that number is growing every year. Players from the Dominican Republic represented an astounding 10.2% of 2014 major league rosters, with Venezuela not far behind with 7.3%. Major League Baseball is not even unique to the United States, having a franchise in Toronto.

The true sign that baseball is now an international sport is the popularity of the World Baseball Classic. It was established in 2005 by the International Baseball Federation (IBAF). Japan won the first two contests, held in 2006 and 2009; the Dominican Republic captured the 2013 title. A total of 18 countries have participated in at least one tournament.

1934 American League All-Stars touring Japan

10. Which team did the Dominican Republic beat to win the 2013 World Baseball Classic?

1B	Doctor Strangeglove Dick Stuart	P	The Singer Throwing Machine Bill Singer
2B	Death to Flying Things Bob Ferguson	P	Losing Pitcher Mulcahy Hugh Mulcahy
3B	Puddin' Head Jones Willie Jones	P	The Curveless Wonder Al Orth
SS	Wagon Tongue Keister Bill Keister	P	The Wild Elk of the Wasatch Ed Heusser
OF	The Rabbi of Swat Mose Solomon	RP	The Gay Reliever Joe Page
OF	What's the use Chiles Pearce Chiles		
OF	Tomato Face Cullop Nick Cullop		
C	Peach Pie O'Connor Jack O'Conner		
DH	Wild Hoss of the Osage Pepper Martin		

How They Got Their Names

"A chunky, unshaven hobo who ran the bases like a berserk locomotive, slept in the raw, and swore at pitchers in his sleep."
Lee Allen on Pepper Martin

Baseball, more than any other sport, is rich in nicknames, both classy and absurd. Baseball nicknames were much more prevalent, and more colorful, in the early days of the game. Perhaps that's because we're more politically correct these days. After all, how would a moniker like Tomato Face go over today? So let's go over our team and discover how some of them got their names.

Dick Stuart "Doctor Strangeglove" played for the Pittsburgh Pirates from 1958-62. He earned his nickname due to his ineptness as a first baseman. He was also called "Stonefingers" which was a take on the popular James Bond movie, *Goldfinger*. He led the major leagues in errors a record seven straight times (1958-64).

Bob Ferguson "Death to Flying Things", earned his nickname due to his ability to snatch a line drive out of the air. He was also the first switch hitter.

I once heard Phil Rizzuto say that Willie "Puddin' Head" Jones got his nickname simply because he liked pudding.

Mose Solomon "The Rabbi of Swat" hit 49 home runs in 1923 for the minor league Hutchinson Wheat Shockers. The Yankees were the toast of New York thanks to their power-hitting right fielder Babe Ruth, aka, the Sultan of Swat. The New York Giants bought Solomon's contract in hopes of finding some royalty of their own. A late season call up in 1923, Solomon hit two singles and a double in just two games, but like Dick Stuart and Wagon Tongue Keister, he couldn't field a lick. He never played in the major leagues again.

Pearce "What's the Use" Chiles was a less than savory character who played for the Philadelphia Phillies at the turn of the 20th century. He would taunt opposing players by shouting "what's the use" whenever he was about to catch a pop fly.

Nick "Tomato Face" Cullop played in the majors from 1926-1931, mostly with Cincinnati. He was a great minor league hitter who never lived up to his potential in the big leagues. His face would turn bright red whenever he became angry.

Al Orth "The Curveless Wonder", never relied on the breaking ball throughout a successful 15-year career. Hall of Famer Jack Chesbro taught him how to throw the spitball, and that pitch, along with his change-up and pinpoint control was all that he needed. He was a pretty good hitter as well. He batted over .300 five times, finishing with a career average of .273.

Willie "Puddin' Head" Jones

11. What was the nickname of Pepper
Martin's St. Louis Cardinals of the 1930s?

1B	The Iron Horse Lou Gehrig	P	The Big Train Walter Johnson
2B	Rajah Rogers Hornsby	P	The Ryan Express Nolan Ryan
3B	Charlie Hustle Pete Rose	P	The Rocket Roger Clemens
SS	The Flying Dutchman Honus Wagner	P	Chairman of the Board Whitey Ford
OF	The Georgia Peach Ty Cobb	P	The Big Unit Randy Johnson
OF	The Yankee Clipper Joe DiMaggio		
OF	The Sultan of Swat Babe Ruth		
C	The Duke of Tralee Roger Bresnahan		
DH	The Splendid Splinter Ted Williams		

Pete Rose

" I'd be willing to bet you, if I was a betting man,
that I have never bet on baseball."
Pete Rose

The best nicknames are those that capture an individual's outstanding quality while lending a touch of class, like The Yankee Clipper. Baseball has these names in abundance. Some, like The Iron Horse, The Ryan Express, The Rocket, and The Sultan of Swat reflect the players' prowess on the diamond. Then there are some that are able to combine a player's on- and off-field persona, like Charlie Hustle. Like Shoeless Joe Jackson before him, Pete Rose will forever be remembered as one of baseball's greatest hitters, as well as one of the game's tragic figures.

Pete made his major league debut on April 8, 1963 with the Cincinnati Reds. In spite of a scouting report that said, "Rose can't make a double play, can't throw, can't hit left handed and can't run," he won the Rookie of the Year Award.

Whitey Ford claimed to have given Rose the nickname "Charlie Hustle." In a spring training game, Mickey Mantle hit a towering home run that cleared the fences by a mile. As Mantle was admiring his blast, the right fielder, Rose, was climbing the fence to catch a ball that was hopelessly out of reach. When Mickey rounded the bases and returned to the dugout, Ford derisively sneered, "Hey, who's Charlie Hustle out there?" Others claim Rose earned the nickname by running to first base on a walk, which he copied from one of his boyhood heroes, Enos Slaughter. Regardless of how he got the nickname, it fits him like a glove.

A chronology of Rose's baseball years provides no doubt that he was one of the greatest players of all time. The following table highlights years he either led or tied the National League in a number of different categories:

1965   at bats (670) and hits (209).
1968   hits (210), batting avg. (.335), and OBP (.391).
1969   runs (120) and batting avg. (.348).
1970   hits (205).
1972   games (154), at bats (645), and hits (198).
1973   at bats (680), hits (230), and batting avg. (.338).
1974   games (163), runs (110), and doubles (45).
1975   games (162), runs (112), and doubles (47).
1976   runs (130), hits (215), and doubles (42).
1977   games (162) and at bats (655).
1978   doubles (51).
1979   OBP (.418).
1980   doubles (42).
1981   hits (140).
1982   games (162).

Pete's career numbers are just as impressive. His 3,562 games played, 14,053 at bats, and 4,256 hits are all major league records. He also notched 2,165 runs, 746 doubles, 135 triples, 160 home runs, 1,314 RBIs, 198 stolen bases, 1,566 walks, .303 batting average, and 5,752 total bases. His at bats and games played are major league records. He played on three World Series Championship teams, won one MVP Award, played in 17 All-Star games (at five different positions), won two Gold Glove Awards, one Silver Slugger Award, and one Rookie of the Year Award. He was named the Sporting News' Player of the Decade for the 1970s, and he was voted to the All Century Team.

Rose had a proclivity for doing two things in a superlative way: hitting a baseball and gambling. It's unfortunate that one cannot write about his career without spending considerable time and energy on the gambling scandal that led to his banishment from the game he loved so much. Some people say that not a day went by when Pete was not betting on something, usually the horses. He also bet on baseball, a practice that Major League Baseball expressly forbids. This prohibition is posted in every team's locker room and is verbally drilled into every player. So when Commissioner Bart Giamatti discovered Rose had been betting on his own team as manager of the Reds, he banned Rose from baseball.

One could take either side in the argument about the justice of his banishment for life from the thing he loved above all else. I will instead pose a debate on an even more volatile subject: should Pete Rose be inducted into the Hall of Fame? Those who vote "yes" list several reasons. His career on the field compels him to get in. C'mon, he got more damn hits than anyone who ever played! And by the way, Ty Cobb, the man whose hit record he broke, was a virulent racist and egomaniac whose self interest some say overshadowed the interests of his team. They also point out that Rose never admitted to betting on baseball. Even if he did, he only bet on his own team. Is there anything wrong with betting on your own team? The Hall's motto is, "Preserving History. Honoring Excellence. Connecting Generations." Yet it let Cobb,

Anson and many other neer-do-wells in, so why not Rose?

I choose the less popular opinion. To my way of thinking, Pete Rose does not belong in the Hall of Fame. Baseball's rule against gambling states, "Any player, umpire, or club official or employee, who shall bet any sum whatsoever upon any baseball game in connection with which the bettor has a duty to perform shall be declared permanently ineligible." This rule does not differentiate between betting on your own team or on the opposing team.

So what's wrong with betting on your own team? The answer should be clear to any serious fan. If a manager has a substantial sum, (and testimony suggests that Rose bet substantial sums on a regular basis), on the outcome of a particular game, he may well make a decision to win the game by overextending his starting pitcher or closer, thus jeopardizing the season or even a pitcher's career. He may also give insider information to nefarious characters.

And while Rose steadfastly denied that he bet on baseball, the investigation by the Commissioner's office provided overwhelming evidence to the contrary. In short, Rose should be denied entrance into the Hall of Fame not because he gambled per se, or because he was an unsavory individual, but simply because he broke the most sacred of baseball's rules.

Pete Rose

12. What Hall of Fame pitcher was called "The Mealticket"?

1B	Earl Torgeson	P	"Prince" Hal Newhouser
2B	Cesar Tovar	P	"King" Felix Hernandez
3B	Ray Knight	P	Mel Queen
SS	Jeff King	P	Zach Duke
OF	Earl Clarke	RP	Don Kaiser
OF	"Duke" Snider		
OF	Jim King		
C	Tom Prince		
DH	Elijah Dukes		

The Clown Prince of Baseball

"I came into this world very homely and haven't changed a bit since."
Al Schacht

The Hapsburg Empire had Crown Prince Rudolf, who met with an untimely death while consorting with his mistress. Major League Baseball had *Clown* Prince Al Schacht, who unlike the royal Austrian died at the ripe old age of 92 on July 14, 1984. He was born in 1892 in New York City to immigrant Russian Jewish parents.

Al was an unlikely prospect in 1919 when he broke into the big leagues with the Washington Senators. At 5'11" and 142 pounds, he was hardly the physical prototype of a major league pitcher. Through grit and determination, he convinced manager Clark Griffith to sign him. He compiled a 14-10 record over three seasons with Washington, but by 1921 his major league career was over. Pinch running during the 1920 season, Schacht slid into second base and Detroit shortstop Donnie Bush crashed down on him, injuring Schacht's elbow. He was never the same after that.

But where a door closes, a window sometimes opens, and that was the case with Schacht. His antics after his playing days were what made him a baseball icon. He was a natural born entertainer and had a wonderful ability to imitate the ballplayers of his time, as well as other celebrities. During spring training in 1920 he ran into another character named Nick Altrock. Together they formed a famous comedy act that entertained fans across the country. From the first and third base coaching boxes they would perform outrageous parodies of other players or simply start playing musical instruments in the middle of an inning. Umpires were another favorite target. Surprisingly, Altrock and Schacht never really got along and their animosity increased with time. One particular routine called for them to imitate the Jack Dempsey versus Gene Tunney fight. Spectators swore that it was no parody. They were beating the hell out of each other.

Al was proud of his Jewish heritage and often kidded about it. In his autobiography "My Own Particular Screwball," he noted, "There is talk that I am Jewish, just because my father was Jewish, my mother is Jewish, I speak Yiddish, and once studied to be a rabbi and a cantor. Well, that's how rumors get started."

Al Schacht

13. On September 22, 1968, how many defensive positions did Cesar Tovar play for the Minnesota Twins?

Occupations

1B	Joe Judge	P	Jim Hunter
2B	Billy Gardner	P	Jared Weaver
3B	Frank Baker	P	Chris Carpenter
SS	Joe Tinker	P	Steve Barber
OF	Torii Hunter	RP	Mike Marshall
OF	Tris Speaker		
OF	Brett Butler		
C	Walker Cooper		
DH	Billy Butler		

Tris Speaker

"Speaker was Willie Mays before there was Willie Mays."
Baseball historian Richard Johnson

Many baseball people consider Tris Speaker to be the best defensive center fielder of all time. My vote goes to Willie Mays, but Speaker was certainly the best of his era. He holds the record for career assists for an outfielder (449!) and had six career unassisted double plays. He would play such a shallow center field that after snagging a short line drive, he would continue running toward the infield to double up the base runner on second base. Because he played so shallow, he was often used as a fifth infielder in bunt situations, allowing the shortstop to cover third base and the third baseman to charge the bunt. He would also take throws from his catcher, nailing those who took too much of a lead off second base. No one, not even Willie, could accomplish these feats in the live ball era. Sportswriters of the day would say that Speaker's glove is where triples go to die. The Boston Red Sox outfield combination of Duffy Lewis in left, Speaker in center, and Harry Hooper in right is considered by many baseball experts to be the best ever defensively.

Speaker was every bit as great offensively. His career stats are impressive indeed: a .345 batting average (sixth all time), 3,514 hits (fifth all time), 1,529 RBIs, and 792 doubles (first all time). In his first full season he batted .309 and for the next 20 years he failed to hit .300 only twice. Curiously, in 1919 he only batted .296 and overall had one of his worst seasons. His Cleveland Indians finished just behind the infamous Chicago White Sox. It's intriguing to ponder that if Tris had had a normal year at the plate then the Indians might have won the American League pennant and thus there would have been no "Black Sox" scandal.

Speaker was an intelligent baseball man and as a manager was credited for two significant innovations: the platoon system and the infield rotation play. He was inducted into the Hall of Fame in 1937, its second year of accepting nominees.

Tris Speaker

14. What was Tris Speaker's nickname

1B	John Mayberry	P	Charlie Root
2B	Jake Flowers	P	Joe Bush
3B	Graig Nettles	P	Howie Reed
SS	Donie Bush	P	Ted Lilly
OF	Pete Rose	RP	Ron Reed
OF	Estel Crabtree		
OF	Kevin Flora		
C	Buster Posey		
DH	Jim Greengrass		

Charlie Root and the Called Shot

"I gave my life to baseball and I'll only be remembered for something that never happened."
Charlie Root

In 1932 the Yankees played the Cubs in the World Series. There was no classic rivalry between these two teams, but for that one year they hated each other. Joe McCarthy, the Yankee skipper, had been fired by the Cubs two years earlier. But more galling to the Yankees was the fact that Mark Koenig, their shortstop, who had been traded to Chicago in mid-season, was only voted a half share of the Series money by the Cubs. The third game was in Chicago. Babe Ruth, ever the heckler, shouted to Koenig, "Hey Mark, who are these cheapskates you're playing with?" This got both the Cub players and their fans riled up. They started throwing lemons at Ruth who then threw them right back at the fans. Imagine a player doing that today!

The Babe hit a three run homer in the first inning, and when he came to bat in the fifth, the drama reached a fever pitch. The first pitch was a called strike, after which Ruth raised a finger, which a newspaper three days later said was him predicting a home run. Gabby Hartnett, the Cubs Hall of Fame catcher, said that when Ruth raised his finger he was telling the Cubs bench that "it only takes one to hit it out." When the count went to 2-2, Root taunted the Babe, who shot back by saying,

"I'm going to knock the next pitch right down your goddamned throat." Ruth hit the most famous home run in the history of Wrigley Field on the next pitch. The Yankees went on to sweep the Cubs four games to none.

Charlie Root was born on St. Patrick's Day in Middleton, Ohio in 1899 and died in Hollister, California in 1970 at the age of 71. He joined the Cubs in 1926 and retired in 1941, having played his entire career with Chicago. Although he was one of the more dominant pitchers of his era, he is remembered as the answer to a trivia question because of the called shot incident. In 1927, he led the majors with 26 wins. He holds the Cubs record for games pitched, innings pitched, and wins with 201. With the way players, and especially pitchers, change teams today, that last record may stand for a long time.

Later in his life Babe Ruth admitted that he did not call the shot. In fact, Root said: "If he pointed to the bleachers, I would have put one in his ear and knocked him on his ass." The lie bothered him for years after his retirement.

Charlie Root

15. What slugger said, "If a horse won't eat it, I don't want to play on it" with regard to artificial turf?

1B	Deron Johnson	P	Walter Johnson
2B	Davey Johnson	P	Randy Johnson
3B	John Kennedy	P	Billy Pierce
SS	Travis Jackson	P	Mudcat Grant
OF	Joe Jackson	RP	Josh Johnson
OF	Hack Wilson		
OF	Joe Carter		
C	Gary Carter		
DH	Reggie Jackson		

Presidents as Fans

"Not making the baseball team at West Point was one of the greatest disappointments of my life, maybe my greatest."
Dwight Eisenhower

U.S. Presidents have been fans of baseball and its antecedents since George Washington. That's right, I said George Washington. His soldiers wrote of the future president playing rounders at Valley Forge. John Adams was said to have played a game called "bat and ball." Skip over the Virginia patricians Jefferson, Madison, and Monroe, and we find Andrew Jackson playing a game of "one ole cat," another early variant of today's game. Abraham Lincoln was said to have liked the game so much that one cartoonist portrayed him on a baseball diamond! His successor, Andrew Johnson was the first to host a baseball team in the White House, followed by Ulysses S. Grant who was the first to host a professional team, the Cincinnati Red Stockings.

In 1910, William Taft was the first president to throw out the first pitch, a tradition that has continued uninterrupted to this day. Five presidents stand out as being serious fans: Dwight Eisenhower, Richard Nixon, Ronald Reagan, George H. Bush, and George W. Bush (all Republicans, interestingly enough). Eisenhower dreamed of emulating Honus Wagner, George W. Bush longed to be Willie Mays, and Richard Nixon's dream was to be a sportswriter. Ronald Reagan was a radio announcer for the Chicago Cubs. George H. Bush was a stellar first baseman and captain of the Yale baseball team, and George W. Bush was a managing partner for the Texas Rangers.

The Baseball Almanac has compiled an impressive list of presidential baseball quotes. Some of my favorites are:

Herbert Hoover: "Next to religion, baseball has furnished a greater impact on American life than any other institution."

Franklin D. Roosevelt: "If I didn't have to hobble up those steps in front of all those people, I'd be out at that ballpark every day."

Gerald Ford: "I had a life-long ambition to be a professional baseball player, but nobody would sign me."

Ronald Reagan: "I really do love baseball."

Dwight Eisenhower throwing out the first pitch - 1953

16. Which president ushered in the 20th century?

1B	Mark Grace	P	Preacher Roe
2B	Johnny Temple	P	Jim Abbott
3B	Larry Parrish	P	Charlie Bishop
SS	Max Bishop	P	Bubba Church
OF	Dave Pope	RP	Travis Baptist
OF	Jeff Abbott		
OF	Bob Christian		
C	Lance Parrish		
DH	Wally Moses		

Baseball Sins

"I try not to break the rules, but merely to test their elasticity."
Bill Veeck

Thou shalt not steal. Tell that to Rickey Henderson. O.K., stealing bases is legitimate, but what of gambling, cheating, performance enhancing drugs, etc. Fixing games is obviously cheating, but what about some other less clear-cut types of gaining an advantage?

My friend Bob and I played high school baseball. Bob played third base. I still remember a particular game when Bob pulled a stunt that won the game for us. We were leading by one run in the bottom of the ninth against our biggest rival, with one out and a man on third. Unfortunately for Bob, said runner was also the toughest player on their team. High school baseball generally uses only one umpire, who takes his place behind the plate. When the batter hit a fly ball to right field, the umpire watched to make sure the ball was caught before the runner could tag up and race for home. Bob waited until the last second and then grabbed the belt of the runner. The enraged runner started to pummel Bob, who acted as if he was the victim. Since the umpire did not see Bob's subterfuge, he ordered the runner to remain on third base. The next batter struck out and we won the game. Did Bob cheat, or was he simply playing "heads up ball"? Ty Cobb, Rogers Hornsby and others pulled tricks like that all the time.

Of course, Bob cheated. But just because his action was blatant shouldn't make it more egregious than other less obvious incidents.

What about the catcher who "frames" the pitch that was actually outside in order to fool the umpire into thinking that it nipped the corner? What about the first baseman who "accidentally" interferes with the base runner trying to make it to second base?

Gil Hodges, one of the most upstanding gentlemen to ever wear a uniform, pulled a similar stunt in the 1969 World Series when managing the New York Mets. In *Gil Hodges* by Tom Clavin and Danny Peary, the authors describe how Hodges used trickery to convince home plate umpire Lou DiMuro that Cleon Jones was hit by a pitch. It was the fifth (and ultimately clinching) game of the series against the Baltimore Orioles. Jones claimed that Dave McNally's pitch hit him on the foot before bouncing into the Met dugout. Hodges walked out of the dugout holding a ball that had shoe polish on it. He convinced DiMuro that this was incontestable proof that Jones was indeed hit on the foot. Jones was awarded first base and scored on a Donn Clendenon home run. Jerry Koosman claimed years later that Hodges told him to pick the ball up and rub it on his shoe in order to get polish on it. We may never know for sure what happened.

Whether it's holding a runner's belt, tricking an umpire, or throwing illegal pitches, "cheating" will always play a role in Major League Baseball. Some would say it adds an element of strategy to the game. What needs to be rigorously enforced are gambling, the use of performance enhancing drugs and deliberate throwing at batters.

Gil Hodges as Manager of the New York Mets

17. Who was the ace of the Chicago Black Sox pitching staff that was complicit in throwing the 1919 World Series?

1B	Wade Boggs	P	David Wells
2B	Eddie Lake	P	Tim Hudson
3B	Brooks Robinson	P	Charlie Ripple
SS	Ernie Banks	P	Ernie Shore
OF	Vernon Wells	RP	Joe Lake
OF	Curt Flood		
OF	Mickey Rivers		
C	Steve Lake		
DH	Jason Bay		

Curt Flood

"I am pleased that God made my skin black,
but I wish that he had made it thicker."
Curt Flood

Today's multi-millionaire ballplayers should collectively build a shrine to Curt Flood. His challenge of Major League Baseball's reserve clause paved the way for free agency and players' ability to "follow the money."

Flood was born on January 18, 1938 in Houston, Texas and made his major league debut in 1956 with the Cincinnati Reds. The Reds already had a promising center fielder by the name of Vada Pinson, so they sent Flood to the St. Louis Cardinals, where he played all but 13 games for the rest of his career. He was a great defensive outfielder, winning seven Gold Gloves. Not bad when you consider his contemporaries included Pinson, Willie Davis, Roberto Clemente, and an aging Willie Mays. In 1966 he handled 396 chances without an error. He was selected to three All-Star teams.

In spite of his borderline Hall of Fame career, Flood will always be remembered more for his role in eliminating the reserve clause. At the end of the 1969 season, he was told that he had been traded to the Philadelphia Phillies for their moody slugger, Richie Allen, who had been trying to get out of Philadelphia for two years, even going so far as to wage a 26-day strike. Allen was delighted with the trade, but Flood was not and refused to go. He sat out the 1970 season and challenged the reserve clause in federal court. Curt made an impassioned speech when pleading his case, even quoting from Frederick Douglass, "If there is not struggle there is not progress. Those who profess to favor freedom, and yet depreciate agitation, are men who want crops without plowing up the ground. Power concedes nothing without a demand. It never did and never will."[3]

In many ways Flood's life was bittersweet. He entered professional baseball when Jim Crow laws were still prevalent. Like Jackie Robinson, Hank Aaron, and Larry Doby before him, he was subjected to racial taunts, denied hotel rooms and bathroom facilities. As the Ken Burns documentary "Baseball" illustrated, his team would not even wash his clothes in the same vat as the white players' clothes.

After losing the reserve clause lawsuit, Flood went bankrupt. But in spite of his travails, he remained optimistic. In an interview with San Francisco Chronicle reporter Joan Ryan, published shortly after Flood's death, he reflected on his contributions to the game: "People try to make a Greek tragedy of my life, and they can't do it. I'm too happy. Remember when I told you about the American dream? That if you worked hard enough and tried hard enough and kicked yourself in the butt, you'd succeed? Well, I think I did."

In 1998, Congress passed the Curt Flood Act, officially eliminating the reserve clause (although the players, through creative collective bargaining, had already made the clause obsolete). And the 1998 Act did not entirely overturn baseball's exemption from antitrust regulations. As a result, players in their first six years in the major leagues are still bound to their teams.

Curt Flood

18. Where do baseballs end up when hit over the right field stands at San Francisco's AT&T Park?

Third Inning

Surnames

1B	Chris	P	Storm
2B	Crash	P	Doug
3B	Jumbo	P	Curt
SS	George	P	Dixie
OF	Chili	RP	Wade
OF	Willie		
OF	Eric		
C	Spud		
DH	Tommy		

Willie

"Willie Davis is so fast, his head's three feet behind the rest of him."
Jocko Conlan

In 2010, as I was reading Willie Davis' obituary, I was astonished at how good he was. I suppose with all the great stars of his era, it was easy to overlook him. There are players in the Hall of Fame with lesser credentials.

Davis was born on April 15, 1940 in Mineral Springs, Arkansas. He made his major league debut at the end of the 1960 season with the Los Angeles Dodgers. Just like Mickey Mantle had to earn the New York fans' support after replacing the inimitable Joe DiMaggio, Willie replaced the much-loved Duke Snider in center field. He was the antithesis of the type of rookie the Dodgers signed just two years prior: the slow, hulking power hitter Frank Howard. The Dodgers were about to re-invent themselves from the power team of Snider, Hodges, Campanella, and Furillo to a team of speed, defense and pitching. Davis, along with teammate Maury Wills, was the epitome of speed and defense, and Sandy Koufax and Don Drysdale provided the pitching. A typical Dodger victory of those years would feature Wills and/or Davis getting on base, stealing second and being driven in by Tommy Davis (see DH above), and winning 1-0 on a Koufax or Drysdale shutout.

Willie was a good hitter and a great center fielder. He only won three Gold Gloves, but he was competing with Mays, Clemente, Curt Flood, and Vada Pinson. If he had played in the American League he may have won 10. Ironically, he set a World Series record by making three errors in two consecutive plays.

He had a lifetime batting average of .279, 2,561 hits, 182 home runs, 1,053 RBIs, and 398 stolen bases. In 1969 he broke Zach Wheat's Dodger record when he hit safely in 31 consecutive games. He also had 138 triples, fourth best since 1945, after which triples became as rare as the Cubs playing in the postseason.

Willie was a devout Buddhist, whose theory of life was reflected in this gem: "If you step on people in this life, you're going to come back as a cockroach."[4] He played his last game on September 30, 1979 as a member of the California Angels.

Willie Davis

19. Which team did Hall of Famer George Davis play most of his career for?

1B	Deron	P	Walter
2B	Davey	P	Randy
3B	Howard	P	Josh
SS	Bob	P	Ken
OF	Alex	RP	Syl
OF	Bob		
OF	Bill		
C	Cliff		
DH	Lou		

Randy

*"Randy Johnson when he was good.
It's hopeless. It's like a hopeless feeling."*
Adam Dunn, when asked in 2012 who the best
pitcher he ever faced was

The Johnson team has arguably the best righty/lefty combination of starting pitchers of any team in history. But we'll get to Walter in another section. If I had to describe Randy Johnson in one word, that word would be *intimidating.* Batters had to be scared out of their wits when they faced the 6'10" flamethrower (his fastball was clocked at 100 mph), who had significant control problems in the beginning of his career. How do you dig in against someone like that? Left-handed batters were particularly vulnerable. In a famous and comical scene at the 1983 All-Star Game Johnson threw a zinger over John Kruk's head. The terrified left-handed hitter swung at two pitches out of the strike zone and promptly struck out.

The "Big Unit" was born on September 10, 1963 in Walnut Creek, California and made his major league debut on September 15, 1988 with the Montreal Expos. He was offered a contract by the Atlanta Braves six years earlier, but chose instead to accept a full athletic scholarship from USC, where he also starred in basketball.

What if he had accepted the Braves offer? Imagine the rotation of Johnson, Maddux, Glavine, and Smoltz throughout the '90s!

Like Sandy Koufax before him, Johnson was extremely wild when he first came up, prompting the Expos to make one of the worst trades in their history by dealing him to the Seattle Mariners for Mark Langston. Langston played one year with Montreal and then became a free agent; Johnson went on to win a Cy Young Award with Seattle, not to mention four more in Arizona.

During the Diamondbacks' 2001 World Series championship season, he went 21-6 with a 2.49 ERA and struck out 372 batters. Oh, and he won three games in that World Series (including game 7 in relief) to share Most Valuable Player honors with Curt Schilling.

In 2015, Johnson was elected to the Hall of Fame, appearing on 534 of the 549 ballots cast. One has to wonder what those 15 people who didn't vote for him were thinking. He was a 10-time All-Star, pitched two no-hitters (one of them a perfect game), compiled a 303-166 won-lost record, and a .3.29 ERA. His five Cy Young Awards are second only to Rogers Clemens, and his career total of 4,875 strikeouts is second only to Nolan Ryan.

Ryan, by the way, was instrumental in getting Randy to change his pitching style, a modification that had immediate and profound results. In 1995, Johnson broke Ryan's record of strikeouts-to-innings ratio for a season when he struck out 12.35 batters for every nine innings. He is one of only two pitchers (the other being Pedro Martinez) to strike out more than 300 batters in a season in each league, and in 1995 his record of 18-2 is the second-best winning percentage in American League history.

Randy Johnson

20. Davey Johnson never hit more than 18 home runs in a season for the Baltimore Orioles. How many did he hit in his first year after being traded to the Atlanta Braves?

1B	Nippy	P	Gordon
2B	Dalton	P	Randy
3B	Chipper	P	Sad Sam
SS	Cobe	P	Sam
OF	Cleon	RP	Todd
OF	Andruw		
OF	Adam		
C	Bill		
DH	Fielder		

Chipper

*"If Todd Van Poppel doesn't want to play for the Atlanta Braves,
I'll be more than happy to take his place."*
Chipper Jones

I was tempted to dedicate this section to Sad Sam Jones, one of baseball's more colorful characters, but since Chipper is the only real star on this team, he gets the nod. Born on April 24, 1972 in Deland, Florida, Jones made his major league debut on September 11, 1993. He was a first round pick of the Atlanta Braves in 1990 and played his entire 19-year career with them. The Braves actually wanted to sign Todd Van Poppel before Jones, but Van Poppel refused to sign with them. Sometimes luck trumps judgment. Van Poppel went on to have a mediocre 13 year career, but he was no Chipper Jones.

Jones, along with Mickey Mantle, Eddie Murray, and Pete Rose may well be the four best switch hitters ever. Jones epitomized the modern ballplayer, especially the corner infielder. At 6'5" and 210 pounds, he dwarfed most of the third basemen of previous generations. I grew up thinking third basemen like Eddie Mathews and Al Rosen were giants at their position, but they would be of average size today.

Jones's career stats are impressive, ensuring him a plaque in Cooperstown as soon as he becomes eligible in 2018. He hit .303 with 468 home runs, 1,512 walks, 1,623 RBIs, and 2,500 games played. He played in eight All-Star games, was voted National League MVP in 1999, won two Silver Slugger awards, was a World Series champion in 1995, won the batting title in 1998, holds the record for all-time on base percentage for a Brave with a .402 average, is number three in career home runs for a Brave, and is second in RBIs for a switch hitter.

There is one more list of statistics that I must mention if for no other reason than to point out the company Jones is in. He joins four other great hitters in amassing at least 2,500 hits, 1,500 walks, 500 doubles, 450 home runs, 1,500 RBIs, a .300 batting average, a .400 on base percentage, and a .500 slugging percentage. The others are Babe Ruth, Lou Gehrig, Ted Williams, and Stan Musial!

Chipper Jones

21. Sad Sam Jones was traded to the Boston Red Sox along with Fred Thomas and $50,000 for what future Hall-of-Famer?

1B	Tino	P	Pedro
2B	Jose	P	Ramon
3B	Edgar	P	Dennis
SS	Teddy	P	Carlos
OF	Carmelo	RP	Tippy
OF	Julio (J.D.)		
OF	David		
C	Buck		
DH	Victor		

Pedro

*"In my era, you've got Roger Clemens, Randy Johnson, and Greg Maddux—
but as far as I'm concerned, Pedro's the best."*
Bret Saberhagen

Major league baseball has produced some outstanding brother combinations: Dizzy and Daffy Dean, Gaylord and Jim Perry, Stan and Harry Coveleski, and Phil and Joe Niekro. All four brother combinations feature one Hall of Famer and one very good pitcher. But in my opinion, Pedro and Ramon Martinez may be the best sibling combo of them all.

Pedro came out of Santo Domingo, where he was born in 1971, to join brother Ramon in the Dodger organization, making his major league debut on September 4, 1992. He showed signs of greatness from the beginning, but Tommy Lasorda, the Dodger manager, couldn't think out of the box. "How can a 5"11" 170 pound power pitcher expect to last in the major leagues?" wondered Lasorda. So the Dodgers traded him to the Montreal Expos for DeLino DeShields in yet another of baseball's many lopsided trades. Maybe this was Montreal's way of compensating for trading Randy Johnson for Mark Langston. What a one-two punch they would have had with both Pedro and Randy!

Martinez did not disappoint his new owners in Montreal. He exceeded expectations, and won a Cy Young award in 1997. He was traded to the Boston Red Sox after the 1997 season for $75 million, the highest amount ever paid for a pitcher at the time. In Boston, Pedro's accomplishments were spectacular, including participating in their first world championship in almost a century. In both 1999 and 2000, Martinez had two of the best years any pitcher has ever had.

In 1999, Pedro won pitching's triple crown, compiling a 23-4 win-loss record, 2.07 ERA, and 313 strikeouts. In the All-Star game, he struck out Barry Larkin, Larry Walker, Sammy Sosa, Mark McGwire, and Jeff Bagwell in succession, recalling Carl Hubbell's performance at an All-Star game 50 years earlier.

In 2000, he posted a 1.74 ERA. That was more than three runs lower than the park-adjusted ERA of 4.97 for the rest of the league. No other pitcher has ever had such a large differential. His 0.74 WHIP (walks plus hits per innings pitched) that year broke Walter Johnson's 87-year-old record. Bear in mind that Johnson pitched in the dead ball era, while Martinez pitched in the steroid-fueled era. While with Boston from 1998 to 2004, Pedro compiled a 117-37 win-loss record, the highest percentage any pitcher has had with any team in history.

His career stats include a 219-100 win-loss record, 2.93 ERA, 3,154 strikeouts, eight All-Star appearances, one World Series championship, three Cy Young awards, and an All-Star MVP award in 1999. Sports Illustrated's Joe Posnanski said of him: "There has never been a pitcher in baseball history who was more overwhelming than the young Pedro."

Pedro Martinez

22. Buck Martinez spent 17 years as a catcher in the Major Leagues. What team did he manage after his retirement?

1B	Hughie	P	Bob
2B	Dots	P	Wade
3B	Bruce	P	Bob
SS	Eddie	P	Jake
OF	Bing	RP	Stu
OF	Rick		
OF	Norm		
C	Otto		
DH	Doggie		

Marvin

"Workers of the world unite!"
Karl Marx

Marvin Miller died just a month before I started writing this chapter. He was 95 years old. As I listened to the talking heads, I'm astonished that too many still think that he did baseball a huge disservice. Are they kidding? In the Ken Burns documentary, "Baseball," Red Barber is quoted as saying, "Babe Ruth, Jackie Robinson, and Marvin Miller are among the three most important men in the history of Major League Baseball." No less a baseball legend than Hank Aaron said Miller was "just as important to the history of baseball as Jackie Robinson."

Miller left his position as staff economist for the United Steelworkers Union in 1966 to become the Executive Director of the Major League Baseball Players Association (MLBPA). He wasted no time in turning professional baseball on its head. In 1968 he organized the first collective bargaining agreement between the owners and players that resulted in an increase from $6,000 to $10,000 as a minimum salary. In 1972 he organized a players strike that won additional concessions. At this point, the owners waged a propaganda war against him. Ironically, the venom that spewed from owners such as Charlie Finley, August Busch, and Ray Kroc, turned the fans in favor of the players. Kroc notoriously said about his players: "I won't subsidize idiots." In 1974, with Miller pulling the strings, Catfish Hunter won an arbitration hearing against Finley for Charlie failing to honor an annuity clause in his contract. Hunter was declared a free agent and signed with the Yankees, opening the door for others to follow.

An even bigger breakthrough came in 1975, when under Marvin's guidance, pitchers Andy Messersmith and Dave McNally refused to sign mandatory one-year contract extensions--known as the reserve clause, with their existing teams. Arbitrator Peter Seitz invalidated the reserve clause, allowing both pitchers (and all subsequent players at the end of their contracts) to become free agents. The reserve clause was dead. Sadly, the decision came six years too late to benefit Curt Flood.

Miller was head of the MLBPA from 1966 to 1982. During that time average salaries soared by 2,000 percent! The minimum salary alone more than quintupled in his tenure. And free agency has forced the owners to share their unprecedented riches with the game's stars. In 2014, for example, the Miami Marlins signed their star outfielder Giancarlo Stanton to a 12-year contract worth $325,000,000; that's more than twice what Marlins owner Jeffrey Loria paid in 2002 for the entire franchise.

Those who wax nostalgic about baseball in the "good old days," say they preferred the game before it became a business. Those people need to get real. Baseball has always been a business and always will be. It's only since Marvin Miller's contributions that the players have been allowed to treat it as the business that the owners have always considered it.

Many fans, including myself, feel that Marvin Miller belongs in the Hall of Fame. He will make it some day but it's too bad he won't be alive to appreciate it. Bob Costas said of Miller, "There is no non-player more deserving of the Hall of Fame."

WAF 041001 4/10/72 WASHINGTON: Representatives of the baseball players and the club owners met 4/10 with the government's chief mediator amid fresh hope for settlement of the 10-day strike that has snarled up the opening of the 1972 season. Shown at the meeting (left to right): John Gaberin, representing the owners; J. Curtis Counts, federal mediator; and Marvin Miller, exec.dir. of the Baseball Players Association. (UPI) rkm/dh   SEE WIRE STORY 113A

Marvin Miller(right) in 1972

23. What unusual event happened to pitcher Stu Miller in the 1961 All-Star
    game, causing him to balk in the tying run?

1B	Randy	P	Mike
2B	Eddie	P	Earl
3B	Junior	P	Ray
SS	Harry	P	Whitey
OF	Gene	RP	Donnie
OF	Terry		
OF	Joe		
C	Charlie		
DH	Johnny		

Donnie

"He could not live with himself after Henderson hit the home run."
Dave Pinter, agent for Donnie Moore

The setting is Anaheim, California, 1986. It's the ninth inning of the American League playoff series between the Angels and the Boston Red Sox. The Angels are leading the series three games to one and are leading this game 5-4. They need just one more out to win the first pennant in their history. Gene Mauch, the Angels manager, lifts Mike Witt, their ace, and brings in Gary Lucas to pitch to Rich Gedman. Lucas hits Gedman with the pitch, putting the tying run on first base. Mauch relieves Lucas and brings in Donnie Moore, who's been their best reliever all year. Moore gets two strikes on Dave Henderson. One strike away from their first pennant! Then Henderson hits the next pitch into the left field stands, putting Boston ahead six to five. The Angels tie the game in the bottom of the ninth, but lost in extra innings and then lost the series.

Donnie Moore was inconsolable after giving up that home run to Henderson. He would tell friends that he did not want to be remembered like Ralph Branca was—as the guy who blew the pennant. He put the blame on himself, but one could just as easily blame Lucas for hitting Gedman. We blame athletes too much in my opinion. For one thing, Moore was pitching hurt with a rib injury.

Secondly, maybe Henderson was simply "in the zone." If I had to blame someone, it would be Gene Mauch for lifting Witt, putting in Lucas, and most importantly not heeding Moore's injury. Mauch is lionized by many as a great baseball mind. I disagree. I remember 1964, when he was managing the Philadelphia Phillies. They had the pennant all but wrapped up. They had a six and one-half game lead on September 20 and needed only one more victory. Then they were swept by the second place Cincinnati Reds. Mauch panicked and pitched his two aces, Jim Bunning and Chris Short, each on two days' rest. It didn't help. The Phillies were swept in St. Louis, bringing their losing streak to 10 games, and the Cardinals went on to win the National League pennant, and ultimately the World Series.

The Angels released Moore in August of 1988. He went to the Royals but was out of baseball in 1989. On July 20 of that year he shot his wife (she survived), then killed himself. Many say it was that home run pitch that pushed him over the edge. Maybe so, but he was wrestling with demons, including a history of violence and alcohol abuse, for years before 1986.

Different people handle similar situations in completely opposite ways. Branca was ultimately able to accept his role in the 1951 pennant, and even embrace it, appearing alongside Bobby Thomson in countless re-enactments of the "shot heard 'round the world." Moore, on the other hand, didn't live long enough to come to grips with his failure.

Donnie Moore

24. Donnie Moore was the goat of the 1986 ALCS. Who was the goat of the ensuing World Series?

1B	Ed		P	Johnny
2B	Daniel		P	Tom
3B	Soldier Boy		P	Ed
SS	Yale		P	Danny
OF	Eddie		RP	Con
OF	Dwayne			
OF	Dale			
C	Morgan			
DH	David			

Dale

"We're 24 morons and 1 Mormon."
John Kruk

2013 was Dale Murphy's last year of eligibility for making the Hall of Fame and I am disappointed that he did not make it. He'll get voted in by the Veterans Committee some day, but that's a little like kissing your sister: sweet, but not very exciting.

I picked two Hall-of-Famers out of my head and compared their career stats with Murphy's.

	Dale Murphy	Jim Rice	Chick Hafey
Hits	2,111	2,452	1,466
Home runs	398	382	164
RBIs	1,266	1,451	833
Stolen bases	161	58	70
Batting average	.265	.298	.317

So let's compare Murphy with Jim Rice. Rice's offensive numbers are slightly better, but Murphy won five Gold Gloves as a center fielder as well as back to back MVP Awards. Chick Hafey's numbers don't even come close to Murphy's except for the batting average. One must remember however, that batting averages during the 1920s and 1930s were on average considerably higher than they are today (a topic for another section).

The question is: because Murphy's numbers are so much better than Hafey's, and so similar to Rice's while being a better defender, what's going on here? I don't know if I just made an argument to vote Murphy in or to kick Hafey out. Hall of Fame voting "shall be based upon the player's record, playing ability, integrity, sportsmanship, character, and contributions to the teams on which he played." Sounds like the definition of Dale Murphy.

Murphy played for 18 years, mostly with the Atlanta Braves. He was one of the three most dominating players of the 1980s. Only Mike Schmidt had more home runs and only Eddie Murray had more RBIs in the decade. He was traded to the Philadelphia Phillies in 1990, prompting their flamboyant first baseman John Kruk to utter the quote at the opening of this section.

Besides the already impressive stats listed above, Murphy also played in seven All-Star games, and he played in every game for four consecutive years. One interesting footnote: Murphy is one of only three players to win two consecutive MVP awards and not make it to the Hall. The others are Roger Maris and Barry Bonds.

Dale Murphy

25. Which Murphy had the unusual nickname "Grandma"?

1B	Eddie	P	Hank
2B	Jackie	P	Humberto
3B	Brooks	P	Don
SS	Craig	P	Ron
OF	Bill	RP	Dewey
OF	Floyd		
OF	Frank		
C	Wilbert		
DH	Yank		

Jackie

"A life is not important except in the impact it has on other lives."
Jackie Robinson

The two most prominent black baseball pioneers are both named Robinson; Jackie, who broke the color barrier for players, and Frank, who broke it for managers.

When Branch Rickey and Clyde Sukeforth scoured the Negro Leagues for the best possible candidate to break the "gentleman's agreement" to bar blacks from integrating Major League Baseball, they did not pick the best hitter, the best pitcher, the fastest, the strongest or the slickest fielder. They did however, pick the best overall candidate for the trial by fire that awaited the major leagues' first black player. Rickey's criteria for picking the best candidate were that the player should be: 1) well-educated; 2) a fierce competitor; 3) a good ballplayer; 4) courageous, and 5) self-controlled. Robinson would be tested on three of these qualities in his very first interview. Rickey was a man who never used vulgarity, but he called Jackie every vile and racist name in the book in order to gauge Robinson's reaction. Jackie stoically absorbed the abuse, and Rickey knew that he had the right man.

No player in the history of the game endured more taunts and threats than did Jackie Robinson when he first came up. There had certainly been numerous racial insults before Jackie came along, but never to such a despicable degree. Native Americans like "Chief" Bender, the Hall of Fame pitcher for the Philadelphia Athletics and the great Jewish star Hank Greenberg suffered constant insults from the opposing bench, (Greenberg by the way, offered moral support to Jackie when he closed out his career in the National League). But neither of these men were denied basic sleeping quarters, transportation, or dining facilities while traveling with the team. Nor were their lives threatened on a daily basis. Robinson received the most vicious threats, both from letters and in verbal assaults from the fans in the stands, and even opposing players. A typical letter said, "Robinson, we are going to kill you if you attempt to enter a ball game at Crosley Field." Jackie endured this nightmare in silence. He had made a deal with Branch Rickey that he would "turn the other cheek" for the first three years. When the fourth year began, he came out fighting. The insults were significantly reduced.

The Brooklyn Dodgers derived immediate benefit from Robinson's arrival. He won Rookie of the Year in 1947, and the team then quickly signed future Hall-of- Fame catcher Roy Campanella and hard throwing right-hander Don Newcombe. This triumvirate, along with established stars like Duke Snider, Gil Hodges, and Carl Furillo made them the dominant team of the 1950s in the National League.

In Jackie's 10 years with the Dodgers they won six pennants and one World Series championship. Robinson won the MVP Award in 1949 by winning both the batting title and the stolen base title, a feat that stood for 51 years until Ichiro Suzuki won both titles in 2000. Campanella won three Most Valuable Player Awards and Newcombe is one of only two players to win a Cy Young Award, a Most Valuable Player Award, and a Rookie of the Year Award (Justin Verlander of the Detroit Tigers is the other).

The American League, with the exception of the Cleveland Indians, was much slower to sign black ballplayers. The last team to sign a black player was the Boston Red Sox who signed Pumpsie Green in 1959. The Red Sox actually had the first shot at Robinson in 1945 but turned him down. They then turned down a young Willie Mays in 1949. A Boston team of Robinson, Mays and Ted Williams most certainly would have stemmed the Bronx Bomber tide of the 1950s and '60s!

Ironically, baseball was Jackie's fourth best sport in his tenure at UCLA. He excelled at football, where he averaged 11 yards per carry in his junior year; basketball, where he led the conference in scoring; and track, where he was the NCAA broad jump champion. As great an athlete as he was, Jackie was also an exceptionally noble man, who could win over even his most ardent adversaries. When he was sent to Montreal to get a year's worth of Minor League experience, Royals' manager Clay Hopper asked Branch Rickey, "Do you really think a nigger is a human being?". By the end of the year Hopper was Jackie's biggest fan. At the end of Robinson's 1947 rookie season, a poll was taken that placed Jackie second to Bing Crosby as the nation's most admired man.

At the conclusion of the 1956 season, the Dodgers traded Robinson to the New York Giants. Rather than go to the team that all Dodger players hated, Jackie hung up his spikes. After 10 years in the major leagues he retired with a .311 batting average, 1,518 hits, 137 home runs, 734 RBIs, and 197 stolen bases. He was inducted into the Hall of Fame in 1962. Sadly, he died at age 53 of diabetes and heart failure. The stress he endured during his early years probably contributed to his early death. In 1997 Major League Baseball took the extraordinary step of having all teams retire his number (42).

Martin Luther King is rightly regarded as the greatest black American emancipator. I would argue that Jackie Robinson is a close second. In 1947, when Jackie broke into professional baseball, it truly was the national pastime, so the entire nation was focused on Rickey's brave experiment. If Jackie had failed, if he had not played at the highest level, if he had lost his temper in the early years, the experiment itself would have failed and its failure would have slowed the growing civil rights movement. In the words of Roger Kahn, "He bore the burden of the pioneer and the weight made him more strong. If one can be certain of anything in baseball, it is that we shall not look upon his like again."

Jackie Robinson

26. How many Gold Gloves did Brooks Robinson amass in his career?

1B	Paul	P	Bob
2B	Billy	P	Al
3B	Charlie	P	Sherry
SS	Ozzie	P	Frank
OF	Lonnie	RP	Lee
OF	Reggie		
OF	Elmer		
C	Earl		
DH	Seth		

Ozzie

*"He plays like he's on a mini-trampoline out there
or wearing helium kangaroo shorts maybe."*
Andy Van Slyke on Ozzie Smith

To the casual baseball fan, the most enduring memory of Ozzie Smith will be his signature pre-game feat, the back flip. To the baseball purist however, it's his incredible 13 consecutive Gold Gloves at one of the two toughest positions in the game. Ozzie is one of the few players to make it to the Hall of Fame based on his defensive achievements. We need to see more of this, especially for the skilled positions of shortstop, catcher, second base, and center field. Brooks Robinson is rightly lauded for his 16 Gold Gloves and is enshrined in Cooperstown because of his defense. I would argue that 13 Gold Gloves at shortstop is a far greater achievement than 16 at third base.

I've always believed that defense is given short shrift when the Baseball Writer's Association of America casts its votes for the Hall of Fame nominees. Sure, there are plenty of defensive wizards in the Hall: Willie Mays, Roberto Clemente, Tris Speaker, Al Kaline, Mike Schmidt and Pie Traynor to name a few, but they're in because of their offensive numbers. Until 1994, only a handful of players like Luis Aparicio, Brooks Robinson and Pee Wee Reese were enshrined for their outstanding defense. The Veterans Committee's election of Reese in

1984 started to amend this injustice. The selection of Reese begat the enshrinement of Phil Rizzuto (1994), Richie Ashburn (1995), Nellie Fox (1997), and the greatest second baseman ever, Bill Mazeroski (2001). In my opinion, the writers made grave mistakes by not voting in Ashburn, Fox, and Mazeroski during their 15-year eligibility periods. I hope they amend their ways when Omar Vizquel becomes eligible in 2017.

Ozzie made his major league debut with the San Diego Padres in 1978. In 1982 he was embroiled in a salary dispute with the San Diego owner Ray Kroc. Coincidentally, the outstanding St. Louis Cardinal shortstop, Gary Templeton, was having major PR problems with the fans. So the teams decided to swap shortstops. It seemed equitable at the time, but the Cardinals definitely got the better deal in the long run. Ozzie's career numbers are: .262 batting average, 2,460 hits, 793 RBIs, 580 stolen bases, 15 All-Star games and one World Series championship. His number (1) was retired by the Cardinals in 1996.

Ozzie Smith

27. How many career saves did Lee Smith attain?

1B	Frank	P	Tommy
2B	Derrel	P	Bud
3B	Frank	P	Myles
SS	Bud	P	Fay
OF	Roy	RP	Stan
OF	Gorman		
OF	George		
C	Ira		
DH	Pinch		

Frank

"In another 30 years, we may be talking about Frank Thomas in the same way we talk about Ted Williams."

Ken Harrelson in Frank's second year

Dustin Pedroia must be heaving a sigh of relief now that "The Big Hurt" is retired. Imagine the anxiety, no make that fear, of waiting for your shortstop to flip you the ball as you hear what sounds like a herd of thundering bison barreling toward you to break up the double play.

Frank Thomas may not have had Ty Cobb's anti-social ferocity, but the former Auburn tight end intimidated middle infielders by his sheer size and fierce determination. Thomas was indeed selected for Auburn as a football player, but after an injury, he switched full time to baseball, which he preferred anyway.

Frank was born on May 27, 1968 in Columbus, Georgia. He made his major league debut on August 2, 1990 with the Chicago White Sox, a team that he would spend almost his entire career with. He wasted no time establishing himself as a star in his first full year, when he batted .318, hit 32 home runs, batted in 109 runs, and walked a league-leading 138 times. He also won a Silver Slugger award and finished third in the MVP voting.

His breakout year was 1993, when he batted .317, smashed 41 round trippers, knocked in 128 runs, scored 196 times, and walked 112 times. He was the unanimous choice for the AL MVP Award.

Nicknamed "The Big Hurt," he nearly duplicated those numbers in 1994 to win his second consecutive MVP Award; his league-leading OPS was 1.217.

Thomas is arguably the greatest player to wear a White Sox uniform, greater than Shoeless Joe Jackson, Luke Appling, Eddie Collins, or Nellie Fox in my opinion. He holds several career club records including: runs (1,327), home runs (448), doubles (447), RBIs (1,465), extra base hits (906), walks (1,466), total bases (3,949), slugging percentage (.568), and on base percentage (.427).

Frank's career totals are: five All-Star games; four Silver Slugger awards; two MVP awards; 1997 batting champion (.347); .301 batting average; 521 home runs; 1,704 RBIs; 1,494 runs; 2,468 hits; .419 on base percentage; and a .555 slugging percentage.

Thomas is the only player to have seven consecutive seasons with at least a .300 average, 100 walks, 100 RBIs, 100 runs scored, and 20 home runs. Ted Williams is second with six consecutive years. There are only five players in history to exceed Thomas's numbers in both batting average and home runs: Hank Aaron, Babe Ruth, Willie Mays, Jimmie Foxx, and Manny Ramirez. Thomas was inducted into the Hall of Fame in 2014. His number was retired by the White Sox, who erected a statue of him in the outfield of Cellular Field.

Frank Thomas

28. The "other" Frank Thomas set the Met season home run record in 1962 with 34. Who broke his record in 1975 with 36 round trippers?

1B	Curt	P	Bill
2B	Todd	P	Luke
3B	Gee	P	Jerry
SS	Oscar	P	Tom
OF	Dixie	RP	Roy
OF	Harry		
OF	Larry		
C	Rube		
DH	Tilly		

Larry

Most Hall of Famers don't have the kind of year Larry Walker had in 1997. Then again, no Hall of Famer ever played home games in the rarefied air of Coors Field. Coors Field notwithstanding, a .366 batting average, 49 home runs, 130 RBIs, and 409 total bases was a year for the ages for Larry. Those 409 total bases by the way, were the most since Stan the Man had 429 in 1948. (Barry Bonds had 411 in 2001.) Walker also stole a career-high 33 bases that year. He was the obvious choice for the MVP award, his only one.

Born on December 1, 1966 in Maple Ridge, British Columbia, Walker, like most Canadian boys, aspired to be a professional hockey player when he grew up. But after failing to make the grade on skates, he turned to baseball, making his major league debut on August 16, 1989 with the Montreal Expos.

Playing for 17 seasons, Walker compiled the following career stats: 1,355 runs scored, 2,160 hits, 471 doubles, 383 home runs, 1,311 RBIs, and 913 walks. He was the MVP in 1997, captured three batting titles, won seven Gold Gloves, and was selected to five All-Star squads. Does he belong in the Hall? Bill James has developed a mathematical set of formulas called the Hall of Fame monitor list. The average player in the Hall has a score of 100. James gives Walker an astounding 148!

Dixie

"Stupidest thing I ever did was that petition."
Dixie Walker

"The People's Cherce," as he was known in Brooklyn, was an outstanding right fielder for 18 years in the big leagues. His career totals include: a .306 batting average, 105 home runs and 1,023 RBIs. He led the league in batting in 1944 with a .357 average, and the following year he led in RBIs with 124 and runs scored with 218.

Despite an outstanding career however, he will always be remembered for one of the most infamous capers in the history of the game. Several ballplayers on the 1947 Brooklyn Dodgers were opposed to playing with Jackie Robinson, but Walker took it a step further. He organized a group of his teammates to sign a petition stating that they refused to play if Jackie joined the team. It was blatant racism at its worst. Leo Durocher, the combative Brooklyn manager, with full support from team president Branch Rickey, told Dixie that he and the other signers would be traded if they did not relent. The petitioners ultimately gave in and agreed to play alongside Robinson. Nevertheless, the Dodgers traded their All-Star outfielder to the Pittsburgh Pirates the following year.

Dixie Walker

29. Dixie Walker's brother Harry won the batting title in 1947 with a .363 average. What team did he play for?

1B	Cy	P	Woody
2B	Davey	P	Stan
3B	Matt	P	Charlie
SS	Otto	P	Lefty
OF	Billy	RP	Mitch
OF	Bernie		
OF	Walt		
C	Earl		
DH	Ted		

Ted

"A man has to have goals, mine was to have people say there goes Ted Williams, the greatest hitter who ever lived."

A strong case can certainly be made to substantiate Williams's goal to be the greatest hitter who ever lived. His .344 lifetime average is only the sixth-best all time, but it's the highest in the live ball era. His lifetime total of 521 home runs, 1,839 RBIs, and 2,654 hits, impressive as it is, falls short of many who are in the Hall of Fame. However, those in the Hall did not miss nearly *five* years in their prime due to military service.

Had Williams not missed those years in the service, he would most likely place first or second in career runs scored, RBIs, total bases, extra base hits, and possibly home runs. Nor were these numbers aided by performance-enhancing drugs. His career slugging percentage of .634 is second only to Babe Ruth, and his .482 on-base percentage is the highest ever. He won six batting titles (and came in second four more times), four home run titles, nine slugging titles, two Triple Crowns and two Most Valuable Player Awards. He missed out on another Triple Crown by losing the batting title to George Kell by .0002. Williams placed second in the Most Valuable Player voting four times. One could easily make the case that he should have won all of those, especially in 1947, when he lost to Joe DiMaggio by a single point. The Sporting

News named him Player of the Decade for the 1950s. He was a first ballot inductee to the Hall of Fame in 1966 and was named by Major League Baseball to the all-time team.

Ted made his Major League debut with the Boston Red Sox in 1939, and when his teammates said, "Wait until you see Jimmie Foxx hit," he responded with "Wait until Foxx sees me hit." He backed up his cockiness by collecting 145 RBIs, a record for a rookie. In 1941 Ted became the last player to hit over .400, hitting .406. Back then sacrifice flies counted as an at bat. Under today's rules, where they do not count as an at bat, he would have hit for about a .417 average! He also had an astounding .553 on-base percentage.

Williams actually came in second in the MVP voting that year to Joe DiMaggio, who had that incredible 56-game hitting streak. Many would argue that Ted's 1957 season was even more incredible than his 1941 season. At age 39, Ted led the league with a .388 average. When you consider that he surely lost multiple "leg" hits, he could have batted .400 yet again. He also set a major league record that year by reaching base 16 consecutive times.

Williams completely terrorized American League pitchers during the 22 years he spent in the league. They would seek guidance from their coaches and teammates with respect to how to pitch to him. Said Paul Richards, manager of the Chicago White Sox, "Best thing to do against Williams was to let him do his thing and then concentrate on the next batter." When Bobby Shantz of the Yankees asked how to pitch Ted, he was told, "He won't hit anything bad, but don't give him anything good." Williams's reluctance to swing at anything bad enabled him to accumulate 2,021 career walks. These walks, combined with his batting average, enabled Williams to reach base safely an incredible 48 percent of the time!

Many baseball men, including Ty Cobb and Al Simmons, criticized Williams for taking all those walks. They argued that with a man in scoring position he should have swung at a close pitch that was just off the corner to try to drive in a run. But Williams refused to contradict his fundamental law of batting, which was to get a good pitch to hit. The man who instilled that philosophy in Ted was none other than the great Rogers Hornsby, who sided with Williams against Cobb and company.

Ted never really had a baseball hero as a kid, but he did try to imitate Bill Terry, which is ironic because Terry was the last man to bat over .400 before Ted did in 1941. Before signing with the Red Sox Williams tried out with the St. Louis Cardinals, who passed on him. He was later offered a contract by the New York Yankees along with a $500 bonus. When his mother insisted that the bonus be $1,000, the Yankees declined. Can you imagine Williams playing in the same outfield with either Musial or DiMaggio for all those years? Twice the Red Sox almost lost Williams. Before the 1947 season he was offered the princely sum of $300,000 to jump to the fledgling Mexican League. He turned down the offer and signed with Boston for $70,000. In April of that same year, Red Sox owner Tom Yawkey met with Yankees owner Dan Topping and verbally consummated a trade of Ted Williams for Joe DiMaggio. The trade was nullified the next morning when Yawkey insisted that Topping include Yogi Berra as well.

Williams was as much a hero off the diamond as he was on it. He earned nearly as many military medals for his feats as a fighter pilot in World War II and Korea as he won for his baseball feats. In 1991, he was presented with the Presidential Medal of Freedom. He was the most influential person in helping to raise funds for the Children's Cancer Research Foundation. One of his greatest moments came during his speech for his Hall of Fame induction. In it, he made an impassioned case for the election of the stars of the old Negro Leagues, such as Satchel Paige and Josh Gibson. He was as much a perfectionist in his hobby of fly fishing as he was in hitting a baseball and was inducted into the Fishing Hall of Fame.

Williams had a tumultuous love/hate relationship with the Boston fans and especially with the Boston sportswriters, but when he retired after the 1960 season, (his last at bat was a home run), a noted sportswriter said that Boston now knew how Britain felt when it lost India.

Ted Williams

30. Ted Williams was succeeded in left field by what future Hall-of-Famer who was then subsequently succeeded by what additional Hall-of-Famer?

1B	Owen	P	Earl
2B	Gary	P	Jim
3B	Parke	P	Jack
SS	Jack	P	Don
OF	Mookie	RP	Brian
OF	Willie		
OF	Hack		
C	Dan		
DH	Dan		

Hack

*"Hack Wilson was built along the lines of a beer keg,
and not unfamiliar with its contents."*
Shirley Povich

Hack Wilson looked more like a Bulgarian Olympic weightlifter than a major league ballplayer, but for five years (1926-1930), he was one of the premier sluggers in the National League. Hack made his major league debut on September 23, 1923 with John McGraw's New York Giants. His 5'6" 190 pound frame served him well as a catcher, but he broke his leg before coming up to the big leagues where McGraw moved him to the outfield. He was quite a sight with his beer-barrel frame and 18" neck atop his size 5.5 feet shagging flies in center field. He played well in parts of three seasons for the Giants, but McGraw sent him down to the minors for further instruction. When a front office oversight left him unprotected, the Chicago Cubs picked him up on waivers. His Giants teammate, Hall-of-Famer Ross Youngs, said at the time, "They let go the best outfielder I ever played alongside, and they're going to regret it."

In 1930 he had a year that may never be duplicated. Of course, many other players had phenomenal years in 1930 as well, including Bill Terry, the last man to hit .400 in the National League. Evidently the ball was tampered with that year, much to the chagrin of the pitchers.

Supposedly the seams were flat so that pitchers could not maximize their curve balls, and Australian wool was injected into the core to make the balls more like golf balls than baseballs. The experiment ended after the 1930 season. The lively ball notwithstanding, Wilson hit 56 home runs, which was a National League record until Mark McGwire and Sammy Sosa broke it in 1998. His RBIs total of 191 still stands as the major league season record.

His career plummeted after that astounding 1930 season, and he was out of baseball by 1934. His career stats include a .307 batting average, 244 home runs (leading the league four times), and 1,063 RBIs. He was voted into the Hall of Fame by the Veterans Committee in 1979. Hack was a heavy drinker and brawler while he was playing, and these traits carried over into retirement. He died an alcoholic and a pauper on November 23, 1948 in Baltimore, Maryland. He was 48 years old.

Wilson realized that he squandered his talent through drinking, brawling, and carousing. In a radio interview one week before his death he said, "Talent isn't enough. You need common sense and good advice. If anyone tries to tell you different, tell them the story of Hack Wilson. Don't let what happened to me happen to you."

Hack Wilson

31. What was closer Brian Wilson's iconic trademark?

Fourth Inning

Alphabet Soup

1B	Cap Anson	P	Grover Alexander
2B	Roberto Alomar	P	Johnny Antonelli
3B	Luke Appling	P	Babe Adams
SS	Luis Aparicio	P	Ken Appier
OF	Earl Averill	RP	Hank Aguirre
OF	Richie Ashburn		
OF	Hank Aaron		
C	Sandy Alomar		
DH	Dick Allen		

Hank Aaron

*"Trying to sneak a fastball by Hank Aaron
is like trying to sneak the sunrise past a rooster."*
Curt Simmons

There are many adjectives one could employ in describing Hank Aaron's baseball career, but the best one that comes to my mind is consistency. Like Stan Musial and Willie Mays, he played at the highest level game after game and year after year. The Sporting News once ranked him the fifth best player of all time.

Aaron's consistency is borne out by the fact that he is the only player to hit 30 or more home runs at least 15 times. He holds the major league record of appearing in 25 All-Star games (21 years). He is one of only four players to collect over 500 home runs and 3,000 hits; the other three are Willie Mays, Eddie Murray, and Rafael Palmeiro. Aaron's career statistics are staggering: .305 batting average, 3,771 hits, 755 home runs, 2,297 RBIs, 2,174 runs, 6,856 total bases, 1,477 extra base hits, 3,298 games, one Most Valuable Player Award, and three Gold Gloves. When he retired in 1976 he was the all-time leader in home runs, and indeed many fans still consider him the home run king due to the performance-enhancing drugs used by his successor, Barry Bonds. He still holds the record for most career RBIs, extra base hits, and total bases. Aaron was inducted into the Hall of Fame in 1983 on the first ballot with 97.83% of the vote, second only to Ty Cobb who was elected with 98.2% of the vote. Both Turner Field in Atlanta and Miller Park in Milwaukee have statues of Aaron on the grounds.

Hank made his major league debut in 1954 with the Milwaukee Braves, replacing Bobby Thompson who broke his leg. Bobby would never get his job back. Hank was there to stay. He was the last player to be recruited from the Negro Leagues, where he played shortstop for the Indianapolis Clowns. Curiously, two other teams passed him up before the Braves landed him. At the tender age of 15 he tried out for the Brooklyn Dodgers but didn't make the cut. The New York Giants made him an offer as did the Boston Braves in 1952. Hank later reminisced, "I had the Giants contract in my hand. But the Braves offered $50 a month more. That's the only thing that kept Willie Mays and me from being teammates – 50 dollars." With Aaron to go along with Mays, Willie McCovey, Orlando Cepeda and Juan Marichal, the Giants would have dominated the National League for two decades!

Hank was born into a poor household on February 5, 1934 in Mobile, Alabama. As a young boy he picked cotton, which he said strengthened his hands. He experienced racism in the Jim Crow South as he was growing up, but it was nothing compared to what he endured when he broke into the big leagues, and especially when he mounted his assault on Babe Ruth's career home run record.

Aaron's experience with virulent racism was not unique to him. Most if not all black players who came up to the major leagues during the 1950s suffered the same fate. Nevertheless the experience had a profound effect on Aaron, which he carried throughout his life. He could not stay in the same hotels as his white teammates nor eat in the same restaurants with them while travelling through the south. Spring training was particularly tough.

Hank recalled an incident while he was still with the Indianapolis Clowns and his team was in Washington D.C. This story, perhaps more than any other, demonstrates the awful indignities that he endured for the first few years in organized baseball. "We had breakfast while we were waiting for the rain to stop, and I can still envision sitting with the Clowns in a restaurant behind Griffith Stadium and hearing them break all the plates in the kitchen after we had finished eating. What a horrible sound. Even as a kid, the irony of it hit me: here we were in the capital in the land of freedom and equality, and they had to destroy the plates that had touched the forks that had been in the mouths of black men. If dogs had eaten off those plates, they'd have washed them."[5]

Aaron was the quintessential raw-boned rookie when he first came up. He ate pork chops three meals a day because that was the only dish that he knew how to order. At 6'0" and 180 pounds, he did not look like the man who would shatter the Babe's home run record, but those strong hands and sinewy wrists enabled him to hit a baseball with explosive power. He didn't even hold the bat properly. As a right handed hitter, he placed his left hand on top of his right until his coaches and teammates broke him of the habit. Even after correcting his hand placement, Hank still had an unorthodox batting technique, especially for a power hitter.

George Plimpton, in *One for the Record*, commented on it: "The odd thing about Aaron's attitude at the plate is that there is nothing to suggest any such intensity of purpose. Aaron steps into the batter's box as if he were going to sit down in it somewhere. First of all, Hank Aaron's swing is all wrong. He hits off the front foot. The great hitting text book in the sky says you swing with weight more on your back foot to get more power."

Physical traits alone did not enable Hank to become one of the most prolific hitters in the history of the game. His powers of concentration at the plate were unshakable. Even as he was sitting on the bench he would study the opposing pitcher by looking through a hole in his cap in order to focus only on the pitcher.

Boston Red Sox fans speak about the "Curse of the Bambino,"

referring to the team's failure to win a World Series for almost a century after they sold Babe Ruth to the Yankees. An even greater curse of the Bambino applied to Hank Aaron as he closed in on Ruth's career home run record of 714. He finished one home run short of the record at the end of the 1973 season. What should have been a wonderful winter of 1973-74 became a nightmare for Aaron as thousands of the most vile racist hate mail, including threats on his life, came pouring into the Braves' front office. Ever the gentleman, Hank stated during that terrible winter that, "Even if I'm lucky enough to hit 715 home runs, Babe Ruth will still be regarded as the greatest home run hitter who ever lived." He survived the vitriol and broke Ruth's record on April 8, 1974.

Hank Aaron

32. Name the only player active when Ruth hit his last home run and Aaron hit his first.

B's

1B	Wade Boggs	P	Bert Blyleven
2B	Craig Biggio	P	Jim Bunning
3B	George Brett	P	Chief Bender
SS	Ernie Banks	P	Three Finger Brown
OF	Barry Bonds	RP	Mark Buehrle
OF	Paul Blair		
OF	Lou Brock		
C	Johnny Bench		
DH	Yogi Berra		

Johnny Bench

*"I don't want to embarrass any other
catcher by comparing him to Johnny Bench."*
Sparky Anderson

As you enter the Cincinnati Reds Hall of Fame building in the Great American Ballpark complex you're struck by the larger than life statue of Johnny Bench in the act of throwing out a base runner with his cannon of an arm. The statue speaks to the greatness of Bench as a player as well as the devotion of the Cincinnati fans to one of the greatest players in the history of the franchise.

In 1999 The Sporting News ranked him as the 16th-greatest player ever and ESPN voted him the greatest catcher of all time. Bench had the extremely rare combination of excellence on both offense and defense. In my humble opinion, he and Willie Mays are the only two players who may be the best of all-time at their positions in both departments (although Ivan Rodriguez may have been a tad better defensively than Bench). His prowess behind the plate included the ability to catch or block whatever came his way as well as his superb talent at handling pitchers and throwing out base runners. He also perfected the art of catching with one hand, thus protecting his throwing hand. Like Gil Hodges and Ernie Lombardi, he had enormous hands and every so often caught errant pitches with his bare hand. He has posed for pictures showing him holding seven baseballs in his big paw! In their book "Baseball Anecdotes," Daniel Okrent and Steve Wulf tell of the time Bench actually caught a pitch with his bare hand. On the mound was Gerry Arrigo, a journeyman pitcher who had long ago lost the zip on his fastball. Bench called for a curve ball, knowing that Arrigo could not blow a fast one by the hitter. After Arrigo insisted on throwing his fastball, Bench capitulated. Arrigo's pitch was wide of the plate. Bench displayed his disdain for the mediocre fastball by catching the ball barehanded.

Bench made his major league debut in 1968 and quickly drew the attention of baseball people by winning the Rookie of the Year and a Gold Glove. One of those he impressed in that rookie year was Ted Williams. When Bench asked Ted for his autograph, Williams responded by signing it, "To Johnny Bench, a Hall of Famer for sure". In 1970, in what was perhaps the greatest year ever for a catcher, he led the National League in home runs (45) and RBIs (148), propelling him to the NL MVP Award. He duplicated the feat in 1972, again leading the league in home runs (40), RBIs (125) and winning his second MVP Award. In 1974 he led the league in RBIs (129) and total bases (315). And in the 1976 World Series, he went 8 for 15 with two home runs to win MVP honors.

Bench's career numbers include: 389 home runs, 1,376 RBIs, two Most Valuable Player Awards, 10 consecutive Gold Gloves and 14 All-Star game appearances. He was a first ballot Hall of Famer, garnering 96% of the vote. He played his entire career (17 seasons) with the Cincinnati Reds. Oh, and by the way, he was his high school valedictorian!

Johnny Bench

33. What two consecutive years did Ernie Banks
win the Most Valuable Player Award?

1B	Orlando Cepeda	P	Roger Clemens
2B	Eddie Collins	P	Steve Carton
3B	Miguel Cabrera	P	Stan Coveleski
SS	Joe Cronin	P	Jack Chesbro
OF	Max Carey	RP	Norm Charleton
OF	Ty Cobb		
OF	Roberto Clemente		
C	Roy Campanella		
DH	Rod Carew		

Ty Cobb

"Baseball is a red-blooded sport for red-blooded men....
It's a struggle for supremacy, a survival of the fittest."
Ty Cobb

"**O**nce, on a golf course, I was about to putt on the fifth green when I heard a voice yelling, 'Get out of my way, I'm coming through!' Then came the demand again. So I made way and Ty Cobb played right through me without apology. I guess nobody but the great Cobb would dare do that to a president." So said Dwight Eisenhower in 1964. I chose to start this section with this quote because it reflects Cobb's arrogance, egotism, recklessness, and utter contempt for his fellow man, traits that defined him just as much as his playing ability.

A valid argument can be made that Ty Cobb is one of the greatest players of all-time. Indeed, Charles Comiskey, owner of the Chicago White Sox for 31 years, called Cobb "*the* greatest player of all time." An equally valid argument can also be made that no player ever played with more ferocity than the great Cobb. It was said that he played with a competitive ferocity that bordered on paranoia.

One of the most enduring qualities about baseball is its timelessness. Hence, a boy can argue with his dad whether Albert Pujols is better than Mike Schmidt. His father and grandfather can argue whether Schmidt was better than Willie Mays, who will in turn argue with the historians that Ruth or Cobb was the best.

What is certain is that excluding pitchers, Ty Cobb and Honus Wagner were heads and shoulders above their peers for the first 20 years of the 20th century. Joe DiMaggio was probably the first great five-tool player, a player who excels in hitting, hitting with power, fielding, throwing, and running. Cobb obviously excelled in hitting and running. His fielding and throwing were above average. But because he played in the dead ball era, it's hard to gauge what his power hitting would have been. However, when he wanted to, he could demonstrate power at the plate. In 1925 he predicted to a group of sportswriters that he could hit home runs if he wanted to. He hit five in the next two games! He simply preferred his brand of baseball to that of the power game. So perhaps both Cobb and Wagner would be considered five-tool players if they played 20 years later than they did.

Besides possessing tremendous physical baseball talent, Cobb was also one of the shrewdest players to ever wear a big league uniform. He and teammate Sam Crawford devised several ploys that involved double steals or going from first to third on bunts. Cobb even figured out how to take advantage of the great Walter Johnson. Walter dominated hitters the way Cobb dominated pitchers, but his easy-going demeanor was the antithesis of Cobb's ferocity. When Ty discovered that Johnson was afraid of killing a batter with his blazing fastball, he crowded the plate against him so much that Walter either walked him or gave him a pitch right into his sweet spot.

A chronology of Ty Cobb's major league career is one of the most impressive in history. He led or tied the American League in the following categories:

1907   Batting avg. (.350), hits (212), slugging avg. (.468), RBIs (119), total bases (283), stolen bases (49).

1908   Batting avg. (.324), hits (188), slugging avg. (.475), RBIs (108), total bases (276), doubles (36), triples (20).

1909   Triple Crown (.377, 9 HRs, 107 RBIs), slugging avg. (.517), total bases (296), hits (216), runs (116), stolen bases (76).

1910   Batting avg. (.385), slugging avg. (.554), runs (106).

1911   Batting avg. (.420), RBIs (127), stolen bases (83), slugging avg. (.621), hits (248), runs (147), doubles (47), triples (24), total bases (367).

1912   Batting avg. (.410), slugging avg. (.586), hits (227).

1913   Batting avg. (.390).

1914   Batting avg. (.368), slugging avg. (.513).

1915   Batting avg. (.369), total bases (274), runs (144), hits (208), stolen bases (96).

1916   Runs (113), stolen bases (68).

1917   Batting avg. (.383), slugging avg. (.570), hits (225), total bases (335), doubles (44), triples (24), stolen bases (55).

1918   Batting avg. (.382), triples (14).

1919   Batting avg. (.384), hits (191).

Cobb retired with the following career statistics: 3,034 games played, 11,434 at bats, 2,246 runs, 4,189 hits, 724 doubles, 295 triples, 117 home runs, 1,938 RBIs, 897 stolen bases, 1,249 walks, 5,854 total bases, and a .367 batting average. All of his career numbers have been eclipsed, except for his lifetime batting average, which I believe will never be broken.

In 1936, Cobb was a member of the inaugural class of players--- along with Ruth, Johnson, Wagner, and Christy Mathewson---to be elected to the Hall of Fame. In a detail that surely pleased him, he received a higher percentage of the vote (98.2%) than Ruth (95.1%) or any of his other contemporaries.

Ty Cobb

34. Norm Charlton was one of three relief pitchers for the Cincinnati Reds of the late 1980s and early 1990s dubbed the "Nasty Boys". Who were the other two?

1B	Carlos Delgado	P	Dizzy Dean
2B	Bobby Doerr	P	Don Drysdale
3B	Josh Donaldson	P	Wild Bill Donovan
SS	George Davis	P	Paul Derringer
OF	Larry Doby	RP	Rob Dibble
OF	Joe DiMaggio		
OF	Andre Dawson		
C	Bill Dickey		
DH	Ed Delahanty		

Joe DiMaggio

" You've bought yourself a cripple."
Bill Terry ridiculing George Weiss for purchasing
Joe DiMaggio from the San Francisco Seals

Joe DiMaggio was the first five-tool player in major league history in my opinion. As I stated in the previous section, Ty Cobb probably had all five tools as well, but since he played in the dead ball era, we'll never know what his power numbers would have been. Perhaps Honus Wagner and Tris Speaker would also be candidates. If Babe Ruth could run and Rogers Hornsby could throw, they too would be candidates. Remember that a complete five-tool player is one who excels at hitting, hitting for power, fielding, throwing, and running. Center field is usually the prototypical position for a five-tool player, since you rarely find a slow or weak-armed player patrolling the middle of the outfield. But speed isn't necessarily measured by stolen bases alone. DiMaggio had only 30 stolen bases in his career, but he could run down balls hit into the gap and stretch singles into doubles and doubles into triples better than most of his contemporaries. Indeed, his nickname, "the Yankee Clipper" was due to his speed in the outfield. He was also a smart base runner. In his entire career, he was never thrown out going from first to third!

He was born Giuseppe Paolo DiMaggio on November 25, 1914 of poor immigrant parents who had just arrived in California from Sicily. His father was a fisherman and wanted Joe and his brothers to be fishermen as well, but they would not abide by his wishes. Joe and his brothers Dom and Vince had baseball in their sights. Joe's father called him lazy and a good-for-nothing for choosing baseball over fishing. Fathers don't always know best.

He was a lonely hero who possessed both grace and greed in equal amounts. He was detached, often to the point of rudeness. One of his teammates quipped that he was so private that he led the league in room service. He was a private person who nevertheless was constantly in the limelight. He became an American icon who was the subject of songs, books, shows, movie appearances, and television programs. Ernest Hemingway's "The Old Man and the Sea" has the old salt yearning to have seen the great DiMaggio play. When Paul Simon wrote "Where have you gone Joe DiMaggio? Our nation turns its lonely eyes to you," Joltin' Joe tried to sue Simon for royalties.

Nineteen thirty-six saw two of the game's greatest players make their major league debut: Joe DiMaggio and Bob Feller. DiMaggio set a rookie record by scoring 132 runs. In 1937 he led the league in runs (151) and total bases (418). In 1939 he led the league in batting with a .381 average and was voted MVP. He led the league in batting again in 1940 with a .352 average. His greatest year was 1941. He led the league in RBIs (125), total bases (348), hit in 56 straight games, and won another MVP Award. He captured the MVP a third time in 1947, winning by one vote over Ted Williams, even though Ted won the Triple Crown. Finally, in 1948 he led the league in RBIs (155), home runs (39), and total bases (355).

The aforementioned 56-game hitting streak is DiMaggio's crowning achievement. It is a record that many baseball fans think will never be broken. The streak is an incredible feat, but if Ken Keltner, third baseman for the Cleveland Indians had not made two outstanding plays to end it at 56 games, the streak would have gone to an astounding 73 games! If Joe had extended the streak to just one more game, the Heinz ketchup company would have paid him $10,000. It captivated the entire country. The Ken Burns documentary featured an interview with baseball historian Robert Creamer who remembered being in a backwater grocery store in Montana and overhearing a gentleman come into the store and asking the clerk behind the counter, "Did he get one yesterday?" There was no need to include the who or the what.

At the peak of their careers, Joe DiMaggio and Ted Williams were almost traded for each other. Williams would have feasted on the short right field fence at Yankee stadium, but not as much as DiMaggio would have at Fenway Park, with its shallow "green monster" in left field. Bill James claims that DiMaggio was robbed of more home runs than any other player in history due to the cavernous expanse of Yankee Stadium's left field. Left center field was 457 feet!

The streak, as impressive as it is, is not, in my opinion, DiMaggio's greatest legacy. Rather, it's his contribution to the Yankee's championship teams. In his 13 years as a Yankee, they won 10 pennants and nine World Series. He was the mainstay of those teams.

Joe DiMaggio

35. Joe DiMaggio's 56-game hitting streak was not the longest of his career. What was his longest consecutive game hitting streak, what team did he play for when he got it, and what year was it?

E's

1B	Darrell Evans	P	Carl Erksine
2B	Johnny Evers	P	Scott Erickson
3B	Bob Elliott	P	Shawn Estes
SS	David Ekstein	P	Dock Ellis
OF	Darin Erstad	RP	Dennis Eckersley
OF	Jim Edmonds		
OF	Dwight Evans		
C	Buck Ewing		
DH	Del Ennis		

Dennis Eckersley

"It's like the Kennedy assassination. Everyone I see comes up and tells me where they were and what they were doing when Gibson hit that home run."
Dennis Eckersley

Dennis Eckersley and I have one thing in common: we both grew up idolizing Willie Mays. I followed Willie the New York Giant. Dennis followed Willie the San Francisco Giant. The similarity ends there. Eckersley could hit the outside of the plate at will (with at least one notable exception); I couldn't throw three strikes in a row.

He was one of a select few that redefined the role of the relief pitcher, specifically that of the closer. When I was a kid following Major League Baseball, there was a spattering of relief specialists: Hoyt Wilhelm, Roy Face, Dick Raddatz, and Ryne Duren, to name a few, but with the exception of Wilhelm these pitchers were not stars. For baseball's first 100 years, relievers were usually pitchers who weren't good enough to make the starting rotation. In the 1970s relief pitchers like Sparky Lyle and Ron Perranoski started to change the game in a profound way. The Yankees and Dodgers would bring them in from the bullpen if their teams had a lead in the ninth inning to *close* out the game. Soon afterwards stars such as Dennis Eckersley, Rollie Fingers, Goose Gossage, Bruce Sutter, Lee Smith, Rob Dibble and John Franco became one of the most valuable players on their respective teams. The era of the superstar closer had arrived, culminating in the greatest of them all, Mariano Rivera of the New York Yankees.

Eckersley made his major league debut as a starter for the Cleveland Indians on April 12, 1975. He was quite successful in that role, including a no-hitter against the California Angels on May 30, 1977. Soon thereafter, a controversy arose that precipitated his being traded to the Boston Red Sox before the 1978 season. Supposedly, his wife was having an affair with teammate Rick Manning. The atmosphere in the Cleveland clubhouse was explosive. One of them had to go. Manning was to be the next Mickey Mantle, so Eckersley was traded. Manning never equaled Mantle and Eckersley went to the Hall of Fame.

Like Ralph Branca a generation before him, Dennis Eckersley will be remembered by casual fans as the pitcher who gave up the home run to Kirk Gibson in game one of the 1988 World Series with two outs, two strikes, and the tying run on base in the bottom of the ninth inning. That is grossly unfair. Dennis Eckersley was a six time All-Star, Most Valuable Player and Cy Young Award winner in 1992, had 390 career saves (fifth- best all-time), is one of only two pitchers with both a 20-win and a 50-save season (the other is John Smoltz). He is the only pitcher in history to have more saves than base runners allowed, is a first ballot Hall-of-Famer, and was voted to the Sporting News 100 greatest player list.

Dennis Eckersley

36. Who is the only player to hit a home run on his first time up in the major leagues, and never hit another?

1B	Jimmie Foxx	P	Bob Feller
2B	Nellie Fox	P	Whitey Ford
3B	Frankie Frisch	P	Red Faber
SS	Jim Fregosi	P	Bob Friend
OF	George Foster	RP	Rollie Fingers
OF	Curt Flood		
OF	Carl Furillo		
C	Carlton Fisk		
DH	Prince Fielder		

Bob Feller

"I don't think anyone is ever going to throw a ball faster than Bob Feller. And his curve ball isn't human."
Joe DiMaggio

The late 1930s witnessed the American League debut of three of the greatest players to ever play in that league: Joe DiMaggio, Ted Williams, and Bob Feller. Feller became the mainstay of a Cleveland Indian rotation that was one of the best, if not *the* best ever. Along with Feller it included Bob Lemon, Early Wynn, and Mike Garcia. Feller, Lemon, and Wynn went to the Hall of Fame.

Born on November 3, 1918 in Van Meter, Iowa, Bob Feller was a true baseball prodigy who went straight to the major leagues from high school. After watching his son pitch five no-hitters in seven games in high school, Bob's father recognized his son's phenomenal potential and went so far as to switch from planting oats and corn on his 360 acre farm to wheat because of the shorter growing season, thus affording both father and son the ability to devote more time to the latter's development. Dad went a step further by building a regulation size baseball field complete with seats and a concession stand and invited local semi-pro players to compete so that Bob could get real game experience. This was the real Iowa "Field of Dreams", not the movie version.

Bob made his major league debut with the Cleveland Indians on July 19, 1936 at just 17 years of age. He played his entire career with the them, retiring at the conclusion of the 1956 season. In his first game as a starter, he struck out 15 St. Louis Browns. Three weeks later, he set an American League record by striking out 17 Philadelphia A's. Immediately after his successful rookie season he went back to Van Meter to finish high school!

In 1937, his first full season, he recorded 150 strikeouts in 149 innings. He started to reach his full potential in 1938 when he set another record with 18 strikeouts in a game. His 240 K's led the league. In 1939 he led the league in strikeouts (246), wins (24), and innings (297). No pitcher in major league history got off to a finer start than "Rapid Robert" did in 1940, when he no-hit the Chicago White Sox on opening day. He went on to lead the league in wins (27), innings (320.1), complete games (31), ERA (2.61), and strikeouts (261). He was just as good the following year, when he led the league in wins (25), innings (343), strikeouts (260), and shutouts (6).

Three months after the 1941 season, the Japanese bombed Pearl Harbor and the United States declared war on Japan. Bob Feller enlisted in the United States Navy two days later. He was the first professional athlete to do so. He tried to become a fighter pilot, but did not pass the hearing test. He did become a Chief Petty Officer on the USS Alabama. He earned six campaign ribbons and eight battle stars during the war.

He returned to the Indians for the second half of the 1945 season. A year later he led the league in strikeouts (348), innings pitched (an astounding 371.1), and tied for the lead in wins (26).

Feller's peer, the great slugger Hank Greenberg, used to feast on opposing pitchers in part by having his third base coach steal the signs from the catcher and relay them back to him before the pitch. After his retirement from the game, Greenberg said, "The only pitcher I wouldn't steal the signs from was Bob Feller. If my third base coach told me a curve was coming and he was wrong-- if it was a fast ball-- I could get killed."[6]

Feller made eight All-Star appearances, pitched for the 1948 World Champions, won pitching's triple crown in 1940, threw three no-hitters, led the American League in wins six times, and led the league in strikeouts seven times. He was inducted into the Hall of Fame in his first year of eligibility in 1962, and in 1988 was ranked as the 36th-best player of all time by the Sporting News. The Cleveland Indians changed their Man of the Year Award to the Bob Feller Man of the Year Award in 2010.

Bob Feller

37. In 1936 Bob Feller struck out 17 batters in a game, making him the first pitcher to have the same amount of strikeouts as his age.
Which pitcher repeated the feat with 20 strikeouts?

1B	Lou Gehrig	P	Lefty Grove
2B	Charley Gehringer	P	Bob Gibson
3B	Troy Glaus	P	Lefty Gomez
SS	Nomar Garciaparra	P	Tom Glavine
OF	Goose Goslin	RP	Goose Gossage
OF	Ken Griffey		
OF	Tony Gwynn		
C	Jerry Grote		
DH	Hank Greenberg		

Lou Gehrig

"He was a symbol of indestructibility – a Gibraltar in cleats."
Newspaper columnist Jim Murray on Lou Gehrig

There's an old story about the manager of an American League team back in the 1920s and '30s who was worried about keeping his job because his team had finished in last place. He pleaded with the owner that he was just two players short of finishing in first place. "Is that right," asked the owner incredulously. "That's right," quipped the beleaguered manager, "as long as the two players are Babe Ruth and Lou Gehrig." Indeed, the addition of Ruth and Gehrig to any team in the major leagues in those days could well have propelled that team into first place.

For the better part of a decade Babe Ruth and Lou Gehrig were two of the three most significant players in Major League Baseball (Rogers Hornsby would be the third). What Ruth and Gehrig had in common was that they both played for the New York Yankees and both were absolute monsters offensively. The similarities ended there. Where Ruth was a boisterous, flamboyant, hard-drinking, womanizing hurricane, Gehrig was quiet, humble, soft-spoken, and of high moral character. He made half of Ruth's salary, yet was the second best player in the league. When you see a picture of Lou Gehrig posing with his teammates, you're immediately struck by the difference between him and the others, much like Honus Wagner and Harmon Killebrew stand out in similar fashion in their team pictures. The broadness of their shoulders compared to their teammates is palpable. When Hank Greenberg, who had very broad shoulders of his own, first saw Gehrig he said, "That guy has shoulders a yard wide and legs like mighty oak trees. I'd never seen such sheer brute strength." Gehrig's athleticism and power enabled him to star at fullback for Columbia University.

After scout Paul Krichell saw Gehrig hit a ball over the grandstands in a college game, he wired the Yankee front office saying, "I think I saw another Ruth today." The Yankees signed him soon thereafter and never looked back. When first baseman Wally Pipp complained of a headache on June 1, 1925, manager Miller Huggins substituted Gehrig. That was the beginning of one of baseball's most enduring records; a string of 2,130 consecutive games played, a record that stood for 56 years until broken by Cal Ripken. Gehrig led the American League in the following years and categories:

1927	RBIs (175), doubles (52), and total bases (447). (Gehrig also won the Most Valuable Player Award. Ruth had a better year, but the rules back then stipulated that no player could win it two years in a row.)
1928	Doubles (47), RBIs (tied with Ruth with 142).
1931	RBIs (184), hits (211) runs (163), total bases (210), and tied for home runs (46).
1934	Triple Crown (.363 batting average, 49 home runs, and 165 RBIs).
1935	Runs (125) and walks (132)
1936	Home runs (49), runs (167), on base percentage (.478), slugging average (.696), walks (130). (Gehrig won his second Most Valuable Player Award.)

In 1938 Gehrig had his 13th consecutive season of 100 or more RBIs.

This was a record he shared with Jimmie Foxx until Alex Rodriguez surpassed it in 2010. It was an off year for him, although most players would have loved to have those statistics. He batted .295, drove in 114 runs, accumulated 170 hits, and hit 29 home runs. At the beginning of the 1939 season it was clear that something was dreadfully wrong with him physically, and on May 2 he asked to be taken out of the lineup for the first time in 14 years. He never played again. Amyotrophic Lateral Sclerosis, the disease to become known as Lou Gehrig's Disease, had invaded the great warrior's body. He died of the disease two years later at the age of 37.

At his retirement, Lou Gehrig had played in seven All-Star games and six World Series. He won two Most Valuable Player Awards and one Triple Crown. In 1969 he was voted the greatest first baseman of all time by the Baseball Writer's Association and was the leading vote-getter on the All-Century team chosen by fans in 1999.

Lou Gehrig

38. What Hall-of-Famer grew up in the same small Pennsylvania town as Ken Griffey Jr. and shares a birthday with him to boot?

1B	Todd Helton	P	Carl Hubbell
2B	Rogers Hornsby	P	Catfish Hunter
3B	Stan Hack	P	Waite Hoyt
SS	J.J. Hardy	P	Orel Hershiser
OF	Rickey Henderson	RP	Trevor Hoffman
OF	Bryce Harper		
OF	Harry Heilmann		
C	Gabby Hartnet		
DH	Babe Herman		

Rogers Hornsby

"I don't like to sound egotistical, but every time I stepped up to the plate with a bat in my hands, I couldn't help but feel sorry for the pitcher."
Rogers Hornsby

Rogers Hornsby and Babe Ruth were to the 1920s in their respective leagues what Honus Wagner and Ty Cobb were to theirs up to the 1920's. They were the dominant stars of the National and American Leagues, head and shoulders above their peers.

The great Giants manager, John McGraw, would become apoplectic whenever anyone talked of Ruth as the best player in the game. He would retort that the National League had the best player in Hornsby. In fact, McGraw tried to persuade the Giants owners to buy Hornsby from the St. Louis Cardinals for the stupendous amount of $300,000 in 1920. That was three times what the Yankees paid for Ruth just the year before and was more than many major league franchises were worth! In any event, Hornsby was not for sale.

Like Cobb and DiMaggio, Rogers Hornsby was not the kind of guy one wanted to pal around with. He was aloof, gruff and a loner. His nickname, the Rajah, was said to be in deference to his imperious manner. Baseball was his only passion, although he also liked betting on the horses. Unfortunately, the latter got him in trouble with Major

League baseball, and it also kept him in debt for much of his career. He lost much more than he won.

Hornsby was so dedicated to the game he loved, and especially to hitting, that he would not read or go to the movies for fear that either would diminish his batting eye. For 22 years that famous batting eye never failed him. His lifetime batting average of .358 is second only to Cobb. He won seven batting titles, including six in a row from 1920-25. He led the National League in slugging percentage nine times, a record that still stands. He won the MVP Award twice and the Triple Crown twice.

In 1924 Hornsby set a record that I believe will never be broken. He hit an astounding .424! But he did not win the MVP Award that year because Jack Ryder, a Cincinnati sportswriter who hated Hornsby's style of play, left him off the ballot completely. The affront was so egregious that in 1962 the Baseball Writers Association presented him with an award retroactively recognizing him as the MVP for that year. He was selected to the All-Century and All-Time teams by Major League Baseball. He was elected to the Hall of Fame in 1942 in his first year of eligibility.

Many baseball historians consider Hornsby the greatest right-handed hitter of all-time. But he could also turn the double play at second base with the best of them, and he was considered one of the fastest base runners in the league, turning singles into doubles, doubles into triples. In a 10-year period, he had 30 inside-the-park home runs. Christy Mathewson called him the fastest man in baseball going from home to first. If Hornsby had a weakness it was catching pop flies. Ty Cobb refused to put him on his all-time team at second base because of this fault, but that was perhaps professional jealousy. There's a popular story of the irascible Cobb throwing Ted Williams out of his office, never to speak to him again, because Ted had the temerity to place Rogers on *his* all-time team.

After a decade of starring with the Cardinals, St. Louis had had enough of Hornsby's bickering with management as a player and a manager. After the 1926 season he was traded to the Giants for Frankie

Frisch, one of the most talked about trades in baseball history. This marked the beginning of Hornsby's nomadic years, in which he would both play and manage for the Giants, Braves, Cubs, and Browns. He also managed for the Reds. As a manager, the players generally hated him. Billy Herman, the Cubs second baseman said that Hornsby "ran the clubhouse like a Gestapo camp." He would fine his batters $50 if they took a third strike with runners on second or third. If one of his pitchers had a 0-2 count, he would fine them if the batter got a hit or if the pitcher didn't knock him down. Like most great players, he simply could not tolerate mediocrity in his players.

Rogers Hornsby

39. How many batting titles did Harry Heilmann attain in his career?

1B	Joe Judge	P	Walter Johnson
2B	Davey Johnson	P	Randy Johnson
3B	Chipper Jones	P	Ferguson Jenkins
SS	Derek Jeter	P	Tommy John
OF	Joe Jackson	RP	Addie Joss
OF	Adam Jones		
OF	Jackie Jensen		
C	Charles Johnson		
DH	Reggie Jackson		

Walter Johnson

"You can't hit what you can't see."
John Francis Daley on batting against Walter Johnson

"First in war, first in peace, and last in the American League." So went a popular refrain with respect to the nation's capital and its baseball team during the 1910s and 1920s, the same years that Walter Johnson pitched for the hapless Senators. Washington had such difficulty fielding a bona fide professional team during Johnson's career that when their stadium was partly destroyed by a fire during the off-season in 1910 and the local fire chief speculated that the blaze, which occurred behind third base, was probably started by a plumber's blowtorch, Joe Cantillon, manager of the Senators, quipped, "The chief is probably right, and the plumber was probably playing third base."

From 1907 to 1927 Johnson won an astonishing 417 games. Over that same period, the Senators won just 1,559 games, meaning that Johnson was responsible for more than one-fourth of all their victories over a 21-year span. Cy Young, who pitched from 1890-1911, is the career leader in total victories with 511; he lost 316 games, also a career record. If the Big Train had played his entire career with the Chicago White Sox, New York Giants, Detroit Tigers or any of a half dozen more successful teams of his era, he might have surpassed Young's career win record. Neither pitcher's win record will likely ever be broken.

A traveling salesman discovered a young Walter Johnson in the backwoods of Idaho. He bombarded Washington manager Cantillon with calls about the phenomenal pitcher he saw playing semi-pro ball. Cantillon finally relented when one of the missives said: "This boy throws so fast you can't see 'em, and he knows where he is throwing, because if he didn't there would be dead bodies all over Idaho." Cantillon sent an ex-catcher to verify the story and Johnson was signed soon thereafter.

Johnson made his Major League debut against Ty Cobb's Tigers who razzed him mercilessly, telling Cantillon to send him back to the farm. He was a strange sight, with his extraordinary long arms dangling half way down his legs. But after just a few innings the Tiger players were absolutely terrified to step into the batter's box. No one in Major League Baseball had ever seen a pitcher with such a blazing fastball. They did not have radar guns back then, but Walter probably threw his fastball at 100 mph.

In my opinion, Walter Johnson is the greatest pitcher of all-time. He led the league in wins six times, strikeouts 12 times, and ERA five times. He won the Most Valuable Player Award twice, won three pitching Triple Crowns, holds the American League record for most games pitched (802), has the second-most wins in major league history and holds the major league record for most shutouts with 110, a record I believe that will never be broken. His mark of 3,508 strikeouts was a record for over half a century, and those strikeouts came in an era when strikeouts were much rarer than they are today. Back then most hitters were slap hitters, just trying to meet the ball. Very few batters swung from the heels in the dead ball era. He may have had 500 more strikeouts if he pitched today with all those free swingers.

Johnson could also hit. His .433 batting average in 1925 is a record for pitchers with at least 75 at bats. In 1913 he had a 1.00 fielding average, another record for a pitcher. Perhaps Johnson's greatest honor came in 1936 when he was one of the first five players voted into the

Hall of Fame. He was named to the All-Century and All-Time teams.

Walter Johnson

40. "Shoeless" Joe Jackson holds the third-best career batting average in major league history. What was his average?

1B	Ted Kluszewski	P	Sandy Koufax
2B	Jeff Kent	P	Clayton Kershaw
3B	George Kell	P	Jim Kaat
SS	Harvey Kuenn	P	Jerry Koosman
OF	Ralph Kiner	RP	Craig Kimbrel
OF	Matt Kemp		
OF	Al Kaline		
C	Jason Kendall		
DH	Harmon Killebrew		

Sandy Koufax

"Koufax is the greatest Jewish athlete since Samson."
George Jessel

Sandy Koufax made his major league debut as a bonus baby with the Brooklyn Dodgers on June 24, 1955. He retired immediately after the 1966 season. From 1955 thru 1960 he showed signs of excellence but was otherwise average. From 1961 thru 1966, however, he put together the greatest six-year span of any pitcher in history. In those six years he dominated the National League, and he did it by pitching for a team that scored runs like politicians tell the truth, rarely. The Dodgers were such punchless hitters that Jim Murray of the Los Angeles Times wrote that if Koufax had pitched for the 1927 Yankees, he would have gone down as the only undefeated pitcher ever.

Even a perfectly pitched game did not guarantee success. After hearing that Koufax had thrown a no-hitter, teammate Don Drysdale once famously quipped, "Did he win it?" I find it ironic that perhaps the two greatest pitchers of all time, Koufax and Walter Johnson, toiled their entire careers for teams with such anemic offenses. Koufax achieved a remarkable 165-87 record by using his pinpoint control of just two pitches. It helped that those two pitches were a 100 mph fastball that actually rose as it crossed the plate, and a devastating

12-to-6 curveball that was more like an exaggerated sinker. Batters said the pitch looked like the ball was falling off a table.

The bonus baby rules of the 1950s were a mixed bag. On the one hand, they guaranteed the ballplayer both a tidy sum of money, as well as a spot on the team. (The player who was displaced by Koufax's signing, coincidentally, was Tommy Lasorda, who was furious at Koufax and the system that dictated the move). One of the most famous bonus babies, Al Kaline, won the batting title as a rookie for the 1955 Detroit Tigers.

But there could be a downside as well, and Koufax was a victim of it for his first six years. Sandy had the misfortune to come up to the Dodgers as a bonus baby when Walter Alston managed the team in Brooklyn. Because Koufax had no minor league experience, and also because Alston was signed to a string of one year contracts, and was thus in constant fear of losing his job, he never gave Koufax a chance to develop his control and confidence. He would start Sandy, a run would score, and Alston would yank him and not pitch him again for weeks. Koufax offered a different reason for not getting enough pitching time in his early years: it was because he was Jewish.

Frustrated by Alston's refusal to play him on a regular basis, Koufax threatened to quit after the 1960 season. Luckily for the Dodgers, he decided to give it one more try. During the winter of 1960-61, he worked extra hard to get in shape and reported to spring training in better physical condition than he had been in prior years. He also worked with backup catcher, Norm Sherry, who convinced Koufax to take something off his fastball in order to gain better control. The result was pin-point control with no loss of velocity!

Thus, began the six-year string of unrivaled pitching dominance not seen in the National League since Christy Mathewson. He retired after the 1966 season not because he couldn't deliver anymore, but rather because he feared that his arm would be irreparably damaged if he continued. He won the Cy Young Award that year with 27 wins, 27 complete games, 317 strikeouts, 323 innings pitched, and a league-leading 1.73 ERA. Now that's going out in style!

Koufax retired with 165 wins and 87 losses, a winning percentage of .655, the highest in half a century. He was the first pitcher to lead the league in ERA for five consecutive years, ending with a career ERA of 2.76. He had 137 complete games, 40 shutouts, three Cy Young Awards, four no hitters, including a perfect game, seven All-Star games (six years), four World Series championships, and one MVP Award in 1963. He is one of five pitchers to have more strikeouts than innings pitched. He was also voted to Major League Baseball's All-Century and All-Time teams.

The numbers tell a powerful story, but the comments from his peers are perhaps even more compelling. Jane Leavy, in her wonderful biography of Koufax, quotes from dozens of players.

"He was a meteor streaking across the heavens." said his former roommate Dick Tracewski.

Hall of Famer Billy Williams claimed "There was a different tone when people talked about Sandy Koufax."

Hank Aaron said "You talk about the Gibsons, and the Drysdales, and the Spahns. And as good as those guys were, Koufax was a step ahead of them."

Lou Johnson, another teammate, called him "Michelangelo and Picasso rolled into one."

Both Casey Stengel and Bob Feller said Koufax was the best they ever saw. He was the youngest player ever elected to the Hall of Fame.

Besides his on-field exploits, Koufax is fondly remembered by the Jewish community for refusing to pitch the first game of the 1965 World Series because it fell on Yom Kippur. One of the most significant and far-reaching acts Koufax did was to collude with Don Drysdale to hold out for more money after the 1965 season. The ploy worked and helped to lay the groundwork for collective bargaining activities in later years.

Sandy Koufax

41. What two teams passed on offering Koufax a contract before the Dodgers signed him?

L's

1B	Derek Lee	P	Ted Lyons
2B	Nap Lajoie	P	Bob Lemon
3B	Freddie Lindstrom	P	Mickey Lolich
SS	Barry Larkin	P	Cliff Lee
OF	Greg Luzinski	RP	Sparky Lyle
OF	Kenny Lofton		
OF	Fred Lynn		
C	Ernie Lombardi		
DH	Evan Longoria		

Barry Larkin

The Cincinnati Reds have a knack for acquiring, and then keeping, quality shortstops. From 1951-2004, excepting the single year of 1969, when Woody Woodward was the shortstop, just four men played the position for the Reds on an everyday basis. And each was a defensive standout. Roy McMillan began the lineage, averaging 135 games a year until 1960. He was succeeded by four-time all-star Leo Cardenas. After Woodward kept the position warm in 1969, Dave Concepcion brought his talents to the position in 1970, winning five Gold Gloves over a 19-year career. He spent the last three of those years as a utility man, training his replacement, Barry Larkin, who went on to be the best of the bunch.

Larkin was born on April 28, 1964 in Cincinnati, but unlike Pete Rose, who was also born there, he did not leave, despite receiving numerous offers from other teams. Loyalty meant more to Barry Larkin than raking in a few more million dollars.

Bill James, the dean of baseball historians, called Larkin the sixth-best shortstop of all time. He also ranked Larkin high on his list of complete ballplayers. He is one of only a handful of shortstops in history that could be called five-tool players.

Known for his leadership as well as his prowess on the diamond, Larkin finished his distinguished career with three Gold Gloves, nine Silver Slugger awards, an MVP Award in 1995, a World Series championship in 1990, and 12 All-Star appearances. In 1988 he led the major leagues by striking out only 24 times in 588 at-bats. Even though he won the MVP Award in 1995, he had a better year in 1996, when he became the first shortstop in history to join the 30-30 club with 33 home runs and 36 stolen bases. He was considered by his teammates to be so valuable that in 2000, when he was involved in a minor salary dispute, Ken Griffey offered to defer some of his own salary to keep Larkin on the Reds.

In his third year of eligibility, Barry Larkin was elected to the Hall of Fame. His career numbers are: 2,180 games played, 1,329 runs scored, 2,340 hits, 441 doubles, 76 triples, 198 home runs, 379 stolen bases, and a .295 batting average.

Barry Larkin

42. How many games did Mickey Lolich win in the 1968 World Series?

1B	Eddie Murray	P	Christy Mathewson
2B	Joe Morgan	P	Greg Maddux
3B	Eddie Mathews	P	Juan Marichal
SS	Marty Marion	P	Pedro Martinez
OF	Mickey Mantle	RP	Mike Marshall
OF	Willie Mays		
OF	Stan Musial		
C	Joe Mauer		
DH	Willie McCovey		

Willie Mays

" There have been only two authentic geniuses in the world,
Willie Mays and Willie Shakespeare."
Tallulah Bankhead

Willie Mays is simply the best that ever played Major League Baseball. One could argue that Ruth had more power, Ted Williams was a better hitter, Clemente had a stronger arm, Rickey Henderson was faster, and Ozzie Smith was a better fielder, but no one combined the five tools better than Mays. Ruth was more dominant, but in my opinion, Mays was the more complete ballplayer.

William Howard Mays (he was named after President Taft, who had died the year before), was born in Westfield, Alabama in 1931 and started playing baseball soon thereafter. At the tender age of two he was playing catch with his dad, "Cat" Mays. At 12 years of age, he fell out of a tree and broke his arm. He threw side-armed before the fall, but when the cast came off he was forced to throw from a three-quarters angle, which strengthened his throwing arm. That arm was so strong that as a quarterback in high school, he could throw the football 80 yards! At 14 he was playing with the Birmingham Black Barons in the Negro Leagues against opponents who were just as good as those in the major leagues. Once Jackie Robinson proved the value of black ballplayers, a handful of major league teams started to raid the Negro Leagues for their star players.

At just 20 years of age, Willie was the youngest black player to reach the majors. The New York Giants signed him for the 1951 season, but it's fascinating to play "what if" games had the following teams not dismissed him after scouting him with the Black Barons. The reasons for not selecting Mays were either due to miserliness or bigotry. The Pittsburgh Pirates could have signed Mays but decided not to spend the $2,000 to hold him. Imagine Willie and Roberto Clemente in the same outfield for almost two decades! Likewise the Boston Braves rejected Willie because they did not want to spend $7,500 to hold him. They recognized their mistake and grabbed Hank Aaron the following year. Imagine Willie and Hank in the same outfield for two decades!

The Brooklyn Dodgers also had a shot at Mays after Roy Campanella alerted them to him, but they decided that they had too many black players. Imagine Willie in the same outfield as Duke Snider! Both the Boston Red Sox and the New York Yankees scouted the young Mays, but decided that their fan base and teammates were not ready for a black player. So once again, imagine Willie in the same outfield with either Ted Williams or Mickey Mantle!

When Mays finally joined the Giants he had a terrible start. He went 1-for-his-first-26 plate appearances and didn't think he was good enough to play at the big league level. Luckily he had Leo Durocher for a manager. Durocher became a father figure to Willie and restored his confidence; he soon started playing to his full ability and won the Rookie of the Year Award for the 1951 season.

Another rookie by the name of Mickey Mantle joined a New York team that year, and together with an already established young center fielder in Brooklyn became part of the storied "Willie, Mickey, and the Duke" triumvirate. Having three future Hall-of-Fame center fielders on the three New York teams at the same time epitomized the golden age of baseball and established New York as the geographical center of the game.

Willie Mays and New York City were perfect for each other, and the Polo Grounds, where the Giants played, with its cavernous outfield, was the ideal venue to showcase Willie's speed and strong arm. Joe DiMaggio said that Willie had the strongest arm that he had ever seen. That arm was aptly displayed in the first game of the 1954 World Series when Willie not only made a miraculous catch of the 400-foot plus line drive off the bat of Cleveland's Vic Wertz, but then whirled and made a spectacular off balance throw to hold the runners. Baseball historian Donald Honig said that, "putting Mays in a small ballpark would have been like trimming a masterpiece to fit a frame."

Mays and Mantle established a new archetype for the complete ballplayer. They were the first to combine the speed and batting skills of Ty Cobb and Tris Speaker with the power of Babe Ruth into one player. Only a handful of players have been able to do the same since. As impressive as Willie's physical talents were, he was also one of the best students of the game ever. He would watch opposing outfielders taking practice throws before a game in order to gauge their arm strength, much like a cheetah will survey its potential prey to see which gazelle may be a hair slower than the others. In one game, Aaron was on first base when the batter hit a long line drive to Mays in center field. Hank had already rounded second base when Willie caught the ball. Mays threw to his second baseman and told him to touch second base. He did, and Hank was called out. How did Mays know that Aaron had failed to retouch second base on his way back to first? He noticed that Hank was shaking his head for having missed the bag!

In 1958 the Giants moved to San Francisco and New York lost its greatest player. No more would Harlem see Willie playing stickball in the street with the local kids. The Dodgers moved to Los Angeles the same year and only Mantle remained of the famous center field trio. San Francisco did not initially embrace Willie the way that New York did. Firstly, the fans swooned over their 1958 Rookie of the Year, Orlando Cepeda, whose popularity exceeded even Willie's. Secondly, Candlestick Park, the Giant's quirky stadium did not favor either Willie's offensive or defensive talents. The notorious outfield winds played havoc with fly balls and those same winds, which typically blew in from left field, significantly hampered right-handed power hitters like Mays.

Some baseball historians estimated that playing almost 900 games at Candlestick, missing all of the 1953 season due to military service, and playing a 154-game schedule for 10 years deprived Willie of about 165 home runs. Had he played in the Giants' current home park for his entire career, he might have hit 815 home runs over his career, making him the all-time home run king. The drawbacks of playing in Candlestick Park were obvious to Willie's peers. Ozzie Smith said, "Until I played at Candlestick, I never realized how great Willie Mays was. My God, what would he have done in a real ballpark?"[7]

Mays was blessed with an extraordinary talent for playing baseball. In his prime he was a muscular 5"11" and 185 pounds. He had huge hands. As mentioned earlier he was the ultimate five-tool player, but he also worked very hard to perfect his craft. He also kept his body clean, never drinking or smoking.

His career numbers are: 2,992 games played, 10,881 at bats, 2,062 runs scored, 3,283 hits, 523 doubles, 140 triples, 660 home runs, 1,903 RBIs, 1,464 walks, 338 stolen bases, .302 batting average, .384 on base percentage, and a .557 slugging average. He played in 24 All-Star games (20 years), won a World Series championship, earned 12 straight Gold Gloves, won two MVP Awards, was voted to the All-Time team, and was elected to the Hall of Fame on the first ballot with 94.7% of the vote, the most since Ty Cobb, Babe Ruth, and Honus Wagner were elected.

Willie Mays

43. Willie Mays holds a quirky record that will most likely never be broken. What is it?

1B	Mike Napoli	P	Hal Newhouser
2B	Dave Nelson	P	Phil Niekro
3B	Graig Nettles	P	Don Newcombe
SS	Skeeter Newsome	P	Joe Niekro
OF	Bill Nicholson	RP	Joe Nathan
OF	Otis Nixon		
OF	Jim Northrop		
C	Dioner Navarro		
DH	Trot Nixon		

Phil Niekro

"Hitting Phil Niekro's knuckleball is like trying to hit a butterfly."
Pete Rose

Few things frustrate a major league hitter more than trying to hit a knuckleball. They hate it. They don't practice for it. They spend endless hours in spring training and during the off season honing their skills at hitting fastballs, curves, and sliders. But because there are so few knuckleballers, they never work on hitting the floater.

Few pitchers have ever thrown a knuckleball better or more consistently than Phil Niekro. His father taught both him and brother Joe to throw it at an early age. Dad's tutelage paid off, because Phil and Joe won 539 games, the most of any brother combination in major league history, more than the Dean brothers, the Perry brothers, the Coveleski brothers, or the Martinez brothers.

The definition of a knuckleball is: "A baseball pitch thrown so as to minimize the spin of the ball in flight, causing an erratic, unpredictable motion." That unpredictable motion not only drives batters crazy, it has catchers seeking therapy. Indeed, teams that employ a knuckleball pitcher will often carry a catcher on their roster that specializes in catching the demonic pitch. Willie Stargell, the great Pirates slugger, took Rose's analogy even farther. "Hitting a knuckleball is not just like hitting a butterfly; it's like hitting a butterfly with hiccups." Bob Uecker, the catcher turned broadcaster, quipped, "The way to catch a knuckleball is to wait for it to stoprolling and pick it up."

Batters are told to lay off a knuckleball low in the strike zone because of its propensity to drop as it crosses the plate, thus leading to the maxim, "If it's low, let it go, if it's high, let it fly." One would think that if a knuckleball is so hard to hit, why don't more pitchers throw it? The answer *is because it's hard to throw!* And it's even harder to throw for strikes consistently. The Hall of Fame has only elected four knuckleball pitchers to its ranks: Phil Niekro, Hoyt Wilhelm, Jesse Haines, and Ted Lyons. Only Niekro and Wilhelm threw it as their signature pitch.

Niekro signed with the Milwaukee Braves in 1959 for the absurd price of $250. By the end of his career, the Braves had erected a statue of him outside of Atlanta Fulton County Stadium. In his illustrious career Niekro tied with brother Joe for the league lead in wins with 21 in 1979 and went 17-4 at the age of 43 in 1982. He accumulated 318 wins, won five Gold Gloves, was a five time All-Star, pitched a no-hitter on August 5, 1973, and holds the live ball era record for innings pitched with 5,404.33. He was voted to the Hall of Fame in 1997.

Phil Niekro
44. The Braves retired Phil Niekro's number in 1984.
What was the number?

1B	John Olerud	P	Roy Oswalt
2B	Jorge Orta	P	Claude Osteen
3B	Frank O'Rourke	P	Blue Moon Odom
SS	Spike Owen	P	Billy O'Dell
OF	Lefty O'Doul	RP	Jesse Orosco
OF	Tony Oliva		
OF	Mel Ott		
C	Bob O'Farrell		
DH	David Ortiz		

Mel Ott

"Nice guys finish last."
Leo Durocher, describing Mel Ott's record as manager of the Giants

Mel Ott walked into Giants manager John McGraw's office in April of 1926, carrying a straw suitcase, a true hick from Gretna, Louisiana. He was only 17 years old, and stood a mere 5'9" and weighed about 150 pounds. McGraw agreed to see him only because his millionaire friend, Harry Williams, insisted that he do. McGraw was unimpressed by the youngster standing in his office, but nevertheless told him to go out and hit with the team. Ott impressed not only McGraw, but the entire Giants team by smacking sizzling line drives and long fly balls. He did so while employing one of the oddest batting stances ever.

McGraw decided immediately that not only would Ott make the team, but he would bypass the usual development time in the minor leagues. He did not want to take the chance that the coaches in the minors would alter his stance. Thus Mel Ott became one of the youngest players in history to make it to the major leagues. The Giant players immediately took a liking to him, and nicknamed him "Master Melvin" due to his age.

Starting in the majors so early enabled Ott to become the youngest player to establish several batting records, including: the youngest player (17), to get a pinch hit, as well as the youngest player (20) to hit 40 home runs. He won or tied for the National League home run title six times, and was among the leaders in RBIs, runs scored, walks, and slugging percentage for almost two decades.

He was the first National Leaguer to reach 500 home runs. In fact, when he retired, he had over 200 more home runs than his closest challenger! This statistic, by the way, lends credence to the speculation that the National League used a less lively ball than the American League for several years during his tenure. Ott played his entire 21 years with the New York Giants. His career statistics are: .304 batting average, 2,876 hits, 511 home runs, 1,860 RBIs, 488 doubles, 72 triples, 89 stolen bases, .414 on base percentage, .533 slugging average, 12 All-Star games, and a World Series championship (1933). He was also an excellent right fielder. He was voted into the Hall of Fame in 1951 on the third ballot and was voted to the Sporting News All-Time team. Ott owns a particular record that will most likely never be broken: he led his team in home runs for 18 consecutive years!

Ott was loved and respected by fans and players alike. Pie Traynor, the Hall of Fame third baseman for the Pittsburgh Pirates, called him the greatest player he ever saw.

Mel Ott

45. Who preceded Mel Ott as manager of the New York Giants?

1B	Abert Pujols	P	Jim Palmer
2B	Dustin Pedroia	P	Gaylord Perry
3B	Tony Perez	P	Eddie Plank
SS	Johnny Pesky	P	David Price
OF	Vada Pinson	RP	Dan Quisenberry
OF	Kirby Puckett		
OF	Dave Parker		
C	Buster Posey		
DH	Mike Piazza		

Jim Palmer

"I don't want to win my 300th game while he's still here.
He'd take credit for it."
Jim Palmer on Earl Weaver

In 49 years of married bliss, as far as I know, there were only two men whom my wife would possibly have left me for. One is Elvis, but he's dead. The other is Jim Palmer, he of the Jockey underwear ads and Hollywood good looks. Palmer is still around and is six months younger than I, so I'm still on guard.

Palmer was born on October 15, 1945 in New York City. He was adopted soon after he was born, and when his adoptive father died, his family moved to California, where he excelled in baseball in high school and various youth leagues. He made his major league debut with the Baltimore Orioles on April 17, 1965 and never played for another team, retiring on May 12, 1984. In one of baseball's myriad "what if" scenarios, Palmer hurt his arm early in his career and was put on waivers for the 1968 expansion draft. Both the Kansas City Royals and the Seattle Pilots passed on him, fearing that his injured arm was too risky. The Orioles reluctantly put him back on the roster.

One of the most contentious relationships in the history of baseball was between Palmer and his fiery manager, Earl Weaver, hence the quote at the beginning of this section. Earl was forever giving Jim unwelcome pitching advice, which prompted Palmer to quip, "The only thing you know about pitching is that you can't hit it". One particularly funny incident occurred when the 5'7" Weaver was literally jumping up and down while berating the 6'3" Palmer when the latter, having heard enough, said, "Why Earl, I've never seen you so tall!"[8]

A hot stove league argument posits that Palmer never would have achieved the career numbers he put up were it not for the spectacular defense behind him for most of his career. He had the incomparable Brooks Robinson at third (16 Gold Gloves), Mark Belanger at shortstop (eight Gold Gloves), and Paul Blair in center field (eight Gold Gloves). He also had defensive wizards Bobby Grich, Luis Aparicio, and Al Bumbry for much of his career. Perhaps there is merit to this argument, but there are dozens of similar arguments. Would Ernie Banks have amassed as many home runs in a park other than Wrigley Field? What about Mel Ott in the Polo Grounds or Duke Snider in cozy Ebbets Field? Would Babe Ruth have had so many pitches to swing at if Lou Gehrig hadn't been hitting behind him? As Bill Belichick, head coach for the New England Patriots is famous for saying, "It is what it is."

Palmer's career statistics are indeed impressive. He played in six All-Star games, and on three World Series championship teams. He won three Cy Young Awards and four Gold Gloves, pitched a no-hitter, had his number (22) retired, won 268 games, compiled 2,212 strikeouts, was voted to the Hall of Fame in 1990 on the first ballot, and was ranked among The Sporting News's 100 greatest players. He had the most wins of any pitcher in the 1970s (186), won 20 games in eight different seasons, is the only pitcher in history to win a World Series game in three different decades, and was the youngest to pitch a shutout in a World Series. He did so in 1966 at the age of 20. Palmer's 2.86 ERA is the third best in the live ball era, behind Whitey Ford and Sandy Koufax.

Jim Palmer

46. In 1971 Jim Palmer was one of four pitchers to win 20 games for the Baltimore Orioles. Who were the other three?

1B	Pete Rose		P	Nolan Ryan
2B	Jackie Robinson		P	Robin Roberts
3B	Brooks Robinson		P	Red Ruffing
SS	Cal Ripken		P	Eppa Rixey
OF	Frank Robinson		RP	Mariano Rivera
OF	Edd Roush			
OF	Babe Ruth			
C	Ivan Rodriguez			
DH	Alex Rodriguez			

Babe Ruth

"If it wasn't for baseball, I'd be either in the penitentiary or the cemetery."
Babe Ruth

Babe Ruth is the Paul Bunyan of baseball. He is the most dominant player ever to play the game. Baseball morphed from a "small game" of beating out base hits, getting sacrificed to second, and scoring on a bloop single to a game of home runs and power in large part due to Ruth's style of play. Everything about him was larger than life. He had the size and strength of an NFL tackle, the hand/eye coordination and batting rhythm of Ted Williams, the throwing arm of Roberto Clemente, the pitching prowess of Lefty Grove, and the carnal appetite of Henry the VIII.

At the age of seven George Herman Ruth was sent to the Saint Mary's Industrial School for Boys, an institution for the "incorrigible." He left there to play for the minor league Baltimore Orioles at age 19. It was with the Orioles by the way, that Ruth got his nickname "Babe." The older players on the team thought he was owner Jack Dunn's "baby." That same year he left the Orioles and joined the Boston Red Sox. He was as raw a rookie as there ever was, a "man child" without much of an education and totally lacking in the social graces. Once he discovered that the team would pay for his meals, he would routinely have up to 18 eggs for breakfast and wash them down with six bottles of soda! Then came a lunch of half a dozen hot dogs, again with soda. We mistakenly think of Ruth as always the big-bellied caricature that he became, but when he first joined the Red Sox he was a strapping 6'2", 200 pounds of muscle.

Ironically, the greatest slugger in history came up to the big leagues as a pitcher. And what a pitcher he was! He was easily the best southpaw of his day, and perhaps second only to the great Walter Johnson. Harry Hooper, the Boston center fielder and team captain, recognized Ruth's importance as a hitter and convinced manager Ed Barrow to convert the Babe from pitcher to full-time outfielder in 1919, five years after his debut. In his first year as an everyday player, Ruth led the league in home runs (29), runs (103), RBIs (114), slugging average (.657), on base percentage (.456), and total bases (284). His amazing performance in 1919 was simply a prelude of much bigger things to come.

Two events occurred in 1920 that shocked the major league establishment. The first was the revelation that the Chicago Black Sox had thrown the 1919 World Series. The damage to baseball's image as our national pastime was significant. Everyone associated with the game was desperate for something or someone to save the game.

The second event that shook the baseball world was the consummation of the worst deal between two teams in the history of Major League Baseball. The Boston Red Sox sold Babe Ruth to the New York Yankees because Boston owner Harry Frazee needed the money to fund a Broadway play. Frazee's name will live in infamy forever in Boston. One could argue that Ruth saved baseball from itself that year. He hit an astounding 54 home runs for his new team, more than the total home run production of 14 other teams! He was the prime reason for the 40% jump in American League attendance from the prior year.

Ruth had already led the league in several batting and pitching categories before 1920, but now he really went on a tear. In 1921 he led the league in home runs (59), RBIs (171), total bases (457) and runs scored (177). In 1923 he trained extra hard in the off season, lost 20 pounds and led the league in home runs (41), walks (170), on base percentage (.545), RBIs (131), runs scored (151), slugging average (.764), and total bases (399), won the MVP Award and finished second in batting with a .393 average. From 1923-31 Ruth won eight home run titles, and was near the top in most other offensive categories. His 47 home runs in 1926 were 28 more than the American League runner-up and 26 more than National League leader Hack Wilson. Ruth's 60 home runs in 1927 were more than any other American League team!

I personally rank Babe Ruth and Willie Mays as the two top players ever. Mays was the ultimate five-tool player, but Ruth, in his younger days, was also a five-tool player. He could certainly hit for power and his lifetime .342 average attests to his ability as a pure hitter. He possessed a powerful throwing arm from right field, was an excellent fielder, and was a smart base runner with moderate speed. And oh, by the way, he was an outstanding pitcher with a lifetime record of 94 wins versus 46 losses, and a 2.28 ERA.

Ruth's life was a classic rags-to-riches story, the very personification of the American dream. He went from Saint Mary's Home for incorrigible boys to become the most popular and dominant figure in American sports history. He was so feared by opposing pitchers that he was walked 2,062 times, even though he had Lou Gehrig batting behind him! Even with his .342 lifetime batting average, his home run to at bat ratio of 11.8 is the highest ever. These statistics are even more amazing when you consider that he had a different woman almost every night on the road, and consumed prodigious amounts of alcohol and bad food.

The Babe finished his career as the all-time leader in home runs, RBIs, and walks, and while others have since surpassed him in those categories, he still owns the game's highest slugging percentage and on base plus slugging percentage (OPS). He was one of five players elected to the Hall of Fame's inaugural class; in 1969 The Sporting News ranked him as the greatest player ever.

Babe Ruth

47. Who struck out Babe Ruth, Lou Gehrig, Jimmie Foxx, Al Simmons, and Joe Cronin in succession in the 1934 All-Star game?

1B	George Sisler	P	Warren Spahn
2B	Ryne Sandberg	P	Tom Seaver
3B	Mike Schmidt	P	Don Sutton
SS	Ozzie Smith	P	John Smoltz
OF	Duke Snider	RP	Bruce Sutter
OF	Tris Speaker		
OF	Ichiro Suzuku		
C	Ted Simmons		
DH	Al Simmons		

Mike Schmidt

*"Just to have his body (Mike Schmidt's),
I'd trade mine and my wife's and throw in some cash."*
Pete Rose

One could argue who's a better first baseman, Lou Gehrig or Stan Musial; second baseman, Rogers Hornsby or Ryne Sandberg; shortstop, Honus Wagner or Cal Ripken; left fielder, Ted Williams or Barry Bonds; center fielder, Willie Mays or Ty Cobb; right fielder, Hank Aaron or Babe Ruth; or catcher, Johnny Bench or Yogi Berra. I don't think there is a similar argument over third base. Mike Schmidt stands alone as the all-time best third baseman. If his batting average were just a little better than a career .267, he would be an unquestioned five-tool player, rare indeed for the hot corner. Only George Brett, Alex Rodriguez, and Chipper Jones come close to being a five-tool third baseman. What makes Schmidt stand out is that besides his impressive career offensive stats, he also won 10 Gold Gloves! He was Brooks Robinson and Eddie Mathews rolled into one.

Schmidt made his major league debut in 1972 with the Philadelphia Phillies and had an inauspicious beginning, batting a mere .197 with 151 strikeouts in 401 at bats in parts of two seasons. But he soon removed all doubts as to his ability in 1974 when he led the National League in home runs with 36. The home runs continued at an astounding rate until he retired in 1989 with 548, having led the league in eight separate seasons. He also led the league in RBIs four times, was selected to 12 All-Star games, and won six Silver Slugger awards, to go along with those 10 Gold Gloves. He won a World Series in 1980, (winning the Series MVP), and captured the National League Most Valuable Player Award three times, matching the accomplishments of Stan Musial and Roy Campanella.

He was one of the most feared hitters of his day. Roger Angell, writing for The New Yorker, wrote, "During a game Mike Schmidt brings such formidable attention and intelligence to bear on the enemy pitcher that one senses that the odds have almost been reversed out there, it is the man on the mound, not the one up at the plate, who is in worse trouble from the start."

Schmidt played his entire career, (1972-1989), for the Philadelphia Phillies. In the era of free agency, it's a rarity for a player of Schmidt's caliber to play for only one team; for that team to be the Philadelphia Phillies is incredible. Any sports figure who has played in that town can attest to the fact that its fans are notoriously difficult to please (Boston is right up there as well).

In their wonderful book, *Baseball Anecdotes*, Daniel Okrent and Steve Wulf talk about Schmidt's love-hate relationship with his fans and the Phillies penurious owner. They mention that after the Phillies lost the 1983 World Series, Schmidt got on a school bus to check on his daughter when the other schoolchildren starting yelling, "Choke, Choke, Choke." Schmidt could laugh that one off, but he had no love for the city's sportswriters. Of them he said, "Philadelphia is the only city in the world where you can experience the thrill of victory and the agony of reading about it the next day."

Schmidt was voted into the Hall of Fame on the first ballot in 1995. He was voted the greatest Phillie ever by the same fickle fans that once booed him. His 548 home runs are the most by any player who spent his entire career with one team. He is # 28 on The Sporting News list of the 100 greatest players ever, and was voted to the All-Century team. The Sporting News also named him as the best player of the 1980s. There is a statue of him at Citizens Bank Park, located fittingly, adjacent to third base.

Mike Schmidt

48. Who did the Phillies trade to the Milwaukee Brewers to make room for Mike Schmidt?

1B	Bill Terry	P	Luis Tiant
2B	Manny Trillo	P	Dizzy Trout
3B	Pie Traynor	P	Frank Tanana
SS	Troy Tulowitzki	P	Virgil Trucks
OF	Sam Thompson	RP	Kent Tekulve
OF	Mike Trout		
OF	Bobby Thomson		
C	Joe Torre		
DH	Frank Thomas		

Bill Terry

"He once hit a ball between my laigs so hard that my center fielder caught it on the fly backing up against the wall."
Dizzy Dean on Bill Terry

B ill Terry was born on October 30, 1898 in Atlanta, Georgia. His was a difficult childhood, punctuated by grinding poverty and a dysfunctional family. Like Babe Ruth and so many other ballplayers of his era, he escaped a hard life, whether it was toiling in the mines, performing backbreaking work in the fields, or the drudgery of the factory floor, by signing with a big league club.

Money was the driving force in Terry's life, right up to his death in 1989 at the ripe old age of 90. Being strong for his age, he dropped out of school at the age of 13 and worked loading sacks of flour onto trucks. He also had the brains and business acumen to complement his brawn, and soon had a sales position with Standard Oil of Louisiana. He needed the money, because even though he was still a teenager, he was already a husband and father.

It was this early recognition of the importance of money that gave him the reputation, probably deserved, that he viewed baseball as strictly a business rather than a source of joy. Carl Hubbell, his teammate for several years, said, "Bill played the game and managed as if he were running a business. There's some question in my mind whether Bill ever enjoyed baseball as the All-American boy enjoys it. I don't think he ever played for fun but for whatever he could get out of it."[9]

John McGraw, the pugnacious manager of the New York Giants got a taste of this dispassionate attitude when he went to see Terry at his home after getting a tip from a scout about the hard-hitting youngster. McGraw was used to young recruits jumping at the chance to play major league ball. When he asked Terry if he wanted to play for the Giants, Bill stoically responded by asking how much the job paid. An average recruit would not have been given a second chance after an answer like that, but McGraw recognized the diamond in the rough sitting in front of him. So for $800 a month, Bill Terry became a Giant. He made his major league debut on September 24, 1923, and played his last game 14 years later, almost to the day. He spent his entire career with the Giants, both as a player and a player/manager.

Like Rogers Hornsby before him and Ted Williams after him, Terry did not suffer fools and had little patience with sportswriters. On one occasion, when managing the Giants, he was taken to task for a questionable pitching change by a horde of reporters after the game. He snapped back, saying, "I don't know who you guys think you are. No goddamn 40-buck-a-week reporter tells me what to do." His antagonism with the reporters cost him. Not only was he constantly criticized in the press, but after retirement, his election to the Hall of Fame took 13 years, when arguably, he should have been a first ballot choice.

Despite his trials and tribulations with the press, his exploits on the diamond were spectacular. He was a devastating line drive hitter, preferring to hit up the middle or into the alleys in left and right center field. Opposing pitchers, such as Dizzy Dean, (see quote above), were terrified to face him. Many baseball historians speculate that if he had chosen to pull the ball and take advantage of the short right field fence in the Polo Grounds like his teammate Mel Ott did, his power numbers would be among the top all-time.

In 1930 he led the league in batting with a .401 average, a mark that has not since been equaled in the National League. The following year he lost the batting title by .0003. For his career, Terry batted .341, hit 154 home runs, accumulated 1,078 RBIs, and had 2,193 hits. He has the highest career batting average for a left-handed batter in the National League. Not bad when you consider Stan Musial is in the same category. He was also the last National Leaguer to get nine hits in a doubleheader. He turned this trick on June, 18, 1929. Besides his batting feats, he managed the Giants to three pennants and one World Series championship. He was also a slick defensive first baseman. Terry was voted into the Hall of Fame in 1954.

Bill Terry

49. Who squeaked by Bill Terry to win the
batting title in 1931 by .0003?

1B	Mickey Vernon	P	Dazzy Vance
2B	Chase Utley	P	Justin Verlander
3B	Robin Ventura	P	Fernando Valenzuela
SS	Arky Vaughn	P	Johnny Vandermeer
OF	Justin Upton	RP	Frank Viola
OF	Andy Van Slyke		
OF	Shane Victorino		
C	Jason Varitek		
DH	Joey Votto		

Fernando Valenzuela

"Every game that Fernando pitched became a fiesta."
Rick Monday

When Fernando Valenzuela wound up to pitch it was downright spooky. How did batters dare to dig in against a pitcher whose eyes rolled back inside his skull as he delivered to the plate? It was like hitting against Regan from "The Exorcist". You almost expected his head to do a 180.

Valenzuela was born on November 1, 1960 in Navajoa, Mexico, the youngest of 12 children. Like so many ballplayers before him, Major League Baseball was his ticket out of grinding poverty.

He made his major league debut with the Los Angeles Dodgers on September 15, 1980, throwing 17.2 scoreless innings in relief. His official rookie season was 1981, and what a season it was! Fernando became the first player in history to win both the Rookie of the Year and the Cy Young Awards in the same season. He led the league in strikeouts, shutouts, and complete games. He was no slouch at the plate either, winning the Silver Slugger award in his rookie year and again two years later. He was also a major contributor to the Dodgers' 1981 World Series win over the dreaded New York Yankees!

Like Fred Lynn before him, Valenzuela was an overnight sensation. He won his first eight games (five of them shutouts). Some consider

Fernando's heroics on the mound as the one bright spot in an otherwise disappointing strike-interrupted season.

When Walter O'Malley moved the Dodgers west from Brooklyn to Los Angeles in 1958, the city of Los Angeles built a brand new ballpark in a neighborhood that once housed a sizable Mexican/American population. Yet, Mexicans were nowhere to be found on the Dodgers' roster.

Bobby Castillo, a marginal pitcher, was one of the first Mexicans to wear the Dodgers' uniform. His most notable achievement was to teach the young Valenzuela how to throw the screwball. It became Fernando's most devastating pitch. He used that pitch, by the way, to duplicate another famous screwball artist when he struck out five consecutive batters in the 1986 All-Star game, just as Carl Hubbell had done in 1934.

After his remarkable rookie year, Valenzuela became an icon in L.A.'s sizable Mexican-American community, and to a lesser extent around the country as well. Whenever he pitched Dodger Stadium would be filled with Mexican flags and banners. He attracted more customers to stadiums all over the National League.

He even appeared on the cover of both Time and Newsweek. The Ritchie Valens hit song, "La Bamba" was changed to "Fer, Nan, Do, Va, Len, Zue, La" and played all over Southern California. He was Elvis and Babe Ruth rolled into one charismatic pitcher. He was even mentioned in the box office hit movie, "Bull Durham," when Annie Savoy tried to help minor league pitcher "Nuke" LaLoosh, by telling him to imitate Valenzuela's pitching delivery.

Hall-of-Fame catcher Johnny Bench combined Valenzuela's Mexican heritage with his overwhelming pitching when he quipped, "You feel like Jim Bowie waiting for Santa Ana to crush you." Fernando was more than just a great pitcher. He was a superb athlete, who was often put into the game to pinch hit, and occasionally played outfield or first base.

For his career, Fernando played in six All-Star games, was on one World Series championship team (1981), won a Cy Young Award, and was Rookie of the Year. His won-lost record was 173-153. He had a 3.54 ERA, and 2,074 strikeouts, and threw a no-hitter in 1990, his last season as a Dodger. In 2005 Major League Baseball named him one of the three starting pitchers on the Latino Legends Team.

Fernando Valenzuela

50. What team did Fernando Valenzuela finish his career with?

1B	Bill White		P	Early Wynn
2B	Lou Whitaker		P	Ed Walsh
3B	Matt Williams		P	Rube Waddell
SS	Honus Wagner		P	Bucky Walters
OF	Billy Williams		RP	Hoyt Wilhelm
OF	Paul Waner			
OF	Dave Winfield			
C	Matt Wieters			
DH	Ted Williams			

Honus Wagner

*"That god-damned Dutchman is the only man
in the game I can't scare."*
Ty Cobb speaking about Honus Wagner

Most serious baseball historians consider Honus Wagner to be the best shortstop ever. Some put up arguments for Cal Ripken, Ernie Banks, Ozzie Smith, or Derek Jeter, but I'm not one of them. I vote for Johannes Peter Wagner, known to us as Honus, Hans, or more descriptively, "The Flying Dutchman." Some baseball experts like John McGraw and Sam Crawford, both Hall of Famers themselves, even go so far as to say that he was the greatest *player* ever. His teammate, Tommy Leach, said that Honus was the greatest shortstop, third baseman, second baseman, first baseman, and outfielder that he ever saw!

Wagner didn't look like a typical ballplayer. He had a wrestler's chest, massive shoulders, extremely bowed legs, and arms so long that Yankee pitcher Lefty Gomez once joked that "He can tie his shoelaces without bending down." He also had huge hands. His first basemen would recall that when he threw to them, they would receive not only the ball, but clods of dirt and pebbles as well.

Like many, if not most, ballplayers of his era, Wagner's childhood was one of extreme poverty. He was one of eight children born to

German immigrant parents. He quit school at 12 years of age to work in the coal fields at $3 per week and never forgot the value of a dollar. He was plucked out of obscurity by Ed Barrow and signed by the Louisville Colonels in 1897. He started his career as an outfielder and immediately showed his prowess as a hitter, a fielder, and a base runner. The owner of the Colonels, Barney Dreyfuss, moved his team to Pittsburgh when the league contracted from 12 teams to 8, and brought Honus along with him.

The turn of the century saw Wagner blossom into the best player in the National League. In 1900 he led the league in batting (.381), doubles (45), triples (22), and slugging percentage (.573). He never batted below .299 until he turned 40, and led the league in hitting eight times, RBIs five times, and stolen bases five times.

Bill James, noted baseball guru, posits that the best single season ever for any player was Wagner's 1908. The league ERA of 2.35 was the lowest of the dead ball era, and was also about half of today's ERA postings. Yet Wagner hit .354 that year with 109 RBIs at a time when half as many runs were scored as today. James asks, "If you had a Gold Glove shortstop who drove in 218 runs, what would he be worth?" Compared to his peers in the National League during his playing days, Honus was 97 points above the average batting percentage and an astounding 200 points above the average slugging percentage!

Wagner has always been compared to Ty Cobb, his counterpart in the American League during the dead ball era. Cobb was the better hitter, and possibly the better base runner, but Wagner had him beat in all other categories and was just a smidgeon behind him in batting and base running.

If their playing abilities were similar, however, their personalities could not have been more different. Where Cobb was vicious, Wagner was gentle: where Cobb was arrogant, Wagner was humble: and where Cobb was despised, even by his own teammates, Wagner was beloved. Another sad difference between the two greats was that after retirement from the game, Cobb became a millionaire, while Wagner struggled with financial issues and alcohol.

Wagner was the first player to endorse a commercial product, the Louisville Slugger baseball bat. He is also the subject of the most famous and expensive baseball card in history. He didn't want his picture used to sell cigarettes, so he halted production of a card issued by the American Tobacco Company, and only a handful remain in circulation. A prized copy of the card sold for $2.8 million in 2007 to Ken Kendrick, owner of the Arizona Diamondbacks.

Wagner's career numbers are as follows: .329 batting average, 3,430 hits, 1,732 RBIs, 101 home runs, 640 doubles, 252 triples, and 722 stolen bases. He was one of the five charter members of the Hall of Fame, along with Babe Ruth, Ty Cobb, Walter Johnson, and Christy Mathewson. There is a life-size statue of him outside the front gate of Pittsburgh's PNC Park.

Honus Wagner

51. Which team did Honus Wagner's Pirates lose to in the 1903 World Series?

1B	Rudy York	P	Cy Young
2B	Don Zimmer	P	Barry Zito
3B	Eddie Yost	P	Carlos Zambrano
SS	Michael Young	P	Tom Zachary
OF	Carl Yastrzemski	RP	Jordan Zimmerman
OF	Robin Yount		
OF	Ross Youngs		
C	Steve Yeager		
DH	Ryan Zimmerman		

Yaz

"Baseball is the discipline of a Carl Yastrzemski ...."
George W. Bush

I became a Red Sox fan in 1967, the year of the "Impossible Dream." Hailing from New York, I had been a Giants fan. Then they moved to the Left Coast and I was a Giant fan no longer, even though Willie Mays was and still is my favorite player. So after living in baseball limbo since 1958, I was ripe for another team to claim my loyalty. I, along with millions of other baseball fans, became transfixed in the summer of 1967, when no less than four teams-- the Boston Red Sox, Minnesota Twins, Detroit Tigers, and Chicago White Sox bludgeoned each other for the American League Pennant. The Red Sox won it on the last day of the season.

Carl Michael Yastrzemski was born on August 22, 1939 in Southampton, New York, the son of a potato farmer. He made his major league debut with the Boston Red Sox on April, 11, 1961. All but two of the then 16 major league teams pursued him. The Cincinnati Reds offered him $125,000, but he decided to go with Boston for $100,000. He was scouted by several teams while playing shortstop for the Lake Ronkonkoma Cardinals. His father, Carl Sr., played third base. Junior batted third and hit .375 in 1958. His father batted fourth and hit .410. Yaz always said that his father was the better athlete of the two.

Shortstop was Carl's natural position, but the Red Sox needed a replacement for their legendary left fielder, Ted Williams, so they moved Yaz to the outfield. Like Mickey Mantle before him, who had to deal with the pressure of filling Joe DiMaggio's shoes, the young Yastrzemski had to deal with the same pressure in replacing Teddy Ballgame. He proved up to the task quickly enough. After two fair seasons, he broke out in 1963, leading the league in batting (.321), hits (183), doubles (40), walks (95), and on base percentage (.418). In 1965 he led the league in on base percentage (.395), slugging average (.536), and doubles (tied with 45). He also won the first of his seven Gold Gloves.

It was 1967 however, that made Carl Yastrzemski a legend. He had a year for the ages. As mentioned earlier, one of the wildest pennant races in history saw three teams controlling their own destiny on the season's final day. Few players ever had the kind of pressure placed on them as Yaz did that year, as he virtually carried the Red Sox on his back for the entire season. To be fair, Rico Petrocelli, George Scott, Tony Conigliaro, and pitcher Jim Lonborg contributed their share.

Yastrzemski won the Triple Crown, (he tied with Harmon Killebrew for most home runs), the Most Valuable Player Award, the Hickock Belt for the top professional athlete, and Sports Illustrated's Sportsman of the Year. Time and again throughout the season he came through in the clutch for the Red Sox. In the last 12 games of the season, with four teams all within a game or two of the lead, Yaz batted .523, hit five home runs, and had 16 RBIs. With two games left in the season, the Twins were in first place by a game when they traveled to Fenway Park for a series that would end up deciding the pennant. Carl went 7-for-8 with 5 RBIs to lead the Sox to first place and the World Series. They lost the series in a heartbreaking seven games to Bob Gibson and the St. Louis Cardinals, but Yaz, ever the clutch player, hit .400 with three home runs and 21 total bases.

Yastrzemski was one of the earliest players to stay in shape during the off season and was usually the first to show up for batting practice during the year. This determination along with his natural athleticism enabled him to finish his career with the following numbers: a .285 average, 3,419 hits, 452 home runs, 1,844 RBIs, 18 All-Star games, seven Gold Gloves (no one played Fenway's Green Monster better than Yaz), and one Most Valuable Player Award. He was inducted into the Hall of Fame on the first ballot in 1989. Only Pete Rose played more games than Yastrzemski (3,308), and only Rose and Hank Aaron have more career at-bats (11,988). He is tied with Brooks Robinson for the most years (23), with the same team. If you visit Fenway Park, you will see a statue of Captain Carl outside the stadium.

Carl Yastrzemski

52. Carl Yastrzemski succeeded a Hall-of-Famer (Ted Williams), in left field for the Boston Red Sox. What Hall-of-Famer succeeded him?

Fifth Inning

Real Teams

This section is comprised of the all-time best players, in my opinion, at each position from their respective franchises. In general, I tried to assign players to the teams to which they played the majority of their career. So even though Frank Robinson won the Triple Crown for the Baltimore Orioles, he had more playing time for the Cincinnati Reds. Hence he's on the Cincinnati team.

But I made a few exceptions to my rule. Carlton Fisk for example, had slightly more playing time with the Chicago White Sox than he had with the Boston Red Sox. But, I put him on the Boston team because he chose to wear the Boston cap for his Hall of Fame plaque. I considered the entire history of a franchise, regardless of how often it changed cities and even nicknames. For example, the St. Louis Browns became the Baltimore Orioles, so they have both George Sisler and Eddie Murray on the team. Likewise, the original Senators and Minnesota Twins are one team, so they get to have both Walter Johnson and Kirby Puckett.

Each of baseball's original 16 teams has been in existence for over 100 years, and therefore boasts a long list of Hall of Fame players to choose from. The expansion teams, by contrast, have far less history. Therefore, I decided to put together all-time teams that are a combination of the first, second, and third/fourth waves of expansion.

1B	Mark McGwire	P	Lefty Grove
2B	Mark Ellis	P	Catfish Hunter
3B	Frank Baker	P	Eddie Plank
SS	Bert Campaneris	P	Chief Bender
OF	Ricky Henderson	RP	Dennis Ekersley
OF	Al Simmons		
OF	Reggie Jackson		
C	Mickey Cochrane		
DH	Jimmie Foxx		

Triple Play: Mack, Finley, Beane

" We run our club like a pawn shop, we buy, we trade, we sell."
Charles O. Finley

Few if any teams in major league history have had more ups and downs on the field than the Athletics of Philadelphia, Kansas City, and Oakland. Connie Mack took the helm of the fledgling team upon its founding in 1901. The next year the team won the pennant.

Cornelius McGillicuddy, born during the Civil War in East Brookfield, Massachusetts, shortened his name to Connie Mack so that it would fit into a box score during his playing days as a catcher for Pittsburgh. His playing career was uneventful, although his penchant for tipping the hitter's bat with his mitt led to a rule making such an action an interference play, and awarding the batter a free pass to first base. Otherwise Mack's contributions to the game were as a manager and an elder statesman to the game, not as a player.

During the 1910s, Mack and John McGraw of the New York Giants were the two most respected and successful managers in the game. Otherwise, they were as different as night and day. Where McGraw was boisterous, hard drinking, cigar smoking, argumentative, short and stout: Mack was a deeply religious teetotaling non-smoker who never swore. He was the "Tall Tactician" to McGraw's "Little Napoleon."

The two teams were the most successful in their respective leagues during that era. McGraw called Mack's 1911 Athletics the best team ever. It included the famous $100,000 infield of Stuffy McInnis, Eddie Collins, Frank "Home Run" Baker, and Jack Barry. Two future Hall of Famers formed the nucleus of the pitching staff: Eddie Plank and Chief Bender. Between 1902 and 1914, the Athletics won six pennants and three world championships.

Financial problems eventually caused Mack to sell off his stars, including three from his famous infield. The result was a 15-year span of futility (including seven straight last-place finishes) until 1929, when he built what many baseball historians feel is the greatest team ever, surpassing even his 1911 team. Four of baseball's all-time greatest players were on this team: Jimmie Foxx, Al Simmons, Mickey Cochrane, and the flame throwing Lefty Grove. This team won three straight pennants from 1929–31 and two World Series championships in 1929 and 1930. Pretty impressive when you consider they were playing at the same time as the Yankees of Ruth and Gehrig.

The Great Depression took its toll on attendance in Philadelphia, and once again Mack felt compelled to sell off his star players. Foxx, Simmons, Cochrane, and Grove were sold between 1933 and 1935 and the A's never finished above fourth place for the rest of Mack's tenure as manager.

Mack spent 64 years in Major League Baseball, 11 as a player in both the National League and Players League, and 53 as both manager and front office executive with the Athletics (including three years with the Pirates). He built and dismantled two of the greatest teams in major league history. He won nine pennants and five world championships. Rube Bressler, who played for Mack, was featured in Lawrence Ritter's wonderful book, *The Glory of Their Times*. In it he says: "Connie Mack did more for baseball than any other living human being, by the example he set, his attitude, the way he handled himself and his players."

Mack died a year after he moved the Athletics to Kansas City in

1955. Insurance baron Charles O. Finley purchased the franchise in 1960, and almost immediately tried to move the team to Dallas, alienating the Kansas City fan base. After years of butting heads with other owners and local politicians, he finally succeeded in 1968 in gaining approval to move the franchise to Oakland. Finley's dealings with the city of Kansas City were so acrimonious that once the move was finally approved, Missouri Senator Stuart Symington, said, "The loss of the A's is more than recompensed by the pleasure of getting rid of Mr. Finley."[10]

Upon arriving in Oakland, Finley went from alienating the fans to alienating his own players. His tenure as the A's owner (1968-81), was marked by bizarre publicity stunts, innovative changes to the game, and mostly by his penurious attitude toward his players.

In order to attract more fans to the stadium, he had his players wear bright gold and green uniforms, encouraged them to grow their hair long and grow mustaches, and tried to persuade his fellow owners to use orange baseballs for better visibility. He was an early proponent of nighttime World Series play, the designated hitter, and even the designated runner.

But, his players hated him. Future Hall of Famers like Catfish Hunter, Reggie Jackson and Rollie Fingers, along with stars like Vida Blue, Sal Bando, and Joe Rudi had to go through excruciating sessions at contract time. When Catfish Hunter discovered a flaw in his contract, he used it as an escape clause to jump ship to the New York Yankees.

Like Mack before him, Finley was able to obtain some of the most talented players in the league. His Athletics matched the Yankees of the 1930s, and 1950s by winning three World Series championships in a row (1972-74). But also like Mack, Finley was constantly concerned about the team's finances, and periodically sold off his top players. By 1977 Finley had jettisoned all of the stars from the team, and Oakland finished with a dismal 63-98 record. It would be another 11 years before the A's again appeared in the World Series.

The Athletics of the late 1980s once again fielded championship teams. Tony La Russa managed a squad that included Rickey Henderson, Dennis Eckersley, Mark McGwire, and Jose Canseco. But after making it to three straight World Series appearances (1988-90), the team again traded away or sold its star players and the losses returned.

In 1997 a new leader emerged, and he would change the dynamics of drafting players, scouting players, and even the tactics of the game itself. His name was Billy Beane. He was drafted in 1984 by the New York Mets. He was probably the most talented prospect of the year, but he didn't make it as a player. However, he exceeded expectations as a General Manager. Beane became GM of the Oakland A's in 1997, inheriting a team noted for its mediocrity. His biggest challenge was to build a winning team with a budget one-third that of the New York Yankees, who were in the midst of creating a new dynasty.

Another challenge was trying to convince his scouts and coaches to change their traditional ways of recruiting and calling plays on the field. Necessity is the mother of invention, and Beane's limited funds forced him to invent new ways of obtaining talent for the least amount of money. He adopted and indeed perfected the use of sabermetrics, which is loosely defined as "the search for objective knowledge about baseball" when scouting and drafting players. He hired computer nerd Paul DePodesta, who was also a disciple of sabermetrics, to help him track down current players and draft candidates whose talents weren't immediately apparent, and could plug holes in Oakland's lineup at discount prices.

Beane went against the grain of most of the old school coaches by eschewing the sacrifice bunt, among other things. His thought process was that a team only has 27 precious outs; why waste one? He also had an incredible talent for getting the better end of trades. Three years after Beane took over as general manager, the A's made the playoffs four years in a row. And after trading away all of the stars that propelled the team, Oakland again made it to the postseason every year from 2012-14. They have yet to win another World Series since 1989, but most teams in the major leagues now emulate Beane's style of "moneyball."

Connie Mack

53. Ricky Henderson holds the career stolen base record.
How many did he steal in 25 years?

Braves

1B	Fred McGriff	P	Warren Spahn
2B	Felix Millan	P	Greg Maddux
3B	Chipper Jones	P	Phil Niekro
SS	Rabbit Maranville	P	Tom Glavine
OF	Wally Berger	RP	John Smoltz
OF	Dale Murphy		
OF	Hank Aaron		
C	Joe Torre		
DH	Eddie Mathews		

A Tale of Three Pitchers

"Maddux just never gives you anything to hit. He just keeps changing speeds and painting the corners. It makes for a long day."

Tony Gwynn

The Braves are the only team in major league history to win a World Series championship in three different cities: Boston in 1914, Milwaukee in 1957, and Atlanta in 1995. Alas, those were the only three championships in franchise history. The Boston Red Stockings, not to be confused with the Red Sox, changed their name to the Beaneaters in 1883, and became an early powerhouse in the National League. The 1898 team's record was an astounding 102-47. The franchise changed its nickname to the Doves in 1907, the Rustlers in 1911, and finally the Braves in 1912. Two years later the "Miracle Braves" came from last place on July 18th to win the pennant and the subsequent World Series. No other team has ever overcome such a deficit.

Shortly thereafter, however, the team's fortunes took a downward drift, attendance fell dramatically over the years, and in 1953 the franchise moved to Milwaukee. In 1957 they won another World Series, led by future Hall of Famers Hank Aaron, Warren Spahn, and Eddie Mathews, along with an impressive supporting cast of players such as Lew Burdette, Joe Adcock, and Del Crandall.

In 1966, the franchise moved once again, this time to Atlanta. After several years of mediocrity, the Braves put together a powerhouse team which won 14 consecutive divisional titles from 1991 to 2005, (the 1994 season had no winner due to a strike). The 1990s Braves also put some great players on the field, including Chipper Jones, David Justice, Fred McGriff, Andruw Jones, and Javy Lopez.

But it was the stellar pitching staff of Greg Maddux, Tom Glavine, and John Smoltz that catapulted the Braves into a dominant role. The best of the trio was Greg Maddux. He came to the Braves from the Chicago Cubs in 1993 where he had won the Cy Young Award the previous year. He then won the award for the next three years, setting a record (since matched by Randy Johnson) by winning it four years in a row.

Maddux was the quintessential cerebral pitcher. Traditional baseball thinking assumes that the batter has the advantage as a game progresses, assuming that the same pitcher is still in the game. They get a "read" on the pitcher so that by the third and fourth time up they know what to expect. Not so with Greg Maddux. He would waste pitches to certain batters so that they would expect the same pitch in a crucial at bat in the eighth or ninth inning, only to be fooled by a pitch they had not yet seen.

Wade Boggs, one of the best hitters of his era, said this about Maddux: "It seems like he's inside your mind with you. When he knows you're not going to swing, he throws a straight one. He sees into the future. It's like he has a crystal ball hidden inside his glove." Maddux and fellow mound mate Tom Glavine were masters at expanding the strike zone as the game wore on. They would start by hitting the outside corner and moving farther off the plate inch by inch. Umpires usually gave them strike calls because of the reputations they earned over the years. Thus by the late innings batters had to either hit an impossible pitch or strike out looking.

Maddux's intelligence, command of the strike zone, and sheer tenacity, rather than a blazing fastball, made him the best pitcher of his day. Baseball analyst Bill James thought that Maddux was the most underrated player *of all time!* Maddux finished his career with 355 victories. Only fellow Brave Warren Spahn had more wins in the live ball era. He is the only pitcher in history to win at least 15 games for 17 consecutive seasons. Beside the aforementioned 355 wins, his career accomplishments include a 3.16 ERA, and 3,371 strikeouts. He played in eight All-Star games and won four Cy Young Awards and an amazing 18 Gold Gloves. His 1994 batting average of .222 exceeded his ERA of 1.56. In 1997, when he became the highest paid player in the major leagues, he went to a 3-0 count only once!

Maddux's left-handed counterpart Tom Glavine made his major league debut with Atlanta on August 17, 1987. He joined a team that was struggling to stay out of the cellar, and did indeed, finish in last place for the next three years. But in 1991, Glavine won 20 games, along with a Cy Young Award, and led the Braves from worst to first to capture the division title. He was an all-around athlete who could have played professional hockey as well as Major League Baseball. He finished his career with 305 wins, a 3.54 ERA, and 2,607 strikeouts. He played on 10 All-Star teams, won four Silver Slugger awards, and two Cy Young Awards.

John Smoltz, a broad-shouldered flame thrower, was the third member of the Brave's triumvirate of the 1990s. His remarkable career included 213 wins, a 3.33 ERA, 3.084 strikeouts, and 154 saves. He was an eight-time All-Star, a Silver Slugger winner, a Cy Young Award winner and a Rolaids Award winner for the best relief pitcher in 2002.

During the 1990s, Maddux, Glavine, and Smoltz won seven Cy Young Awards. In 1996, they were three of six pitchers in the entire National League to have an ERA under 3.00. Maddux and Glavine were elected to the Hall of Fame in their first year of eligibility in 2013, along with their manager, Bobby Cox. John Smoltz joined them a year later. I believe they made up the greatest trio of starting pitchers ever, even eclipsing the great Cleveland Indian staff of Bob Feller, Bob Lemon, and Early Wynn.

Tom Glavine and Greg Maddux at their Hall of Fame Induction - 2013

54. What teams did Greg Maddux, Tom Glavine, and John Smoltz finish their careers with?

1B	Albert Pujols	P	Bob Gibson
2B	Frankie Frisch	P	Dizzy Dean
3B	Ken Boyer	P	Chris Carpenter
SS	Ozzie Smith	P	Jesse Haines
OF	Joe Medwick	RP	Lindy McDaniel
OF	Lou Brock		
OF	Stan Musial		
C	Yadier Molina		
DH	Rogers Hornsby		

The Cards of the 1960s

"Bob Gibson never had to put on a game face when he went out to pitch, because he never took his game face off. He intimidated everybody, including his own teammates."
Mike Shannon

Stan Musial, the greatest Cardinal of them all, retired in 1963. That's too bad. It would have been nice to see him play in one more World Series. He came close to finishing his illustrious career not with the Cardinals, but rather with the Philadelphia Phillies. In 1956, Cardinal General Manager Frank "Trader" Lane tried to deal Musial to the Phillies for Robin Roberts. St. Louis owner Gussie Busch nixed the deal, but the attempt left a bad taste in everyone's mouth regarding Lane. The following year Lane had a public altercation with Busch and then had the audacity to ask for a raise. Busch's response was classic for him: he told Lane to "kiss my ass" and promptly fired him. It was fortuitous for the Cardinals because they hired Bing Devine to replace him. Devine then built a Cardinals team that would once again be among the best teams in the National League.

Devine set out to build a Cardinals team based on speed and defense. He moved Ken Boyer to third base from the outfield and made a shrewd trade to acquire Curt Flood from the Cincinnati Reds. Cincinnati thought Flood was expendable because they had two other young studs in the outfield: Frank Robinson and Vada Pinson. Another significant move came in 1961 when the Cardinals replaced manager Solly Hemus for Johnny Keane. Hemus was hated by his players, especially the black players. Only his friendship with Gussie Busch kept him at the helm for as long as he lasted.

Devine then acquired Dick Groat in 1962 to shore up the infield. The Cardinals were never in the thick of the pennant race in 1963, but they did win 19 out of 20 games at the end of the season, providing hope going into 1964. But Musial's retirement at the end of the 1963 season left a gaping hole in the outfield.

Both Devine and Keane were high on a young, unproven outfielder with the Chicago Cubs by the name of Lou Brock. They proceeded to trade one of their best pitchers, Ernie Broglio, to Chicago for Brock. At the time of the trade the Cardinals were 28-31 and mired in eighth place. Most people thought the Cubs got the best part of the deal. But Brock found his groove in St. Louis and became, along with Boyer and pitcher Bob Gibson, a significant factor in bringing the pennant and a World Series trophy to St. Louis in 1964. In the 103 games he played for St. Louis Brock batted .348. It was the most lopsided transaction since the Boston Red Sox sold Babe Ruth to the Yankees.

The 1964 National League pennant race was one for the ages, one for which Devine and Keane deserve as much credit as the players. Besides trading for Brock, they "stole" Curt Simmons from the Phillies, which not only helped St. Louis, but hurt the Phillies, who were the Card's chief competition for the pennant. They also called up Mike Shannon to fill another outfield vacancy.

The Phillies had the pennant all but won that season, except their manager, Gene Mauch, foolishly started his two aces, Jim Bunning and Chris Short, each on two days' rest in the last week of the season. The Phillies lost all six games, while the Cardinals won 12 of their last 15 games to take the flag on the last day of the season.

St. Louis met the New York Yankees in the World Series and beat them in seven games. Ken Boyer hit a grand slam in game 4 for a come-from-behind victory. Bob Gibson was outstanding on the mound and won the Series MVP Award. Boyer won the NL MVP Award and Bing Devine was voted the Executive of the Year. The insufferable Gussie Busch fired Devine midway through the 1964 season, and Johnny Keane quit after the World Series to join foundering Yankees. Their departures presaged a rebuilding period for the Cardinals, who fell to seventh place in 1965.

In 1966, St. Louis traded Ray Sadeki to the San Francisco Giants for Orlando Cepeda, a slugging first baseman. Cepeda was to fill the gap left by the departed Ken Boyer and, much like the Brock/Broglio trade, the Cardinals got the best of this trade as well. Cepeda went on to win the MVP Award that year and lead the Cards to another World Series championship in 1967. He, along with Bob Gibson, Lou Brock and Yankee castoff Roger Maris, enabled the Cardinals to win the pennant by a commanding 10 games.

They faced the "impossible dream team" of Carl Yastrzemski's Boston Red Sox in the World Series and beat them in seven games. Bob Gibson, who missed a third of the season with a broken leg, was absolutely dominant, winning three complete games. Brock led all players in the Series with a .414 batting average, 12 hits, seven stolen bases, and eight runs scored.

The Card's won the 1968 pennant with virtually the same team. But this time they would face the Detroit Tigers' Denny McLain, who won 30 games that year. As good as McLain's year was, Bob Gibson's was arguably even better. Thirteen of his 22 victories in 1968 were shutouts. He struck out 268 batters and only issued 62 walks. He pitched 304 innings with 28 complete games. Now for the remarkable part: his ERA that year was a stingy 1.12!

Pitching in general was so spectacular in 1968 that Major League Baseball lowered the mound in 1969 from 15 to 10 inches to encourage more offense. Gibson set a World Series record in game 1 by striking out 17 Detroit batters. The series went the distance with Gibson facing Detroit's Mickey Lolich for all the marbles. It was a classic pitcher's duel, but Lolich prevailed, giving Detroit the victory. Brock once again led all players in the Series with a .464 batting average and seven stolen bases.

The lineups for the Cardinals in their three pennant winning years are as follows:

	1964	1967	1968
1B	Bill White	Orlando Cepeda	Orlando Cepeda
2B	Julian Javier	Julian Javier	Julian Javier
3B	Ken Boyer	Mike Shannon	Mike Shannon
SS	Dick Groat	Dal Maxvill	Dal Maxvill
LF	Lou Brock	Lou Brock	Lou Brock
CF	Curt Flood	Curt Flood	Curt Flood
RF	Mike Shannon	Roger Maris	Roger Maris
C	Tim McCarver	Tim McCarver	Tim McCarver
P	Bob Gibson	Bob Gibson	Bob Gibson
P	Ray Sadeki	Steve Carlton	Steve Carlton
P	Curt Simmons	Ray Washburn	Nelson Briles
P	Roger Craig	Dick Hughes	Ray Washburn
RP	Barney Schultz	Joe Hoerner	Joe Hoerner

Bob Gibson

55. How many career hits did Stan Musial have at home and on the road?

1B	Frank Chance	P	Ferguson Jenkins
2B	Ryne Sandberg	P	Mordecai Brown
3B	Ron Santo	P	Charlie Root
SS	Ernie Banks	P	Ken Holtzman
OF	Billy Williams	RP	Bruce Sutter
OF	Hack Wilson		
OF	Kiki Cuyler		
C	Gabby Hartnet		
DH	Sammy Sosa		

Mr. Cub

*" What does a mama bear on the pill have in common
with the World Series? No Cubs."*
Harry Caray

When the late Ernie Banks made his major league debut with the Chicago Cubs on September 17, 1953, not many would have guessed that the wiry 6'1", 180-pound rookie would become a prodigious home run hitter. If they had probed a little deeper however, and felt the power in his wrists, they may have thought otherwise.

Banks skipped the minor leagues and came to the big show straight from the Negro Leagues' Kansas City Monarchs. He joined Willie Mays, Hank Aaron, and several others in the first wave of black ballplayers to take advantage of the opening created by Jackie Robinson. Banks at short and Gene Baker at second base was the first black double-play combination in major league history.

A power-hitting outfielder or first baseman is a valuable asset to any ball club. A power-hitting, Gold Glove shortstop is a rarity indeed, which is why Ernie was coveted by most teams in both leagues. Many tried to pry him from the Cubs, but none succeeded. Banks spent his entire 19-year career with Chicago, never once making it into postseason play. The closest he came was in his penultimate season of 1970, when the Cubs finished five games back. Indeed, Banks holds the dubious record of most games played without a postseason appearance.

Despite playing for perennial losers, Banks nevertheless won two MVP Awards, in 1958 and 1959. He was the first player from a losing club to be so honored. The Cubs' dismal record during Bank's career certainly would have been even worse without him at shortstop. Jimmie Dykes, a prominent manager of the day, once quipped, "Without Banks, the Cubs would finish in Albuquerque."[11]

Banks retired from professional baseball after the 1971 season. His best years were in the late 1950s and early 1960s. During this period he was given the nickname "Mr. Cub", correctly reflecting his role as the face of the franchise. An injury in 1956 ended his streak of consecutive games played, but upon his return to the lineup 16 days later, he reeled off another 717 consecutive games. Banks always came to the ballpark to play.

He won his first MVP Award in 1958 by leading the league in home runs (47), RBIs (129), total bases (379), runs produced (201), and slugging average (.614). His MVP year of 1959 saw him lead the league in RBIs with 143 and in 1960 he led the league in home runs with 41. His competition during these years was the likes of Willie Mays, Hank Aaron, Frank Robinson, Roberto Clemente, and Eddie Mathews.

Banks's accomplishments during his 19-year career include: a .274 batting average, 2,583 hits, 512 home runs, and 1,636 RBIs. He played in 14 All-Star games (11 years), won two MVP Awards, two home run crowns, one RBI title, and one Gold Glove award. He holds the franchise record for games played, at-bats, extra base hits, and total bases.

Banks was voted into the Hall of Fame in 1977 on the first ballot, and named to the All-Century team in 1999. In 2013 he was awarded the Presidential Medal of Freedom. Fittingly, there is a statue of Ernie outside of his beloved "friendly confines" of Wrigley Field. He died January 23, 2015 at the age of 83.

Ernie Banks

56. What year did the Chicago Cubs last win the World Series?

1B	Gil Hodges	P	Sandy Koufax
2B	Jackie Robinson	P	Clayton Kershaw
3B	Maury Wills	P	Don Drysdale
SS	Pee Wee Reese	P	Don Sutton
OF	Zack Wheat	RP	Eric Gagne
OF	Duke Snider		
OF	Matt Kemp		
C	Roy Campanella		
DH	Babe Herman		

Dem Bums

" Wait 'til next year!"
Brooklyn Dodger fan mantra

The Dodgers were always colorful, but they were not always good. That changed in the late 1940s when they assembled a powerhouse team to go along with their élan. The Brooklyn Dodgers of the 1940s and '50s was perhaps the most beloved team in the history of the game. In Brooklyn during those years, they were a source of local pride bordering on a sacred institution as they evolved from the lovable bums to perennial pennant contenders.

One cause of extreme loyalty to a group, team, or institution is the level of hatred toward that group's rivals, be it a rival school, a rival town, or a rival country. Both of the Dodgers' rivals during the 1950s played in the same town, exacerbating the feeling of contempt. Within the National League, the Dodgers' biggest rival was the New York Giants, who frequently vied with Brooklyn for the pennant, and whose pitchers, most notably Sal "the Barber" Maglie, often threw at the heads of the Dodger batters.

The Dodgers got the better of the Giants more often than not, but their real nemesis was the elitist New York Yankees, who kept frustrating Brooklyn when the teams met in the World Series. From 1949 to 1964, at least one New York team was in the World Series, and often two. The Dodgers lost the World Series to the Yankees five times

(1941, 1947, 1949, 1952, and 1953), prompting the Brooklyn mantra "Wait 'til next year." Next year finally came in 1955 when the Dodgers defeated the Yankees in seven games in the fall classic.

All teams have their legions of loyal fans, but three factors added to the Dodgers's appeal. First, they played in Ebbet's Field. Many fans considered it a dump, but to the Dodger faithful, it was the most cozy and intimate park in the league. It was said that spectators sitting in the first base seats could hear the conversation between first baseman Gil Hodges and the opposing base runner.

Second, the Dodger lineup tended to remain intact throughout the late 1940s and 50s. Virtually all of their stars were in the lineup year after year. This constancy of familiar faces, so different from today's teams, also added to the fans's feeling of belonging to the team. The third factor was the fact that the Dodgers were the first team to integrate black players. That allowed them to field talent like Jackie Robinson, Roy Campanella, and Don Newcombe. I believe Dodger fans also had a feeling of immense pride that their team was defying the lords of baseball and doing "the right thing" by signing black players.

The Dodger team that finally beat the Yankees in 1955 for the World Series championship had the following lineup:

1B	Gil Hodges	P	Don Newcombe
2B	Jim Gilliam	P	Carl Erskine
3B	Jackie Robinson	P	Johnny Podres
SS	Pee Wee Reese	P	Billy Loes
LF	Sandy Amoros	RP	Clem Labine
CF	Duke Snider		
RF	Carl Furillo		
C	Roy Campanella		

They were 98-55 for the season and finished 13.5 games ahead of the second place Braves. Campanella won his third MVP Award and batted .318. He was fond of saying, "You gotta have a lot of little boy in you to be a good ballplayer." After he was paralyzed in a 1958 car accident, the largest baseball crowd ever to assemble came to pay homage at a benefit game in Los Angeles Memorial Stadium in 1959. Duke Snider was a close runner up to Campy for MVP: he led the league with 136 RBIs and walloped 42 home runs. The "Duke of Flatbush" had one of the strongest throwing arms in baseball: he once threw a ball over the 40-foot-high right field fence at Ebbets Field while standing at home plate, some 350 feet away.

Jackie Robinson contributed as usual to the team's success. During his 10-year tenure, Brooklyn won six pennants and one World Series championship. Carl Furillo, aka the "Reading Rifle" added 26 home runs, a .314 batting average, and stellar fielding to the mix; Gil Hodges chipped in 27 home runs and 102 RBIs. Even utility man Don Zimmer contributed on a part-time basis with 15 home runs and 50 RBIs. The pitching staff was led by Don Newcombe who won 20 games, Billy Loes who won 10 while only losing 4, and by Johnny Podres, who shut out the Yankees in the seventh game of the World Series to finally enable the loyal Dodger fans to proclaim, "This is next year!"

Jackie Robinson and Pee Wee Reese

57. Who succeeded Roy Campanella as the Dodger catcher?

1B	Bill Terry	P	Christy Mathewson
2B	Jeff Kent	P	Carl Hubbell
3B	Fred Lindstrom	P	Juan Marichal
SS	Travis Jackson	P	Gaylord Perry
OF	Barry Bonds	RP	Madison Bumgarner
OF	Willie Mays		
OF	Mel Ott		
C	Buster Posey		
DH	Willie McCovey		

The Shot Heard 'Round the World

"The Giants win the pennant! The Giants win the pennant!"
Russ Hodges, Giants announcer

The Brooklyn Dodgers won the National League pennant in 1949, then lost the 1950 flag to the Philadelphia "Whiz Kids" on a 10th inning home run by Dick Sisler in the last game of the season. Brooklyn was generally considered the National League's best team by far in 1951, and had a comfortable 13 game lead on August 11. All bets were on them to take the pennant again. Then the inexplicable happened. The New York Giants staged one of the greatest pennant comebacks in history, leading to what many consider the greatest game ever played: the "shot heard 'round the world."

After August 11, the Dodgers played 26-22 ball while the New York Giants, under the leadership of their fiery manager Leo Durocher, went 52-12 over the last 62 games. The Giants took a half-game lead on the last day of the season, meaning Brooklyn had to win its final game just to tie and force a three-game playoff. The Dodgers did just that against a good Philadelphia team, courtesy of a 14th-inning Jackie Robinson home run off Robin Roberts, the best pitcher in the league. It was a tough victory, exhausting the Dodgers as they returned home to face the Giants in the first playoff game.

One of the main reasons for the Giants' surge was the addition of perhaps the greatest player of all-time: Willie Mays. The Giants were mired in 5th place when Willie arrived on May 25. He started off terribly, but Durocher stuck with him and gave him the confidence to keep going. He ended the season by winning the Rookie of the Year Award.

The 1951 Giants were not as formidable on paper as the Dodgers, but they nevertheless had some talented ballplayers. Monte Irvin joined the team from the Negro Leagues at the age of 30. Roy Campanella, who played against Irvin in the Negro Leagues, called him the best player he ever saw when in his prime. Monte led the league in RBIs with 121. Scowling, dark, Sal "the Barber" Maglie struck terror in the hearts of Dodger batters due to his propensity to throw at their heads. Outfielder Don Mueller and super-sub Bobby Thomson were what baseball people call "professional hitters."

The stage was set for the three game playoff that would decide which team would face the New York Yankees in the World Series. One sure winner would be the city of New York, which would be home to a Subway Series regardless of the playoff's outcome. Big Jim Hearn won the first game for the Giants, 3-1 at Ebbets Field. In the second game, Chuck Dressen, the Dodger manager, surprised everyone by starting Clem Labine, who cruised to an easy 10-0 win at the Polo Grounds.

The third game was winner-take-all. Curiously, only 34,320 fans came out to watch the Wednesday afternoon contest. Both teams had their aces on the mound: big Don Newcombe for Brooklyn and the menacing Maglie for the Giants. Maglie, who had won 23 games that year, got off to a bad start and the Dodgers took an early 1-0 lead. But he held them in check until the eighth, when the Dodgers pushed across three more runs on four singles and a wild pitch. Meanwhile, Newcombe limited the Giants to just a run on four hits through the first eight innings. The Dodgers took their 4-1 lead into the bottom of the ninth, and it looked like the Giants' remarkable comeback would become nothing more than a footnote to history. Four days earlier,

Newcombe tossed a complete game shutout against Philadelphia, then threw 5.2 innings of scoreless relief in the season-ending win the following day. He complained that he had nothing left in his arm, but Dressen kept him on the mound anyway. Alvin Dark, the Giant shortstop, led off the ninth with a single. Dressen instructed Gil Hodges, his first baseman, to hold Dark on first even though his run was meaningless in a 4-1 game. The next batter, Don Mueller, then singled through the hole vacated by Hodges. Monte Irvin fouled out, but Whitey Lockman doubled, scoring Dark.

The Giants now had runners on second and third and were down by two runs with one out. At this point, Dressen finally removed Newcombe and brought in Ralph Branca, who had pitched eight innings in the first playoff game. Bobby Thomson hit Branca's second pitch into the left field stands to win the game and the pennant. The home run has been known ever since as "the shot heard 'round the world."

Branca immediately saw a priest after the game, asking "why me?" Thomson went on the Perry Como Show. The following day Red Smith of the New York Times wrote these lines: "Now it is done. The story ends. There is no way to tell it. The art of fiction is dead. Reality has strangled invention. Only the utterly impossible, the inexpressibly fantastic, can ever be possible again."

The 1951 Giants lineup follows:

1B	Whitey Lockman	P	Sal Maglie
2B	Davey Williams	P	Larry Jansen
3B	Bobby Thomson	P	Jim Hearn
	Hank Thompson	P	Dave Koslo
SS	Alvin Dark	RP	George Spencer
LF	Monte Irvin		
CF	Willie Mays		
RF	Don Mueller		
C	Wes Westrum		

Bobby Thomson

58. Who was on deck when Bobby Thomson hit his famous home run?

1B	Jim Thome	P	Bob Feller
2B	Nap Lajoie	P	Early Wynn
3B	Al Rosen	P	Bob Lemon
SS	Lou Boudreau	P	Stan Coveleski
OF	Larry Doby	RP	Mel Harder
OF	Tris Speaker		
OF	Rocky Colavito		
C	Victor Martinez		
DH	Earl Averill		

Larry, Lemon, Lou, and Leroy

*"In Cleveland, pennant fever usually ends up
being just a 48-hour virus."*
Frank Robinson

In October of 1948, Bostonians were excited about the prospect of an all-Boston World Series between the Red Sox and the Braves. The only thing standing in the way were the Cleveland Indians. The Red Sox and Indians were tied after the last game of the season, and a flip of a coin had the one-game do-or-die playoff game scheduled for Fenway Park.

Both managers, Lou Boudreau of the Indians, and Joe McCarthy of the Red Sox surprised the baseball world by starting unlikely pitchers for the most crucial game of the season. Boudreau's choice, Gene Bearden, won 20 games that year, but he was a southpaw, and lefties usually had a tough time at Fenway, with its short left field wall, the notorious Green Monster.

McCarthy's choice for a starting pitcher was even more bizarre. In fact, he was haunted by his decision for the remainder of his life. His two aces, lefty Mel Parnell and right-hander Ellis Kinder, were rested and ready to go. Everyone expected Parnell to get the nod, but McCarthy picked journeyman Denny Galehouse, ironically because he was a right-handed pitcher. The Indians won handily 8-3.

The Indians hadn't won a World Series since the 1920 team of Tris Speaker and Stan Coveleski. But the 1948 team was a powerhouse that seemed poised to end that reign of futility. It featured six future Hall-of-Famers as well as several other talented players. Pitchers Bob Feller and Bob Lemon, and player/manager Lou Boudreau were the team's stalwart veterans. Second baseman Joe Gordon came over from the Yankees the year before in a trade for pitcher Allie Reynolds.

Owner Bill Veeck, who tried to integrate the major leagues years earlier, bought the contract of Larry Doby from the Newark Eagles of the Negro Leagues a mere six weeks after Jackie Robinson made his major league debut in 1947 and then at the end of the 1948 season, Veeck acquired the services of Negro League legend, Leroy "Satchel" Paige. As the 1948 season began the six future Hall-of-Famers were now primed for a championship run. Boudreau had a season for the ages. He shone both offensively and defensively and won the American League Most Valuable Player Award as well as the Associated Press Athlete of the Year. He made the All-Star team along with Gordon, Feller, Lemon, and third baseman Ken Keltner.

The Indians beat the Boston Braves in six games to take the World Series. Satchel Paige became the first black pitcher to win a World Series game, and Larry Doby became the first black player to hit a home run in a World Series. The Braves of "Spahn and Sain and pray for rain" were good-- the two aces were the winning pitchers in Boston's two victories-but the rest of the Braves pitching staff came up short.

It's tough to be number two. Jackie Robinson deservedly gets credit for being the dominant force in integrating the major leagues. But Doby, who signed with the Indians just six weeks after Jackie's debut, endured the same insults, physical threats, and disdain from his own teammates that Jackie did. He also did it without the media attention that Robinson had. As a rookie Doby was booed even from his own fans if he struck out or made a bad play.

In one particular game in his rookie year, Doby struck out on three pitches that were out of the strike zone. Joe Gordon was the next batter, an excellent contact hitter. He too struck out on three swings, missing the ball by a wide margin on each pitch. Then in a move reminiscent of Pee Wee Reese putting his hand on Jackie Robinson's shoulder in front of a hostile Cincinnati crowd, he went into the dugout and sat down next to Doby. Doby finished his career a seven time All-Star, a World Series champion, a two-time home run champion, and an RBI champion. He was voted into the Hall of Fame in 1998 by the Veterans Committee. Fittingly, Cleveland was the first major league team to hire a black manager, Frank Robinson, in 1975.

The 1948 Cleveland Indians lineup was:

1B	Eddie Robinson		P	Bob Feller
2B	Joe Gordon		P	Bob Lemon
3B	Ken Keltner		P	Gene Bearden
SS	Lou Boudreau		P	Sam Zoldak
LF	Dale Mitchell		RP	Russ Christopher
CF	Larry Doby			
RF	Thurman Tucker			
C	Jim Hegan			

1948 Cleveland Indians

59. How many games did the 1954 Indians win?

1B	George Sisler	P	Jim Palmer
2B	Davey Johnson	P	Dave McNally
3B	Brooks Robinson	P	Mike Mussina
SS	Cal Ripken	P	Mike Flannigan
OF	Boog Powell	RP	Tippy Martinez
OF	Paul Blair		
OF	Adam Jones		
C	Rick Ferrell		
DH	Eddie Murray		

Weaver's Boys

"Brooks Robinson never asked anyone to name a candy bar after him. In Baltimore, people name their children after him."

Gordon Beard

The Baltimore Orioles of the early to mid 1960s were an average American League team. But they became a great team by 1969 and remained that way throughout the 1970s. A solid young pitching staff provided the foundation for greatness, along with stalwart position players like Brooks Robinson, Boog Powell and Paul Blair, but they consistently lacked sufficient talent to overtake the Yankees, Tigers, and Twins for the pennant.

Two trades and one promotion from the minor leagues significantly changed the Orioles' prospects and put them on the road to becoming a potential dynasty. At the beginning of the 1966 season, the Orioles orchestrated what is perhaps the most one-sided trade in baseball history (Babe Ruth was sold, not traded). They sent Milt Pappas, Jack Baldschun, and Dick Simpson to the Cincinnati Reds for Frank Robinson.

Reds owner Bill DeWitt tried to justify the trade by stating that Robinson was an "old" 30 years of age. Old or not, Robinson won the Triple Crown in his first year with the Orioles, and anchored the great Baltimore teams for the next several years, prompting one scribe to write: "Baltimore belonged to Brooks, but the Orioles were the property of Frank Robinson".[12]

In 1968 the Orioles brought a pugnacious manager up from their minor league system to the parent club. He started as the third base coach, but took the managerial helm in July of that year. His name was Earl Weaver, and he remained as manager for 17 years, retiring on October 5, 1986. Weaver, like Billy Beane a generation later, did not believe in "small ball." He built his Oriole teams around pitching, defense, and three-run home runs. When stressing defense, he told his players, "Let's not give them more outs than they're entitled to."

He also believed that most winning teams score more runs in one inning than the losing team scores in the entire game, hence his distaste for bunts and sacrifices. When asked about his philosophy he said, "I've got nothing against the bunt in its place. But most of the time, that place is at the bottom of a long forgotten closet."

Weaver was a master at setting his lineups based on matchups, so he often benched a slugger like Boog Powell against a particular pitcher that the gargantuan first baseman had a history of hitting poorly. This was at a time when most big league managers couldn't even spell the word statistics. He had a love/hate relationship with his players, especially the temperamental ace of his staff, Jim Palmer. Daniel Okrent and Steve Wulf, in their book, "Baseball Anecdotes," tell the story of a tour that the Orioles took to Japan. A sumo wrestler visiting the team wanted to show how strong he was by lifting the diminutive Weaver over his head with just one hand, whereupon the entire team yelled in unison, "Drop him."

Only once in 17 years did a Weaver-managed Oriole team finish below .500. He was ejected over 100 times, yet his career won-lost record is 1,480-1,060. He won four pennants and one World Series championship and was voted into the Hall of Fame in 1996. Peter Angelos, managing partner of the Orioles, said this about him: "Earl Weaver stands alone as the greatest manager in the history of the Orioles' organization, and is one of the greatest in the history of baseball."

When Weaver arrived in Baltimore, he inherited a team with a good pitching staff, but it needed just a little more depth. The second significant trade made before the 1969 season was to secure the services of the veteran screwball pitcher Mike Cuellar from the Houston Astros. Like Robinson, Cuellar paid immediate dividends, winning 23 games and sharing the Cy Young Award with the Tigers' Denny McLain. He would win 20 games three more times by 1974.

Robinson, Weaver, and Cuellar put an already strong Oriole team over the top. The Orioles won the pennant in 1969 with a record of 109-53, 19 games ahead of the second place Detroit Tigers. Dave McNally won his first 15 decisions. Baltimore swept the Minnesota Twins in the playoffs, but lost to the "Miracle" New York Mets in the World Series.

In 1970 they again won the pennant, again swept the Twins in the playoffs, but this time beat the Cincinnati Reds in the World Series, which showcased Brooks Robinson's amazing defense at third base. They went 108-54 and finished ahead of the second place New York Yankees by 15 games. The 1970 team featured three 20-game winners in Cuellar, McNally, and Palmer, and three Gold Glovers in Brooks Robinson, center fielder Paul Blair, and second baseman Davey Johnson, (shortstop Mark Belanger just missed the award). Boog Powell won the Most Valuable Player Award with 35 home runs and 114 RBIs. Frank Robinson contributed with a .306 batting average and 25 home runs, and Brooks Robinson added 94 RBIs. Merv Rettenmund, who replaced Blair after a beaning, hit .322 with 18 home runs in 106 games.

The 1971 season brought a third straight pennant, putting this group of Orioles in the company of the great Yankee teams of the 1950s and Athletic teams of the 1920s. They again swept their opponents in the playoffs, only this time the victims were the Oakland A's. Baltimore's 101-57 record placed them 12 games ahead of the second-place Tigers.

Pat Dobson, who the Orioles had acquired in a trade over the previous offseason, joined McNally, Palmer, and Cuellar in the 20-win club. It was only the second time in major league history that four members of a team's pitching staff had achieved that goal (the 1920 Chicago White Sox staff was the first to accomplish the feat). Alas, the four aces lost to Roberto Clemente and the Pittsburgh Pirates in the World Series.

The starting players and the pitching staff stayed essentially the same from 1969-1971 The lineup follows:

1B	Boog Powell	P	Jim Palmer
2B	Davey Johnson	P	Dave McNally
3B	Brooks Robinson	P	Mike Cuellar
SS	Mark Belanger	P	Tom Phoebus/Pat Dobson
LF	Don Buford	RP	Pete Richert
CF	Paul Blair/Merv Rettenmund		
RF	Frank Robinson		
C	Elrod Hendricks/Andy Etchebarren.		

Earl Weaver

60. How many career Gold Gloves did Paul Blair win?

1B	Ryan Howard	P	Steve Carlton
2B	Chase Utley	P	Grover Alexander
3B	Mike Schmidt	P	Robin Roberts
SS	Dave Bancroft	P	Curt Schilling
OF	Ed Delahanty	RP	Jim Konstanty
OF	Richie Ashburn		
OF	Chuck Klein		
C	Darren Daulton		
DH	Dick Allen		

Lefty

"When you call a pitcher Lefty and everybody in both leagues knows who you mean, he must be pretty good."
Clint Hurdle on Steve Carlton

Every team and every city celebrates when they win a World Series championship, but the 1980 Philadelphia Phillies and their fans had a special reason for exuberance after they beat the Kansas City Royals to win the title.

The Phillies had never won a championship in 98 years of existence! They had just finished a grueling playoff series with the Houston Astros, including multiple-extra inning games; the Royals, meanwhile had four days of rest after easily dispatching the New York Yankees. A special treat for the fans watching the Series that year was the fact that they were able to watch two third basemen who were perhaps the two best ever at that position: Mike Schmidt and George Brett. They both played well, but Schmidt took the World Series MVP honors. The Phillies had a good all-around team in 1980, but three players stood out: Schmidt, the newly acquired Pete Rose, and their ace pitcher, Steve Carlton.

Lefty, as Carlton became known, made his major league debut on April 12, 1965 with the St. Louis Cardinals. He made the All-Star team three times in seven years with the Redbirds, and he struck out a then-record 19 Mets in a game in 1969 (although he lost the game due to two home runs by Ron Swoboda). His breakout year was 1971, when he won 20 games, just a year after losing 19.

At the end of that season, a contract dispute with Cardinals' owner Gussie Busch led to his being traded to the Philadelphia Phillies for Rick Wise. Like Frank Robinson for Milt Pappas, this trade ended up being completely one-sided. Lefty's first year with the Phillies was one for the ages. He won pitching's triple crown with 27 wins, 310 strikeouts, and a 1.97 ERA. He also pitched 30 complete games and toiled for 346 innings. However, his most amazing statistic was that his 27 wins represented 46% of Philadelphia's total wins! If he had pitched for Pittsburgh that year he may well have racked up 35 victories.

Carlton was one of those dominating pitchers whose fastball and slider terrified hitters. His physical appearance alone was enough to unnerve even the most intrepid batters. He stood 6'4", weighed 210 pounds, and kept himself in superb shape by practicing martial arts. He had a routine in which he would fill a five-gallon barrel with rice, and then work his hand to the bottom and then start over again, helping him develop one of the strongest wrists and forearms in the majors. His regimen also helped him attain one of his proudest achievements: in 23 seasons he was never on the disabled list.

Lefty was voted into the Hall of Fame in 1994 on the first ballot, garnering 95.8% of the vote. He treated sportswriters as pariahs, earning their enmity and the nickname, "Silent Steve." By 1978 he had stopped talking to them completely. I have to wonder if the 95.8% of the Hall of Fame vote may have approached 100% if he and the writers got along better.

Carlton finished his career with 329 wins, a 3.22 ERA and 4,136 strikeouts (still fourth all-time). He appeared in 10 All-Star games, was a member of two World Series championship teams, pitched six one-hitters, won one Gold Glove and four Cy Young Awards. He holds a strange combination of records: most career balks (90), and most career pick-offs (144). The Sporting News ranked him #30 on their All-Time team. There is a statue of Lefty just outside of Veterans Stadium in Philadelphia.

The lineup for the 1980 Phillies World Series champions follows:

1B	Pete Rose	P	Steve Carlton
2B	Manny Trillo	P	Randy Lerch
3B	Mike Schmidt	P	Dick Ruthven
SS	Larry Bowa	P	Bob Walk
LF	Greg Luzinski	RP	Tug McGraw
CF	Garry Maddox		
RF	Bake McBride		
C	Bob Boone		

Steve Carlton

61. Which member of the 1980 Phillies was nicknamed "The Bull"?

Pirates

1B	Willie Stargell	P	Rip Sewell
2B	Bill Mazeroski	P	Deacon Phillippe
3B	Pie Traynor	P	Bob Friend
SS	Honus Wagner	P	Babe Adams
OF	Paul Waner	RP	Roy Face
OF	Lloyd Waner		
OF	Roberto Clemente		
C	George Gibson		
DH	Ralph Kiner		

The Great One

*" That night on which Roberto Clemente left us physically,
his immortality began."*
Puerto Rican writer Elliott Castro

V ery few major league ballplayers leave a legacy that transcends their play on the field. Jackie Robinson did it by opening the door to black players. Ted Williams did it with his exploits as a fighter pilot. Lou Gehrig did it with his courage in the face of impending doom.

I would like to add Roberto Clemente to that august list. The Great One, as he was called throughout Latin America, was a pathfinder for other Hispanic players. He was as close as any man in history to being deified throughout that world, especially in his native Puerto Rico.

Clemente's initial years were marked by the same racial issues that Jackie Robinson endured, only they were exacerbated by his inability to speak English. He chose to speak Spanish on national television while being interviewed after his spectacular play in the 1971 World Series. That choice shocked the American viewing audience, but brought pride to millions of Latinos.

He wasn't the first Latino ballplayer to come to the major leagues, but he was the first star. For much of his career he received little attention outside Pittsburgh, but he eventually won wide acclaim due to his spectacular outfield play and consistent hitting, striking fear in pitchers with his vicious line drives up the middle.

Roberto was initially scouted by the Brooklyn Dodgers. Their scout, Al Campanis, said that Clemente was the best free agent he ever saw. In one of the biggest blunders in baseball history, the Dodgers left Clemente unprotected in the 1955 Rule 5 draft, thinking that no other team would pluck him from their roster.*

Branch Rickey, the former Dodger president who was now the Pirates general manager, couldn't believe his luck when he saw Clemente was available and made him the first pick of the draft. Recall that the Dodgers had once passed on Willie Mays. So in hindsight, they could have had Mays, Clemente, and Duke Snider in the same outfield!

At the end of 1954, Clemente was involved in a car crash. He wrenched his neck and spine, which he said bothered him for the rest of his career. One has to wonder how much better he, like Mickey Mantle before him, might have been if not for injury.

Because of the neck injury, Clemente had a ritual at the plate where he would go through all sorts of neck gyrations, cock his bat toward the pitcher, and point his right hand toward the umpire. Soon kids throughout Pittsburgh and Puerto Rico were mimicking him. He was one of the most graceful outfielders in the history of the game, but at the plate he was herky-jerky.

Robin Roberts, the Hall of Fame Philadelphia Phillies pitcher said this of Clemente, "He was the most unorthodox good ballplayer I ever saw. Most good ballplayers are smooth. They do things with rhythm. Well, Roberto had his own rhythm. He looked like he was falling apart when he ran the bases. His stance at the plate was ridiculous. It was a crazy thing. The only thing that made him look sensational was the results."[13]

Clemente was a true five tool player. He could hit (.317 lifetime average), hit for power, field (12 Gold Gloves), run, and throw. He had only 240 home runs, but two factors contributed to that relatively low number. First, he was a natural line drive hitter. Don Drysdale said that he feared for his life whenever he faced Roberto, because of his propensity to hit ferocious line drives up the middle. In 1969, Clemente hit one that nicked Drysdale's ear, drawing blood. He pitched to one more batter, then promptly retired from baseball. Secondly, the first time Clemente saw Forbes Field, the Pirates' home field, he realized that it would be fruitless to try to hit home runs in that cavernous park.

Perhaps his greatest asset was his strong arm. He may have had the strongest arm in major league history. He would deliberately fumble a ball just to make the base runner think that he could advance, whereupon Roberto would fire a bullet to cut him down. Al Kaline, the outstanding right fielder for the Detroit Tigers, played during the same years as Clemente during their prime. He won 10 Gold Gloves (Clemente won 12), and was considered the finest right fielder in the American League. If he had played in the National League, he would have been second best every year.

In Game 2 of the 1971 World Series, Merv Rettenmund of the Baltimore Orioles was on second base when Frank Robinson hit a ball to deep right center field. Clemente caught the ball as he crashed into the wall. Rettenmund figured he could tag up easily. Clemente's throw nearly caught him as he slid into third base. Andy Etchebarren, the Baltimore catcher, said it was the greatest throw he had ever seen. National Leaguers had been seeing throws like that from Clemente for years.

Roberto knew that he was among the premier players of his time and he resented what he thought was a lack of respect by the Pittsburgh sportswriters and fans. A glaring example of this lack of respect, at least in his eyes, came at the end of the 1960 season. The Pirates had awakened from their slumber and beat the mighty Yankees in the World Series. Clemente had a great year and many baseball experts thought he should have won the Most Valuable Player Award. Les Biederman, a writer for the Pittsburgh Press, campaigned heavily for

Roberto's teammate Dick Groat, who won the batting title and was a sparkplug for the team. Not only did Groat win the award, but fellow teammates Don Hoak and Vernon Law finished ahead of Clemente as well. This deeply hurt Clemente for the rest of his life. He felt that if he played in a major media center that he would get the respect afforded to players like Mays, Mantle, and Sandy Koufax.

Clemente's opportunity to play in the national spotlight came again in 1971, when the Pirates faced the Baltimore Orioles in the World Series. He hit safely in all seven games, (he also hit safely in all seven games of the 1960 Series, giving him a 14-game hitting streak in World Series play). The series featured two of the best right fielders of the day, with Pittsburgh's Clemente opposing Baltimore's Frank Robinson. Both stars had stellar performances, but when the Pirates won game 7, Clemente's two homers and .414 average made him the obvious MVP.

When Clemente got his last hit (number 3,000), in 1972, little did people know that it would be his last. Three months later, he died in a plane crash, delivering emergency supplies to the ravaged country of Nicaragua, which had suffered a devastating earthquake. Nicaraguan dictator Anastasio Somoza's soldiers were stealing the supplies and the population was starving. Roberto planned to confront the dictator and force him to distribute the food. As the quote at the beginning of this section says, Roberto's immortality began when the plane went down.

The entire Hispanic world mourned the Great One. The Hall of Fame waived the mandatory five-year waiting period after retirement and immediately voted him into the Hall in 1973. He joined Lou Gehrig as the only two players to be so honored. As a testament to his global appeal, 40 public schools, two hospitals, and over 200 parks are named after him in Puerto Rico, Pittsburgh, and Mannheim, Germany. The Roberto Clemente Award is given annually to the player that best exemplifies the combination of outstanding baseball ability and significant community involvement.

Roberto's 18 year career was spectacular. His .328 batting average was the best in the 1960s. He is tied for the most games in a Pittsburgh uniform. For his career he had a .317 batting average, amassed 3,000 hits, 240 home runs, and 1,305 RBIs. He played in 15 All-Star games (12 years), won two World Series, won 12 Gold Gloves, and four batting titles. He was the Most Valuable Player in 1966, and the MVP of the 1971 World Series. There is a magnificent statue of Clemente outside of PNC Park in Pittsburgh.

The rule 5 Draft allows teams to pick up any unprotected player from another team's roster as long as it keeps that player on the major league 25-man roster for the entire season.

Roberto Clemente

62. Whose record did Clemente tie for most games in a Pirate uniform?

Reds

1B	Ted Kluszewski	P	Eppa Rixey
2B	Joe Morgan	P	Bucky Walters
3B	Pete Rose	P	Jim Maloney
SS	Barry Larkin	P	Don Gullett
OF	Frank Robinson	RP	Norm Charlton
OF	Vada Pinson		
OF	Edd Roush		
C	Johnny Bench		
DH	Tony Perez		

The Big Red Machine

"If there's a runner on second base, there isn't anybody I'd rather see walk to the plate than Tony Perez. He turns mean with men on base."

Sparky Anderson

The Cincinatti Reds of the 1970s possessed one of the most fearsome lineups in baseball history. You can count on one hand the number of teams that have had four future Hall-of-Famers in their lineup during their prime. The 1927 New York Yankees actually had six players make it to Cooperstown: Babe Ruth, Lou Gehrig, Tony Lazzeri, Earle Coombs, Waite Hoyt, and Herb Pennock. Connie Mack's 1932 Philadelphia Athletics boasted such stars as Jimmie Foxx, Mickey Cochrane, Al Simmons, and Lefty Grove.

The great Atlanta Braves teams of the late 1990s and early 2000s featured Hall-of-Famers Greg Maddux, Tom Glavine, John Smoltz, and Chipper Jones, who is certain to be inducted when eligible in 2017. Gary Sheffield, a borderline Cooperstown candidate, played with these four perennial All-Stars from 2002-03.

Technically, the Big Red Machine of the 1970s only has three Hall-of-Famers, but I count Pete Rose because his playing ability merits his election, even if his personal failings rightly keep him out of Cooperstown. The other three were Johnny Bench, perhaps the greatest catcher ever, second baseman Joe Morgan, and first baseman

Tony Perez. Their manager, Sparky Anderson, also has a plaque in Cooperstown.

Anderson came to Cincinnati in 1970 and managed the team to its first pennant of the decade. The Reds amassed 102 victories in their new park, Riverfront Stadium, on their way to the flag, but lost the World Series to Earl Weaver's Baltimore Orioles. Rose, Bench, Perez, and shortstop Dave Concepcion led the attack, with Bench taking the NL MVP Award. The Reds led the league in home runs and slugging average. The pitching was solid with Jim Merritt and Gary Nolan comprising an outstanding one-two starting pitching punch while Wayne Granger set a record with 35 saves. The Big Red Machine was on its way to dominating the National League for the decade.

In 1971 the offense slumped and the Reds lost 29 points off their team batting average as well as a whopping 200 runs off their previous year's production. They significantly increased their offensive punch the following year when they acquired Joe Morgan from the Houston Astros.

To get Morgan, the Reds had to trade their power-hitting first baseman, Lee May, along with second baseman Tommy Helms. In return however, they improved their speed and power with Morgan, their defense with center fielder Cesar Geronimo, and their starting pitching with Jack Billingham.

The trade didn't quite make up for dealing Frank Robinson for Milt Pappas, but it was still pretty lopsided in Cincinnati's favor. Morgan became one of the cornerstones for the Big Red Machine. He was a rare player: a second baseman who could hit for power, possessed great speed, and was a defensive stalwart.

In 1972, Cincinnati's power returned, with Bench hitting 40 home runs, knocking in 125 runs, and winning his second MVP Award. But after defeating the defending champion Pirates for the pennant, the Reds again came up short in the World Series, losing to the Oakland A's, who were building their own dynasty.

The Reds won their division again in 1973, but this time fell to the Mets in the playoffs. Pete Rose won the MVP Award that year with a .338 batting average and 230 hits. Both Rose and Bench once again had outstanding seasons in 1974. Rose led the league in runs (110) and doubles (45), and Bench led with 129 RBIs and 315 total bases.

The magic returned in 1975, when Cincinnati's 108 victories were 20 better than the second-place Dodgers. This time it was Joe Morgan's turn to win the MVP Award, while Rose led the league in runs with 112 as well as in doubles with 47. After defeating the Pittsburgh Pirates in the National League Championship Series, they met the Boston Red Sox in what many experts still consider the greatest World Series of them all. Five games were decided by one run, and two went to extra innings. The Series is remembered, of course, for Boston catcher Carlton Fisk "willing" his home run to stay fair to win game 6 in the 13th inning. But the Reds came back the next day to take game 7. The victory gave Cincinnati its first World Series championship in 35 years.

The Big Red Machine repeated as champions in 1976, making them the first National League team to do so since the 1921-22 New York Giants. They didn't lose a game in postseason play that year, sweeping the Phillies in the NLCS and the Yankees in the fall classic.

Morgan won his second-straight MVP Award that year, Rose led the league in hits (215), doubles (42), and runs (130), and Bench starred in the Series with a blistering .533 batting average, two home runs, and 6 RBIs. Sparky Anderson however, maintained that it was the pitching more than the offense that contributed to Cincinnati's stellar year. An egalitarian group of starters (seven pitchers had double-digit victories) was bolstered by the best relief corps in the league: closer Rawley Eastwick, and setup men Pedro Borbon and Will McEnaney.

Anderson's tenure as skipper during the decade of the 1970s was punctuated by his proclivity to yank starting pitchers at the slightest sign of trouble, earning him the nickname, "Captain Hook". He allowed the starting pitchers of his 1970, 1972, 1973, 1975, and 1976 divisional championship teams to only complete 32, 25, 39, 22, and 33 games respectively. In 1975 the Reds went 45 consecutive games without anyone pitching a complete game, winning 32 of those games.

The Reds did not win another pennant for the rest of the decade, but they were in the thick of it every year. Individual players continued to excel. In 1977, a new member of the Big Red Machine joined the MVP club. George Foster, who first cracked the starting lineup in 1975, led the league with 52 home runs, 149 RBIs, 124 runs, a .631 slugging average, 388 total bases, and 221 runs produced. A year later, Rose hit safely in 44 consecutive games and Foster once again led the league in home runs (40) and RBIs (120). The 1979 Reds won their division but lost the playoffs to the Pirates.

Overall, the 1970s saw the Reds win five divisional titles, four pennants, two World Series championships, and six MVP Awards. Indeed, they were one of the greatest teams ever. But as with all things, the Big Red Machine lost its dominance as the decade came to a close. One by one, beginning with Perez in 1977 and ending with Foster in 1981, Rose, Morgan, and manager Anderson all signed as free agents with other clubs.

The most significant Cincinnati players for the decade of the Big Red Machine were:

1B	Tony Perez	P	Don Gullett
2B	Joe Morgan	P	Jack Billingham
3B	Pete Rose	P	Gary Nolan
SS	Dave Concepcion	P	Pat Darcy
LF	George Foster	RP	Rawley Eastwick
CF	Cesar Geronimo		
RF	Ken Griffey		
C	Johnny Bench		

1975 "Big Red Machine"

63. What two members of the Big Red Machine of the 1970s played their entire career with the Reds?

1B	Carl Yastrzemski	P	Roger Clemens
2B	Bobby Doerr	P	Pedro Martinez
3B	Wade Boggs	P	Cy Young
SS	Joe Cronin	P	Luis Tiant
OF	Ted Williams	RP	Dick Radatz
OF	Harry Hooper		
OF	Jim Rice		
C	Carlton Fisk		
DH	David Ortiz		

End of the Drought

"All you see in Red Sox –Yankee games are fights
and cops dragging people out by the hair."
Don Zimmer

The Boston Red Sox became champions of Major League Baseball in 2004. The last time that had happened, Lawrence of Arabia captured Damascus, the Somme offensive was launched, the Red Baron was shot down and killed, Sergeant Alvin York killed 20 Germans and captured 132, the Spanish Flu killed 21,000 Americans in one week, Poland and Iceland became independent states, the Austro-Hungarian Empire collapsed, and World War I came to an end.

Talk about a losing streak! After losing the World Series in seven often heart-breaking games in 1946, 1967, 1975, and 1986, Bostonians finally had reason to celebrate. An astounding three million fans came out to participate in the victory parade on October 30. Grown men were openly crying in the streets.

The year before, the Red Sox lost the American League Championship to the hated Yankees. They were ahead 5-2 in the eighth inning of the deciding seventh game when Pedro Martinez told manager Grady Little that he still had enough stuff to get the Yankees out, even though he was clearly tired. The Yankees tied the game and went on to win in the 11th inning. The Sox were eager for revenge as the 2004 campaign got under way.

The foundation for the 2004 season was laid in 2002 when John Henry, Tom Werner, Larry Lucchino, and Theo Epstein became principal owner, chairman, president, and general manager respectively. At the beginning of the 2003 season Epstein orchestrated deals that brought David Ortiz and Kevin Millar to the Sox, and acquired the services of pitcher Curt Schilling and manager Terry Francona at the outset of the 2004 season. All four would prove instrumental in the successful run for the championship.

As the season progressed, Epstein made two additional significant trades that finally brought the Sox the talent and the team chemistry they needed to compete in the tough American League Eastern Division. Nomar Garciaparra was the linchpin of the infield and a bonafide superstar at shortstop, as well as a fan favorite, but he was becoming more and more disgruntled. His public remarks as well as his mood swings weren't helping the team's cohesiveness. So, in a surprise move that both shocked and angered Boston fans, Epstein shipped him to the Chicago Cubs in a multi-team deal on the final day of the trading deadline. In return the Red Sox acquired shortstop Orlando Cabrera and first baseman Doug Mientkiewicz. They also traded little known Henri Stanley to the Los Angeles Dodgers for speedster Dave Roberts. All the pieces were now in place.

Soon after these trades were consummated, Boston went on a tear and won 22 out of 25 games. They finished the season in second place in their division, three games behind the Yankees, and good for a wild card berth for the American League playoffs. Thus the stage was set for one of the most improbable and thrilling playoffs in baseball history. After sweeping the Anaheim Angels, the Sox would meet the Yankees for the American League championship.

The Red Sox lost the first three games of the Series, and their prospects were dim for finally besting their hated rivals. In game four, the Sox were down to their last straw, losing 4-3 in the ninth inning. But future Hall of Fame closer Mariano Rivera issued a walk to Kevin Millar, who was taken out for pinch runner Dave Roberts. Roberts stole second base, and scored on a single by third baseman Bill Mueller to tie the game. Boston then won in extra innings on a David Ortiz home run. Game five was another nail-biter. Boston was trailing 4-2 when Ortiz made it 4-3 with a home run in the eighth inning. Catcher Jason Varitek tied the game with a sacrifice fly and Ortiz knocked in the winning run with a single in the 14th inning.

Game six may one day be the topic of a Hollywood movie. Curt Schilling, after being spiked, had suffered a torn tendon in one of the divisional playoff games. Francona nevertheless selected him as his starter. He required three sutures on his ankle, but pitched in pain for seven innings allowing only one New York run. The television camera zooming in on his bloody sock has become an iconic image forever etched in the minds of Boston fans. Part-time second baseman Mark Belhorn hit a three run home run in the fourth inning to give Boston the lead.

The game took an odd turn in the eighth inning. Third baseman Alex Rodriguez hit a ball back to the Boston pitcher, Bronson Arroyo. But as Arroyo tagged him, Rodriguez slapped the ball out of Arroyo's hand. Rodriguez was called safe and ended up on second base, while Derek Jeter scored all the way from first base. But after the umpires huddled to review the play, they called Rodriguez out for interference. Jeter was ordered back to first base, and the riot police were called out to restrain the angry New York fans. The Yankees didn't get another hit the rest of the game, and the Red Sox won.

Boston's Derek Lowe pitched a one-hit gem for six innings in the seventh game, and won with help from outfielder Johnny Damon's two home runs, one of which was a grand slam. The Red Sox became the only team in Major League Baseball history to come back from a 0-3 deficit in a best-of-seven series.

The World Series against the St. Louis Cardinals was almost anti-climatic after the heart-stopping series against New York, even though the Cardinals had the best record in the majors. The Red Sox train just kept on rolling, sweeping the Cardinals in four games.

The usual starting lineup for the 2004 Red Sox was:

1B	Kevin Millar	P	Pedro Martinez
2B	Mark Belhorn	P	Curt Schilling
3B	Bill Mueller	P	Derek Lowe
SS	Orlando Cabrera	P	Tim Wakefield
LF	Manny Ramierez	RP	Keith Foulke
CF	Johnny Damon		
RF	Gabe Kapler		
C	Jason Varitek		
DH	David Ortiz		

Curt Schilling

64. Who caught the ball for the last out of the 2004 World Series?

Tigers

1B	Hank Greenberg	P	Hal Newhowser
2B	Charlie Gehringer	P	Jim Bunning
3B	George Kell	P	Jack Morris
SS	Alan Trammel	P	Justin Verlander
OF	Harry Heilmann	RP	Willie Hernandez
OF	Ty Cobb		
OF	Al Kaline		
C	Lance Parrish		
DH	Miguel Cabrera		

Mr. Tiger

"I have always referred to Al Kaline as Mr. Perfection."
Billy Martin

As far as I know, there are only two other ballplayers besides Al Kaline who are honored by having the nickname Mr. (team name). They are Mr. Cub (Ernie Banks), and Mr. Brave (Hank Aaron). Such a nickname denotes not only an illustrious career, but devotion and loyalty to a particular club. Both Kaline and Banks spent their entire Hall of Fame careers with one team, and Aaron was a Brave for the great majority of his career. Ty Cobb was certainly a better player than Kaline, and Hank Greenberg and Charlie Gehringer were huge fan favorites. But no other Detroit Tiger player is more revered than Al Kaline.

Kaline was born in Baltimore, Maryland on December 19, 1934 to a poor family. He was playing semi-pro ball at the tender age of 14, facing pitchers with minor league experience. He was an outstanding pitcher in the league, but when he showed up to play for his high school team, there was no room for him at that position, so they moved him to the outfield. There he shone, batting .353, .418, and .469 in three seasons.

Kaline's high school exploits did not go unnoticed by the baseball scouts. The Tigers signed him at 18 years of age as a bonus baby right out of high school. He made his major league debut on June 25, 1953.

Two years later he became the youngest player in history to win the batting title, hitting .340 with a league-leading 200 hits, plus 27 home runs and 102 RBIs.

Kaline was the prototypical five-tool player. He could hit for average, he could hit for power, he had a powerful right fielder's arm, he was fast and he was an excellent fielder. When Rawlings introduced the Gold Glove Award in 1957, it originally chose just one player at each position for all of Major League Baseball. That year, Kaline, Willie Mays, and Minnie Minoso were the three outfield choices. He went on to win nine more Gold Gloves. Brooks Robinson, who knows a thing or two about fielding, said, "There have been a lot of great defensive players. The fella who could do everything is Al Kaline. He was just the epitome of what a great outfielder is all about – great speed, catches the ball and throws well." Kaline played 242 consecutive errorless games at the height of his career. He accomplished these feats in spite of a foot that was so deformed from a bout of osteomyelitis as a kid that he was almost a cripple! He played in constant pain.

Al was a fan favorite for many reasons, including his total dedication to the team over himself and his clutch play. The first reason was demonstrated in 1970 when he turned down a $5,000 raise that would have placed him in the rarified air of the $100,000 a year player. He felt he did not deserve it. The second reason was demonstrated over and over again, but never quite as profoundly as when he batted .379 to help the Tigers win the 1968 World Series.

Kaline's career statistics are: .297 batting average, 3,007 hits, 399 home runs, 1,583 RBIs, 18 All-Star games (15 years), 10 Gold Gloves, a batting title, and a World Series championship. He was elected to the Hall of Fame on the first ballot in 1980, and was selected to The Sporting News list of the all-time 100 greatest players.

Al Kaline

65. In 1961 Al Kaline batted .324 and finished second for the batting title. His teammate finished first. Who was the teammate?

1B	Mickey Vernon	P	Walter Johnson
2B	Rod Carew	P	Bert Blyleven
3B	Harmon Killebrew	P	Jim Katt
SS	Cecil Travis	P	Johan Santana
OF	Heine Manush	RP	Joe Nathan
OF	Kirby Puckett		
OF	Goose Goslin		
C	Joe Mauer		
DH	Sam Rice		

1991

"The 1991 World Series is the greatest of all-time."
ESPN

The history of the Minnesota Twins begins with an 1894 Western League franchise known as the Kansas City Blues. When the league changed its name to the American League in 1900 to compete with the more established National League, the Blues moved to the nation's capital, where they became the Washington Senators. The Senators were mediocre or worse during most of their history, prompting the quip, "First in war, first in peace, and last in the American League," but they did win one championship in 1924. They also owned perhaps the greatest pitcher of all-time, Walter Johnson.

In 1961 the Senators moved the franchise to Minnesota and changed their name to the Twins. They quickly became pennant contenders and produced such stars as Harmon Killebrew, Rod Carew, Tony Oliva, Jim Kaat, and Zoilo Versailes. Since moving to Minnesota the Twins have won 10 divisional titles, three pennants, and two World Series championships. From 1964-2009, a Twin has led the league in hitting 14 times, with Rod Carew responsible for half of those titles.

The 1991 World Series was undoubtedly the most thrilling of the Twins' two titles. Their opponents were the Atlanta Braves. Ironically, both Minnesota and Atlanta had finished last the previous year before completing a worst to first turnaround. Before the start of the 1991 campaign, Minnesota's front office made two significant acquisitions. They acquired free agents Chili Davis, who became a devastating designated hitter for them, and Jack Morris, who became an iron man on the mound and the ace of the staff. They faced the Toronto Blue Jays in the American League Championship Series, beating them in five games on the strength of Morris' two victories and center fielder Kirby Puckett's nine hits and five RBIs.

Thus, the stage was set for what ESPN would come to regard as the greatest World Series of all time. Minnesota hosted Atlanta in the first game and pitted war horse Jack Morris against Atlanta's crafty southpaw Charlie Leibrandt. The Twins drew first blood with left fielder Dan Gladden scoring on a single by Chuck Knoblauch in the third inning. They then added three more runs in the fifth on a three-run home run by shortstop Greg Gagne. The Twins won 5-2, with Morris getting the win.

Game Two featured future Hall-of-Famer Tom Glavine on the mound for the Braves, and 16-game winner Kevin Tapani throwing for the hometown Twins. A first inning collision between Braves second baseman Mark Lemke and right fielder David Justice gave Minnesota two unearned runs. Then in the third inning first base umpire Drew Coble called Ron Gant out as he tried to get back to the bag after a single. Replays showed that first baseman Kent Hrbek had pulled Gant off the base, but Coble did not change his call, and the Atlanta threat ended. Scott Leius' eighth-inning homer broke a 2-2 tie to give Minnesota the 3-2 win.

Game three was a topsy turvy affair in which the Braves won in 12 innings 5-4. Twins manager Tom Kelly used up all of his position players by the 12th inning, so he had to use a pitcher, Rick Aguilera, as a pinch-hitter with two outs and the bases loaded. Aguilera flied out, then gave up the winning run in the bottom of the 12th.

Jack Morris took the mound for Minnesota once again in the fourth game, going against John Smoltz for Atlanta. It was another wild game, yet again decided by one run in the final at-bat. Mark Lemke tripled with one out in the Atlanta ninth, and fourth-string catcher Jerry Willard hit a sacrifice fly to complete the walk-off win.

Glavine and Tapani faced off again in the fifth game, which the Braves won in what was the only one-sided game of the Series, 14-5. Lonnie Smith hit his third home run of the Series, David Justice hit his second, and Brian Hunter added a home run of his own.

As the Series shifted back to Minnesota, both teams had reason to be optimistic. The Braves were winning the series 3-2, but the Twins were going home to the Metrodome where they enjoyed a 9-1 record in postseason play. Game Six was another nail-biter, with the Twins prevailing 4-3 in 11 innings. This game was the Kirby Puckett show. He had three hits, including a walk-off home run in the bottom of the 11th. Puckett animatedly pumped his fist as he rounded second base, a memory captured in the statue of him that sits outside Target Field, the new Twins' stadium. Equally important was a spectacular catch he made against the Plexiglas in the third inning to rob Ron Gant of a two run homer.

If game six was the Kirby Puckett show, game seven was the Jack Morris show. Morris went the distance, and then some: he threw a 10-inning shutout, 126 pitches in all, and growled at manager Tom Kelly several times in the late innings when Kelly tried to take him out of the game. The game's only run came in the bottom of the 10th, when Gladden led off with a double and Gene Larkin singled him home.

Morris's last year of Hall of Fame eligibility passed in 2014 without him winning enough votes for enshrinement. Too bad. There are worse pitchers in the Hall.

As stated earlier, the 1991 World Series was arguably *the* most exciting series ever. Five games were decided by one run. Four games were decided in the final at bat. Three games went extra innings, with the final game being won in the eleventh for a 1-0 victory. The 69 innings played remain a modern day World Series record.

The 1991 Twins lineup was as follows:

1B	Kent Hrbek	P	Jack Morris
2B	Chuck Knoblauch	P	Kevin Tapani
3B	Mike Pagliarulo	P	Scott Erickson
SS	Greg Gagne	P	Allan Anderson
LF	Dan Gladden	RP	Rick Aquilera
CF	Kirby Puckett		
RF	Shane Mack		
C	Brian Harper		
DH	Chili Davis		

1991 Minnesota Twins

66. Jack Morris was called up by the Tigers in 1977 to replace their quirky ace. Who did he replace?

White Sox

1B	Paul Konerko	P	Ted Lyons
2B	Eddie Collins	P	Ed Walsh
3B	Luke Appling	P	Red Faber
SS	Luis Aparicio	P	Mark Buerle
OF	Joe Jackson	RP	Hoyt Wilhelm
OF	Minnie Minoso		
OF	Harold Baines		
C	Ray Schalk		
DH	Frank Thomas		

Say it ain't so, Joe

"I done it for the wife and kiddies."
Eddie Cicotte

An awful revelation greeted readers of the sports pages in September, 1920. The Chicago White Sox had fixed the 1919 World Series. From the very beginning, the lords of baseball had worried about the potential for corruption in the game. Petty gambling in the form of office pools and individual bets were and always will be a risk to the game. The natural urge to gamble however, very often gave way to the sure thing: the fix. Hal Chase, one of the best first baseman of the day, was notorious for fixing games. Christie Mathewson suspected him of nefarious dealings, but couldn't prove it, so Chase continued the practice. It's suspected that he played a role in the aforementioned World Series fix, which became known as the Black Sox scandal.

Charles Comiskey, known as "the old Roman," was the owner of the Chicago White Sox from 1901-31. He was one of the most powerful owners in baseball, and he was also one of the most parsimonious. Attendance was down in 1919, so Comiskey was constantly looking for ways to cut costs. Usually that meant shortchanging his players. The White Sox were the best team in the major leagues, yet had one of the lowest payrolls in either league.

The most egregious example of Comiskey's stinginess was his treatment of his ace pitcher, Eddie Cicotte. Cicotte was promised a $10,000 bonus if he attained 30 wins in 1919. His record at the end of the season was 29-7. His 30th win was in the bag when Comiskey gave orders to the manager, Kid Gleason to "rest" him for the final two weeks. The resentment that Cicotte and other shabbily treated players felt toward Comiskey surely affected their judgment when temptation came their way in the form of professional gamblers waving dollar bills under their noses.

Chick Gandil, the Chicago first baseman, was the instigator of the fix. He often associated with various small time hoodlums and ne'er-do-wells. In one such meeting, with Boston gambler and petty gangster Joseph Sullivan, Gandil intimated that he would consider throwing the Series if the money were right. Sullivan took the bait and assured Gandil that he would deliver $100,000 if Gandil could guarantee seven key players to go along.

By persuasion and deceit Gandil was able to add pitchers Cicotte, Lefty Williams, shortstop Swede Risberg, and left fielder "Shoeless" Joe Jackson. He approached third baseman Buck Weaver, who declined. Utility infielder Fred McMullin overheard Gandil and Risberg discussing the fix and threatened to expose them if he was not included, so he was the seventh player to sell out.

Petty hoodlums Bill Burns, Billy Maharg, and Abe Attell became involved as well. The big player however, on the gambler's side, was Arnold Rothstein, a major New York gambler who supplied resources and connections. The odds were set at 3-1 in favor of the White Sox over the National League champion Cincinnati Reds. The gamblers were not certain that the players would actually fulfill their part of the bargain, so a signal had to be sent to ensure them that their money was guaranteed. When Cicotte hit the second Cincinnati batter, they knew the fix was on.

Hugh Fullerton, a reporter for the Chicago Herald and Examiner, smelled a rat from the very first game and was instrumental in exposing the fix. Cicotte lost the first game and Williams lost the second. In both contests, catcher Ray Schalk was infuriated at both pitchers for repeatedly ignoring his pitch signals. Dickie Kerr, who was not in on the fix, pitched the third and sixth games and won them both. Decades later, Red Sox pitcher and "philosopher" Bill Lee noted that Kerr owns one of the greatest records in baseball: he won two games in a World Series even though the rest of his team was trying to lose those games.

Legendary sportswriter Ring Lardner, composed a song that he defiantly sang to the White Sox players on the train back to Chicago. It was titled, "I'm forever blowing ball games." When the players realized that the gamblers were going to stiff them on their payment, they decided to play for real. Eddie Cicotte won the seventh game and Lefty Williams was primed to win the eighth when one of the gangsters threatened to kill him and his family if he won. He threw the game and the Reds won the nine-game Series in eight games.

Ban Johnson, President of the American League, launched an investigation. He and the owners also decided it was time to put some teeth into baseball's governing body. As such, they hired a crusty, hard-nosed judge to become the first Commissioner of Major League Baseball. His name was Kenesaw Mountain Landis, and he agreed to take the job as long as he could have unquestioned authority. The owners reluctantly agreed to his terms. Jackson, Cicotte, and Williams were persuaded to sign confessions as to their involvement. Johnson convinced Bill Burns to testify against the players and the gamblers in front of a Grand Jury. However, the confessions were "lost" and the eight players (the original seven plus Buck Weaver), were exonerated and cleared of criminal charges.

The players were ecstatic after being cleared of all charges and went to an Italian restaurant to celebrate. While they were celebrating however, Judge Landis made an announcement that shook the world of professional baseball. "Regardless of the verdict of juries, no player that throws a game, no player that entertains propositions or promises to throw a game, no player that sits in on a conference with a bunch of gamblers in which ways and means of throwing a game are discussed and does not promptly tell his club about it, will ever play professional baseball."[14]

All eight players were banned for life from playing in the major leagues. Even Buck Weaver, who never took any money, did not agree to be included in the fix, and who had a stellar series, was doomed by the last clause, since he did not report what he knew. Joe Jackson, who had a spectacular series, and was allegedly too simple minded to grasp what was being done, was another unfortunate victim. He would have been a shoe-in for the Hall of Fame if not for the scandal. (Eddie Cicotte might also have made it). But, while Landis's sentence strikes me as too harsh for Jackson and Weaver, it was well-deserved for the other six players. As was Landis' intention, the rough justice served to clean up the sport, and professional gambling on sports took a precipitous fall after the judge's ruling.

"Shoeless" Joe Jackson

67. What players on the 1919 White Sox are members of the Hall of Fame?

1B	Lou Gehrig	P	Whitey Ford
2B	Tony Lazzeri	P	Lefty Gomez
3B	Alex Rodriguez	P	Red Ruffing
SS	Derek Jeter	P	Waite Hoyt
OF	Mickey Mantle	RP	Mariano Rivera
OF	Joe DiMaggio		
OF	Dave Winfield		
C	Yogi Berra		
DH	Babe Ruth		

Dominance (1949-53)

" You kind of took it for granted around the Yankees that there was always going to be baseball in October."

Whitey Ford

Prior to the 1949 season, the Sporting News polled 206 baseball writers for their forecast of the upcoming year for the American League. More than half (119) picked the Red Sox, based on Boston's strong finish the year before, when they missed winning the pennant by one game. Another 79 sportswriters chose the defending champion Cleveland Indians.

Just six sportswriters picked the New York Yankees, even though the Bronx Bombers were just two seasons removed from their last World Series championship. But that was under Bucky Harris, who the Yankees fired when he failed to repeat in 1948. The team's decision to replace Harris in 1949 with Casey Stengel was greeted with derision by many baseball people, including writers, fans, and even some Yankee players, especially the greatest Yankee, Joe DiMaggio.

Stengel was viewed as a clown, which indeed he was for much of his previous managerial stints. He wouldn't become known as "The Old Perfessor" until later in his career. Only once in his previous nine years of managing had he finished over .500. But, when he assumed the helm of the Yankees, he set out to prove the pundits wrong about both himself and the team.

Stengel also inherited problems that were not obvious to the sportswriters or the fans. The biggest was his aging roster of injured veteran stars. DiMaggio, the most famous athlete in America, was 35 and had foot problems that kept him out until June 28. Tommy "Old Reliable" Henrich was 36 and appeared in just 115 games. Charlie "King Kong" Keller was 32 and limited to just 144 plate appearances.

But, there were bright spots too. Yogi Berra had settled in behind the plate after being tutored in the art of catching by ex-Yankee great Bill Dickey, and was hammering the ball to all fields. When asked by a reporter about the progress of his learning process, Yogi inimitably replied, "Dickey is learning me all of his experiences."

The pitching staff, on the other hand, was stellar, second only to the Indians fearsome foursome of Bob Lemon, Bob Feller, Early Wynn, and Mike Garcia. Stengel would never allow his pitchers to throw more than 300 innings, thus, preserving their arms for the postseason, as well as likely extending their careers.

The team got off to a fast start, winning 30 of its first 42 games. They split their next 24 games, but managed to maintain a hold on first place. Then, DiMaggio woke up one morning in midsummer and realized that his foot did not hurt. He inserted himself into the lineup and went on a tear, hitting .346 for the season.

The pennant was decided on the last day, with the Yankees and Red Sox tied for the lead, and facing each other in Yankee Stadium. Joe DiMaggio vs. Ted Williams. The Yankees prevailed, thanks to a four-run outburst in the eighth inning. Stengel's boys then went on to defeat the Brooklyn Dodgers in the World Series, 4 games to 1. Joe DiMaggio became the first $100,000 player that year, and Casey Stengel proved that he was for real.

Ironically, the roster that seemed so old at the beginning of the 1949 season became the nucleus of a team that would dominate the American League for the next decade. The starting rotation of Allie Reynolds, Vic Raschi, and Ed Lopat was not only very good, but very intimidating as well. Opposing batters feared facing them, especially the frowning, big-shouldered Raschi. In 1950, the Yanks added a fourth starter to this troika: Whitey Ford, a homegrown New York kid who won nine out of his first 10 games. They now possessed one of the best starting rotations in history.

On the way to the 1950 World Series, Joe DiMaggio hit three home runs in one game against the Senators on September 10, and Vic Raschi set a record by retiring 32 batters in a row. Their opponents in the fall classic were the "Whiz Kids," the Philadelphia Phillies. New York swept the Phillies, although the first three games were decided by one run. Shortstop Phil Rizzuto was the Series Most Valuable Player.

If people suspected that the Phillies were a team of destiny in 1950, they were absolutely convinced that the New York Giants were similarly fated to win in 1951. The Giants were fresh off their astounding victory against the Dodgers, thanks to Bobby Thomson's "shot heard 'round the world" and took two of the first three games. Because Whitey Ford was inducted into the military before the start of the series, Stengel had no other pitcher to start the fourth game. Luckily for the Yankees it rained, and the game was postponed, allowing Allie Reynolds to start the next game. He pitched a complete game victory, as did Lopat the day after, and the Yankees held on in game 6 to win the series.

Before the start of the 1951 season, the Yankees signed a raw-boned kid from Oklahoma who would eventually replace Joe DiMaggio in center field. His name was Mickey Mantle. In game 2 of the 1951 World Series, Mantle was playing right field, with DiMaggio in center. Willie Mays was the batter for the Giants, and the ensuing play entered the pantheon of epic major league moments, seeing as how it involved arguably the three best center fielders in history.

Stengel told Mantle before the game to, "Take everything you can get in center: the Dago's heel is hurting pretty bad." When Mays hit a blooper to right center, Mantle charged in for the catch as Stengel had instructed him. However, DiMaggio was already camped under the ball. Mantle then tried to get out of Joe's way, and in so doing, tripped on a sewer drain, severely damaging his knee. He suffered torn ligaments and would never play another game without pain. Yogi Berra was the Series Most Valuable Player, and Ed Lopat won two complete games and had a 0.50 ERA.

The Yankees once again faced the Dodgers in the 1952 World Series. They won again, with three players contributing in spectacular fashion. Allie Reynolds won two games and saved one. Johnny Mize, 39 years old, hit three home runs and knocked in six in 15 at bats. The young second baseman Billy Martin made a spectacular play in the seventh game. The Yankees were ahead 4-2 in the seventh inning and the Dodgers had the bases loaded with two outs. First baseman Joe Collins lost a pop up in the sun. If it fell to the ground the game would be tied. Martin made an acrobatic diving catch to retire the side and quite possibly save the series.

The same two teams squared off again in the 1953 fall classic, with the Yankees winning again, this time in six games. Martin led both teams with 12 hits in 24 World Series at bats. During the season, Mickey Mantle, who had replaced DiMaggio in center field the year before, started to amaze the baseball world with his tape measure home runs, and Ed Lopat had an .800 won-lost percentage to go along with his 3.42 ERA.

The best and most representative Yankee players during the five year period 1949-1953 are:

1B	Joe Collins	P	Whitey Ford
	Johnny Mize		
2B	Jerry Coleman	P	Allie Reynolds
	Billy Martin		
3B	Bobby Brown	P	Vic Raschi
	Billy Johnson		
	Gil McDougal		
SS	Phil Rizzuto	P	Ed Lopat
LF	Gene Woodling	RP	Joe Page
CF	Joe DiMaggio		
	Mickey Mantle		
RF	Tommy Henrich		
	Hank Bauer		
C	Yogi Berra		

Six of the above players were elected to the Hall of Fame: DiMaggio, Mantle, Berra, Ford, Rizzuto, and Mize. All but Mize played their entire careers with the Yankees. Casey Stengel also made it into

Cooperstown. When Joe DiMaggio was alive, he was voted the greatest living player, won three MVP Awards, and hit in 56 consecutive games. Mantle also won the MVP Award three times, is regarded as the best switch hitter in history, hit some of the longest home runs ever, and was a five-tool player who before his injury may have been the fastest player in the major leagues at the time. Berra bested them all, winning a total of 10 World Series rings over his career. He won three MVP Awards, and is considered one of the two best catchers of all-time.

Ford, nicknamed "Chairman of the Board," ended his career with a .690 won-lost percentage, the best among modern pitchers with 200 or more victories. Stengel generally used Ford only against the stronger teams; otherwise his career numbers would be even more impressive. Rizzuto was a defensive whiz at shortstop and a team leader during his tenure with the team. Third baseman Billy Johnson said, "You want to know the key to our team, it's Phil Rizzuto."

The Yankee stars were central to their success of course, but they would not have won an incredible five consecutive World Series championships without their manager, Stengel. He won 10 pennants in 12 years and was a master at getting the most out of his players. He was ahead of his time in platooning players and in using his bullpen. It is doubtful, in today's free agent environment, if a team will ever again win five consecutive championships.

1950 New York Yankees

68. Who replaced Casey Stengel as manager of the Yankees?

— Angels/Astros/Mets/Rangers —
First Wave of Expansion

1B	Jeff Bagwell	P	Nolan Ryan
2B	Craig Biggio	P	Tom Seaver
3B	David Wright	P	Dwight Gooden
SS	Michael Young	P	Jered Weaver
OF	Josh Hamilton	RP	Billy Wagner
OF	Mike Trout		
OF	Lance Berkman		
C	Ivan Rodriguez		
DH	Juan Gonzalez		

The Ryan Express

"He's the only guy who puts fear into me. Not because he can get me out but because he could kill me."

Reggie Jackson on Nolan Ryan

The Cincinnati Reds became the first acknowledged professional baseball team in 1869. Other teams and an additional league were added and pretty soon there were 16 professional baseball teams in America. Those 16 teams would change locations and names, but would stay intact for all intents and purposes, until 1961-62, when Major League Baseball expanded to 20 teams.

When I think about expansion baseball teams, I think of Gene Autry, the longtime owner of the Angels baseball club. Long before he considered owning a franchise, however, Autry was The Singing Cowboy, and he had the coolest horse of all the Hollywood cowboys. Champion the Wonder Horse was a sorrel-colored beauty. I got my first bike when I was seven years old, and named it Champion.

Autry was one of the grand old gentlemen of baseball owners, holding the Angels for 38 years. When the franchise moved to Orange County in 1965, the Los Angeles Angels changed their name to the California Angels. A 1997 agreement with the city of Anaheim led to another name change to the Anaheim Angels in 1997: since 2005, despite much derision, they have been known as the Los Angeles Angels of Anaheim.

It took 41 years, but the Angels finally won a World Series in 2002. They made it to the playoffs as a wild card, and defeated the Yankees in the Divisional Series 3 games to 1. This was not a complete surprise, as the Angels are the only team in the American League to have a winning record against the Yankees in the last 20+ plus years. Anaheim then easily handled the Minnesota Twins in the LCS, 4-1.

The Angels faced the San Francisco Giants in the World Series. It was the first World Series between two wild card teams. Barry Bonds of the Giants had broken Mark McGwire's single season home run record that year, walloping 73 round-trippers, and many thought the series would be the Barry Bonds show. Bonds did indeed hit four home runs in the seven-game series, but the Giants were done in by a double dosage of Troys. Reliever Troy Percival had 3 saves and third baseman Troy Glaus had 10 hits and was the series MVP.

The play that is the most memorable in my mind occurred in the fifth game. Giants first baseman J.T. Snow was racing toward home with David Bell hot on his heels, when Darren Baker, the Giants' three-year old bat boy (and son of Manager Dusty Baker) ran to the plate from the dugout to retrieve a bat. Snow scooped the tyke up by his jacket as he crossed the plate, thus avoiding what could have been a serious collision.

The other team to debut in the American League in 1961 was the Washington Senators. The name was old, but the team was new. The original Senators moved west at the end of the 1960 season and became the Minneapolis Twins. The new Senators eventually moved west too. In 1971 they became the Texas Rangers, a franchise that has come close, but as of 2014, is still waiting for its first championship.

The National League followed suit in 1962 by adding two teams of its own: the Houston Colt .45s and the New York Mets. In 1965 Houston made two significant changes. They changed their name to the Astros in honor of their new home, the Houston Astrodome, the so-called "eighth wonder of the world." The building proved to be less than wondrous, however. To reduce glare for the fielders, the team had to paint over the roof's glass panels. That prevented sunlight from shining on the grass, which quickly died. Thus another innovation was born: AstroTurf.

On April 15, 1968 the Astros played a game against the Mets that lasted 24 innings! Tom Seaver of the Mets pitched for 10 innings and Houston's Don Wilson went the first nine. Wilson was a mainstay of the Astros' rotation in the late '60s and early '70s. He was supplanted in 1975 by J.R. Richard, a huge right-hander with a devastating fastball. Bizarre, tragic accidents ended each man's career. Wilson was found in his car dead of carbon monoxide poisoning; Richard suffered a series of strokes in the midst of a 10-4 season, and never pitched in the big leagues again.

Houston fans still chafe when they think of the 1971 trade that sent popular second baseman Joe Morgan and Cesar Geronimo to the Cincinnati Reds for Lee May and Tommy Helms, among others. Morgan and Geronimo became vital cogs for the Big Red Machine: May excelled for the Astros for three years, but was traded again in 1974 for Baltimore's Enos Cabell.

The Astros had their longest sustained run of success from 1997-2005, when they won four division titles and made the playoffs six times, including a 2005 World Series loss to the Chicago White Sox. Those years coincide with the peak performance of the "Killer B's:" Jeff Bagwell, Craig Biggio, Derek Bell, Sean Berry, and Lance Berkman. The Astros never finished any higher than second place after that lone World Series appearance, and from 2011-2013, they lost 100 or more games every year.

The New York Mets were supposed to replace the Dodgers and Giants, the two National League teams that abandoned New York for California five years earlier. The Mets' colors are, in fact, a combination of Dodger blue and Giant orange. As daunting an assignment as that was, they did a remarkable job of achieving their goal. Despite posting a worst-ever 40-120 record, they became lovable losers in New York, a comic antidote to the high-flying Yankees. Los Angeles Times sportswriter Jim Murray once claimed "the only difference between the Mets and the Titanic is that the Mets have a better organist." The early Mets were so awful that their manager, an aging Casey Stengel, reportedly once asked : "Can't anybody here play this game?" Jimmy Breslin made it the title of his book about the Mets' inaugural year.

In 1969, however, the "Miracle Mets" stunned the baseball world by not only getting into the World Series but defeating the powerful Baltimore Orioles. In 1986 they once again won the World Series championship by defeating the Boston Red Sox in stunning fashion. This time, however, they were not a surprise entrant into the fall classic. Their record of 108-54 was one of the best in history.

What do the four expansion teams listed above have in common? They all employed one of the greatest pitchers of all time: Nolan Ryan: (All four teams also employed pitcher Darren Oliver, but he's merely the answer to a trivia question). Ryan made his debut with the Mets on September 11, 1966. He was used as a reliever and spot starter for New York and had a tendency to be wild.

So, in another one of the long list of horrible trades, the Mets dealt him to the Angels in 1971 for Jim Fregosi, an All-Star shortstop. Fregosi got old in a hurry, and was shipped to Texas after a season and a half in New York. Ryan, meanwhile, blossomed with the Angels. In his first year in California, he led the league in strikeouts with 329 and set an American League record by allowing only 5.26 hits per nine innings. In 1974 the Angels finished in last place, but Ryan nevertheless won 22 games.

At the end of the 1979 season, Ryan became a free agent. The Houston Astros then signed him to a $1,000,000 contract, the first player to make it to that milestone.

At the end of the 1988 season, Ryan was 41, and though he had led the National League in strikeouts that year, his career appeared to be on the downswing. The Texas Rangers took a chance on him, and he rewarded them with a 16-10 season, not to mention a league-leading 301 strikeouts. He went on to pitch for another four years with Texas, throwing high-90s fastballs well into his 40s, winning his 300th game and reaching the 5,500 strikeout plateau.

Ryan's achievements on the mound were the stuff of legend. He pitched for 27 years in the major leagues, a record. He pitched seven no-hitters, another record. He struck out 5,714 batters, a record that still exceeds his closest competitor, Randy Johnson, by 839. He averaged the fewest hits allowed per nine innings, 6.56. He threw a 100 mph fastball along with a devastating 12-6 curve ball. On the negative side, he has the record for the most walks issued, 2,795, which is 962 more than runner up Steve Carlton. Put another way, batters walked 50% more often against Ryan than against any other pitcher in history.

Despite his remarkable achievements, Ryan never won a Cy Young Award. He was elected to the Hall of Fame on the first ballot, garnering 98.79% of the vote. Only Jackie Robinson has had his number retired by more teams than Ryan, with the Angels, Astros, and Rangers all doing the honors.

Nolan Ryan

69. Who are the only 2 players to receive more Hall of Fame votes than Nolan Ryan?

— Brewers/Expos/Padres/Royals —
Second Wave of Expansion

1B	Adrian Gonzalez	P	Teddy Higuera
2B	Frank White	P	Bret Saberhagen
3B	George Brett	P	Zack Greinke
SS	Robin Yount	P	Jake Peavy
OF	Ryan Braun	RP	Trevor Hoffman
OF	Andre Dawson		
OF	Tony Gwynn		
C	Gary Carter		
DH	Paul Molitor		

Captain Video

"Tony Gwynn is the best pure hitter in the game. Easily."
Greg Maddux

In 1969 Major League Baseball expanded again by adding four more teams: the Kansas City Royals, Montreal Expos, San Diego Padres, and Seattle Pilots. The Pilots went bankrupt after one year, and in 1970 became the Milwaukee Brewers. They have yet to win a championship, but in 1982, "Harvey's Wallbangers," named for manager Harvey Kuenn's hitters, won the American League pennant.

The San Diego Padres have also never won a championship, although they twice won the National League pennant, in 1984 and 1998. The Montreal Expos were the first major league team to be based outside of the United States. The name "Expos," was derived from the 1967 World Exposition, which was held in Montreal. The franchise has never won a World Series either, although the Expos had the best record in baseball well into the 1994 season when a strike was called and the rest of the season was cancelled. Baseball threatened to eliminate the Expos in 2004, salvaging it only when the league purchased the franchise and moved it to Washington D.C., where the team became known as the Nationals.

Thus, the only team of the 1969 expansion class to win World Series championships (2) is the Kansas City Royals. The first was in 1985, in what was known as the I-70 Series. Their opponents that year were the cross-state rival St. Louis Cardinals. Cardinal fans forever remember that series as the one in which umpire Don Denkinger blew a call at first base, leading to two Royal runs to win game six.

The Royals went into a 29-year long skid after that title, failing to reach the postseason again until their heartbreaking loss to the San Francisco Giants in the 2014 World Series. Their troubles began with the 1989 signing of free agent closer Mark Davis from the Padres. The $13 million they paid Davis over four years was the highest yearly salary ever paid at the time. Unfortunately, Davis never saved more than six games in a season for Kansas City, who shipped him off to Atlanta two years later, and ate a lot of salary.

Ewing Kauffman, the Royals founding owner, never minded spending money on his team, even if it didn't translate to on-field success. But after his death in 1993, new owner David Glass treated the team the way he treated his other business, Wal-Mart, where he was Chief Executive Officer until 2000. Playing in small-market Kansas City, Glass was never shy about keeping his payroll low. In 1994 the Royals had a $40.5 million payroll, the fourth-highest in the major leagues. Two years later, their payroll slipped to $18.5 million, the second lowest in the majors. One major asset of the Royals for much of their existence was their spectacular third baseman, George Brett. Among his many achievements is one that may never be duplicated and certainly never broken: he is the only player to win a batting title in three separate decades.

Brett was part of the World Champion Royals of 1985 as a player. Thirty years later, in 2015 he was once more a member of a Royals championship team, only this time it was as a front office executive. The 2015 Royals ran away with the American League Central Division title by besting the second place Twins by 12 games. Their 95-67 record was the best in the league. Their style of play, exemplified by keeping the ball in play, solid defense, and great pitching, especially out of the bullpen, enabled them to beat the New York Mets in the World Series 4 games to 1.

In the age of free agency, four all-star players nevertheless spent their entire careers with one of the four 1969 expansion teams. Three are in the Hall of Fame: George Brett of Kansas City, Robin Yount of Milwaukee, and Tony Gwynn of San Diego. The fourth player, Frank White of Kansas City is a borderline Hall-of-Famer.

Gwynn made his major league debut on July 19, 1982. His first love was not baseball, but basketball, in which he excelled in high school and college, primarily as a point guard. His many hours of playing hoops served him well once he broke into professional baseball, because dribbling the ball thousands of times helped him develop quickness and strong wrists.

Gwynn, who passed away in 2014, at age 54, was one of the greatest hitters who ever played, and many people will assume it's because of his extraordinary talent. He had talent for sure. But, he also had a relentless work ethic that had him taking batting practice for hours longer than most, and most importantly, becoming a dedicated student of the art of hitting.

George Will, in his wonderful book, "Men at Work," talks about Gwynn watching countless movies of himself batting against every pitcher he faced. He would slow the video down and count the frames from when the pitcher let go of the ball until Tony's shoulder opened up at the plate. This would tell him if he was too far ahead or too far behind in his swing. He would then spend hours at the batting cage correcting even the most minuscule flaw he detected in the video. His nickname, Captain Video, comes from this obsession.

Like Ted Williams and Wade Boggs, Gwynn was a perfectionist. His goal was always to be the best that he could be in the long run. Hence, his mechanics were more important to him than what he did in a particular game. Will highlighted an interview he did with Gwynn after a two-game stretch when he hit a home run in each game. Tony was very disappointed with himself and, thus, was taking extra batting practice because the home runs revealed a flaw in his swing when he reviewed the video. He was, however, delighted with a line drive that he hit in one of those games, even though it resulted in an out.

Like Pete Rose and Rod Carew, Gwynn was primarily a singles hitter. He had a real knack for going the other way and hitting the ball between the shortstop and the third baseman for a base hit. Outfielders would play him deep, despite his lack of big home run numbers, because of his propensity to hit slashing line drives into the gaps. The New York Times called him the purest hitter of his generation. Some baseball people, including some of his own teammates, blasted him for not having more RBIs or home runs, even though he hit in the number three spot. They said that by strictly concentrating on base hits, he was not a team player. But Gwynn insisted that it was important for him to "stay within himself," and not try to turn himself into a power hitter. Dick Williams, who managed Gwynn from 1982-1985, refuted the criticisms when he said, "I don't think I've ever had a ballplayer who worked harder, cared more, and was more deserving of his awards." Most of Gwynn's teammates and managers gave him the highest marks for being a team player. Besides being an outstanding hitter for 20 years, Gwynn was also an excellent base runner and defensive outfielder.

When Gwynn retired, he had earned eight batting titles, tying him for the National League record with Honus Wagner. Only Ty Cobb has more with 12. His career batting average, (.338) is the highest of any player who started his career after World War II. In addition to that impressive average, Gwynn posted 3,141 hits, 135 home runs, and 1,138 RBIs. He played in 15 All-Star games, won seven Silver Slugger awards, and five Gold Gloves. He was inducted into the Hall of Fame on the first ballot in 2007 with 97.6% of the vote.

As you approach San Diego's Petco Park, you will pass Tony Gwynn Drive just before you spot a statue of Tony at the plate just outside of the park.

Tony Gwynn

70. What center fielder was Tony Gwynn's idol when he was growing up?

—— Blue Jays/Diamondbacks/Marlins/—— Mariners/Rays/Rockies
Third and Fourth Wave of Expansion

1B	Todd Helton	P	Randy Johnson
2B	Roberto Alomar	P	Roy Halladay
3B	Evan Longoria	P	Felix Hernandez
SS	Troy Tulowitzki	P	Dave Stieb
OF	Larry Walker	RP	David Price
OF	Ken Griffey		
OF	Ichiro Suzuki		
C	Charles Johnson		
DH	Paul Goldschmidt		

Re-alignment and Wild Cards

"The Giants win the pennant! The Giants win the pennant! The Dodgers win the wild card! The Dodgers win the wild card!"

Bob Costas, mockingly recreating the famous broadcast as it would be announced in today's convoluted playoff format

In 1977, the American League added two additional teams, the Seattle Mariners and the Toronto Blue Jays. The Mariners have struggled since their inception, despite having stars like Ken Griffey Jr., Alex Rodriguez, Edgar Martinez, Randy Johnson, and Ichiro Suzuki on their roster. They posted a losing record in 26 of their first 38 seasons, with no World Series championships. They did however, set an American League record in 2001 by winning 116 games.

The Blue Jays, on the other hand have had more success, though they now play in what is probably the toughest division in baseball. From 1985-93, they won five division titles and back-to-back World Series championships in 1992 and 1993. In '93 they had the American League's top three batters: John Olerud, Paul Molitor, and Roberto Alomar. They are currently the only team based outside of the United States.

Sixteen years later, in 1993, the National League added two teams, the Colorado Rockies and the Florida Marlins. The Marlins would eventually win two World Series titles, but the Rockies had greater success early on. Colorado won the pennant in 2007 after winning a remarkable 21 of their last 22 games, then got swept by the Boston Red Sox in the World Series.

The Marlins won their first World Series in 1997, and then gutted the team. They are the only team ever to lose 100 games after winning the World Series championship the previous year. They won again in 2003 after calling up Dontrelle Willis and Miguel Cabrera from the Carolina Mudcats. In 2012 the Marlins moved to a new stadium in Miami and changed their name accordingly to the Miami Marlins. The Marlins employ a form of entertainment that I, as a baseball purist, find particularly offensive: they actually have cheerleaders, the Miami Mermaids!

In 1998, each league added one more team: the Arizona Diamondbacks in the National League, and the Tampa Bay Devil Rays in the American. The Rays dropped the "Devil" from their name in 2008, en route to their first pennant. The Diamondbacks became the fastest expansion team to win a World Series, just four years after their inception, when they won it all in 2001 in a thriller over the three-time defending champion New York Yankees.

For baseball's first 100 years, that is from 1869-1969, all was right with the world. Yes, we had two horrendous world wars, scores of lesser wars, massive genocide, and displacement of peoples, but at least we had a sane baseball playoff format and memorable pennant races. All of that changed with the second expansion in 1969, which necessitated multiple divisions in each league. We still, nevertheless, had a pennant race, albeit with a somewhat different look and feel. Postseason play now had two rounds, with the winners of each division squaring off to see who would play in the World Series.

Expansion transformed the postseason again, beginning in 1994, when the leagues were split into three divisions: East, Central, and West. To create symmetry between the leagues, the American League's Milwaukee Brewers had to move to the National League so that each league would have an even number of teams. That gave the National League Central Division six teams, while the American League West had four; all other divisions had five. Each division champ advanced to the playoffs, along with a wild card, the team with the next-best overall record.

In 2012, the postseason became even more byzantine as Major League Baseball added a second wild card team in each league. Now there are 10 teams playing in the postseason, which is up to four rounds! The two wild card teams play a one-game contest to determine who advances. In 2013, the Houston Astros moved to the American League West, giving each league 15 teams, and interleague play every day of the season.

So, what's wrong with the wild card format? After all, it has many proponents. Bob Costas, in his book, "Fair Ball" offers several reasons why it's a bad idea. More than any other sport, baseball is intimately linked with its past, its players and its traditions. One of those traditions is the two pennant races each year. The casual fan will argue that even with the wild card format, four rounds of postseason play, and 10 teams involved, you have a pennant race. Are you kidding?

Costas gives two examples as to why the "new and improved" pennant race can't measure up to the races of yore. In 1997, the Marlins were nine games out of first place, yet won the wild card spot, and ultimately the World Series. To advance, they had to beat the first place Atlanta Braves, who had to prove themselves again in a short series, despite a superior performance over the 162-game season? Baseball, more than any other major sport can witness a mediocre team prevail in a short series, which is what the Marlins did. In my opinion, the Braves earned a spot in the World Series, but the Marlins did not.

In 1996, the Dodgers and Padres were tied for first place with one game remaining. Their records were such that the loser of the last game was guaranteed a wild card berth. So instead of a game to rival that of the 1949 Red Sox/Yankees match to determine the pennant winner, the game became meaningless. Both teams rested their ace pitchers in order to set up their rotations for the playoff games.

Proponents of the new system argue that a wild card team deserves to be in the playoffs by virtue of a winning season. WRONG! Sport is about winning, not about finishing in second place. The wild card system devalues supremacy and rewards second best. Remembering who the wild cards were from year to year is like trying to remember the Vice Presidents through history. Nobody cares. And another thing, baseball should not be played in November.

Costas offers an alternative to the chaos, one I can fully support. Why not allow only the three division winners to advance to the postseason? Let the team with the best record get a bye, like they do in football, and let the other two winners battle to see who plays the first place team. Let's stop rewarding second-place finishers.

1992 Toronto Blue Jays

71. Who was the Colorado Rockies manager in their pennant winning 2007 season?

Sixth Inning

Ethnic Teams

I've done my best, but I can't guarantee the ethnic accuracy of all the players in this section. But, this is supposed to be a fun book, not a legal document. In most cases, if a player was at least 50% of a particular ethnicity, I made him eligible for the team. Hence, Roy Campanella would qualify for both the African-American and Italian teams (although Yogi Berra was still the better Italian catcher).

I have used last names or, what I know to be fact as deciding factors when assigning a player to a specific ethnic group. So, a player like Eddie Plank is on the German team because his father's surname is German, even though his mother was Irish. Other players have surnames that are not indicative of their ethnic group even though they are indeed of that group. Al Simmons is on the Polish team because his original name was Syzmanski, and Ted Williams is on the Hispanic team because his mother was Mexican. Jewish, Irish, and French names are tough to pin down, so I researched each of the players on that team as best I could, in order to ensure that they do indeed belong there. For Jewish players, I'm not interested in their religious beliefs, but rather their cultural ethnicity, so Rod Carew doesn't make the team, but he does make the Hispanic team.

1B	Eddie Murray	P	Bob Gibson
2B	Joe Morgan	P	Ferguson Jenkins
3B	Jackie Robinson	P	Vida Blue
SS	Derek Jeter	P	Dave Stewart
OF	Barry Bonds	RP	Lee Smith
OF	Willie Mays		
OF	Hank Aaron		
C	Roy Campanella		
DH	Ken Griffey		

Negro Leagues

"They used to say, 'If we find a good black player,
we'll sign him.' They was lying."
Cool Papa Bell

When Ted Williams gave his Hall of Fame induction speech, perhaps the most significant thing he said was, "I hope that one day Satchel Paige and Josh Gibson will be voted into the Hall of Fame as symbols of the great Negro players who are not here only because they weren't given the chance." Indeed, Major League Baseball's unwritten "gentleman's agreement" kept men of color out of its ranks for the first 80 years of the league's existence. The Civil Rights Bill of 1875 gave hope to black men who aspired to play professional ball, but that hope was extinguished in 1883, when the Supreme Court ruled that the bill was unconstitutional, thus opening the door for segregation in the major leagues.

It wasn't just the courts that formed a barrier to integration. Judge Kenesaw Mountain Landis, Commissioner of baseball from 1920-44, was steadfast in keeping blacks out of the major leagues. Adrian "Cap" Anson, one of the most charismatic and dominant players at the turn of the century, refused to play games if the other team fielded even one black player. He was such an influential figure, that he had the power to tilt the decision one way or the other. Shame on him for choosing the wrong path. Other stars, like Ty Cobb, were also vocal in favor of segregation, but integration had its proponents as well. Honus Wagner, the dominant player in the National League well into the 1920s, was supportive of lifting the ban on black players.

The Cuban Giants were established in 1885. They passed themselves off as Cuban in order to be better accepted among white fans. They spoke gibberish in order to fool the fans into thinking that they were talking in Spanish. In 1920, Rube Foster, a huge, far-sighted power pitcher, assembled the loosely organized black teams and formed the "official" Negro Leagues. Finances were tenuous at best, and the league folded in 1931. However, a second league was started in 1933. Pittsburgh became the hub of the new league. The Pittsburgh Crawfords and the Homestead Grays dominated the league for years.

McDaniels III points out in "Baseball and Philosophy" that even as segregation limited the progress of blacks into mainstream society, the ability of black men to perform on the baseball diamond at the same level (or higher) as their white counterparts endeared them to their communities. He points out that the players would often clown around on the field, much as the Harlem Globetrotters of basketball still do, as this would induce more fans to attend. However, teams like the "Zulu Cannibals" were so extreme in their clowning that they reinforced negative stereotype of blacks as clownish.

McDaniels maintains that the clownish behavior was rooted in the slave culture. The clowning displayed by the players was an active form of what the German philosopher Friedrich Nietzsche described as resentment within the context of traditional black forms of resistance to white supremacy. This is a tradition going back to the gallows humor of slaves in the 19th century. Such humor was used as an act of protest against otherwise unbearable conditions.

Clowning may have been part of their everyday routine, but what really separated the style of play of the Negro Leagues from the major leagues was *speed*. While Babe Ruth, Jimmie Foxx, and Hank Greenberg were ushering in the era of the long ball, Negro League players were perfecting the art of bunting, stealing bases, and going from first to third on a ground ball. Not until Jackie Robinson brought the Negro Leagues style of play with him would the major leagues so openly embrace speed in the game.

The Negro Leagues produced some of the best, and most charismatic stars who ever played the game. Andrew "Rube" Foster, the "father of black baseball," won his nickname by outdueling the great Rube Waddell in a barnstorming game.

Josh Gibson was the greatest non-pitcher to play in the Negro Leagues. He is said to have hit the longest home run ever hit in Yankee Stadium! Connie Mack said that if third baseman "Judy" Johnson were white, "he could name his price." Buck Leonard played 17 years for the Homestead Grays, and was called the "black Lou Gehrig." John Henry Lloyd was dubbed the "black Honus Wagner" and continued playing semi-pro ball until he was 58 years old. Wagner said that he was honored by the comparison. "Cool" Papa Bell may have been the fastest player to ever don spikes. In a game against white major leaguers, he scored from first on a bunt! Oscar Charleston and Martin Dihigo were powerful five tool players.

And then there was Leroy "Satchel" Paige. He was the most famous of the Negro Leagues stars, and was the best pitcher. Besides being immensely talented, Satchel was a master showman. He would routinely intentionally walk three batters to load the bases, and then tell his infield to sit down, whereupon he would then strike out the side. Both Dizzy Dean and Joe DiMaggio called Satchel the best pitcher they had ever seen.

When Landis died in 1944, Albert "Happy" Chandler replaced him as commissioner. Branch Rickey, owner of the Brooklyn Dodgers, had been planning to integrate the majors leagues for some time. World War II was over, blacks had fought for their country, and Rickey thought the time was right. When he approached Chandler with the proposition, he was pleasantly surprised at the Kentuckian's answer.

Said Chandler: "I'm for the four freedoms. If a black boy can make it on Okinawa and Guadalcanal, hell, he can make it in baseball." Jackie Robinson broke the color line in 1947. In so doing, he precipitated the downfall of the Negro Leagues. They were no longer needed.

Despite Robinson's success on the field, Major League Baseball was slow to fully integrate. In 1948 the Dodgers added three more black players, but they were still the only National League team to integrate. By 1953 only six teams fielded black players. It wasn't until 1959, 12 years after Jackie's debut, that the Boston Red Sox finally became the last team to integrate.

Despite their initial hesitance, National League teams that did integrate quickly recognized the value of black players. The abundance of black players in the National League during this time was a major factor in their winning 9 out of 13 All-Star games from 1950-60 (there were two All-Star games from 1958-61). From 1952 to 1959, a black player won the National League MVP Award every year. Throughout the 1950s the New York Giants had more black players than the entire American League!

Ted Williams' wish finally materialized in 1971, when the Hall of Fame recognized the Negro stars by inducting several into the Hall. Satchel Paige was the first to be inducted.

Satchel Paige

72. Who was the first black player to join the American League?

1B	Steve Garvey	P	Nolan Ryan
2B	Daniel Murphy	P	Whitey Ford
3B	Jimmy Collins	P	Joe McGinnity
SS	Joe Cronin	P	Ed Walsh
OF	Ed Delahanty	RP	Tug McGraw
OF	Hugh Duffy		
OF	Paul O'Neill		
C	Tim McCarver		
DH	Mark McGwire		

Big Mac

"I'm in awe of myself."
Mark McGwire

Mark McGwire was born on October 1, 1963 in Pomona, California. He made his major league debut on August 22, 1986 for the Oakland A's, and it was indeed an auspicious beginning. In 1987, his first full season, he shattered the rookie home run record by slamming 49 round trippers and won the Rookie of the Year Award. He also set a rookie record with a league-leading .618 slugging average. He continued thumping home runs, leading the league in 1996 with 52, despite missing 32 games.

Major League Baseball went on strike in 1994-95, souring millions of fans on the game, many forever. Attendance fell dramatically in all cities. Baseball clearly needed something to win the fans back. In 1998, McGwire, Sammy Sosa of the Chicago Cubs, and Ken Griffey of the Seattle Mariners went on a home run tear for the ages. And fans came back by the millions to see their heroes compete with each other to see if any or all of them would eclipse Roger Maris' single season record of 61 set back in 1961.

Griffey ultimately fell off the pace, but McGwire and Sosa battled each other like two gladiators down to the wire. They both broke Maris' record. Big Mac hit 70 and Slamin' Sammy hit 66. Many baseball people give credit to both McGwire and Sosa for "saving" baseball that season. They may be right. McGwire certainly helped save the Cardinals franchise. After Oakland traded the slugger to St. Louis in the midst of the 1997 season, the Cardinals sold about 600,000 more tickets in 1998 than they did in 1997. Big Mac's 70th home run ball was sold at auction for $3,000,000. It was the highest paid single item of baseball memorabilia ever sold. It was sold to Todd McFarlane, a native of Canada, who described himself as a "psycho baseball fan."

In 1999, McGwire nearly duplicated his 1998 heroics, whacking 65 home runs and driving in 147 on just 145 hits. It was the highest RBI-per-hit average ever. In both 1998 and 1999, he had more home runs than singles.

Injuries hampered him in the next two seasons, and he retired after the 2001 season. McGwire ended his career with a .263 batting average, 1,626 hits, 583 home runs, and 1,414 RBIs. He played in 12 All-Star games, and on one World Series championship team, and won one Gold Glove and three Silver Slugger awards. He is one of only four players to hit a ball over the roof of Tiger Stadium. He led the majors in home runs five times and hit 50 or more home runs four years in a row. He was voted to the major league All Century Team.

McGwire's career will forever be tainted by his steroid abuse. In a 1998 Associated Press Article by Steve Wilstein, McGwire confessed to using androstenedione, a supplement that was not banned by Major League Baseball. During the 2005 Congressional hearings on steroid use in baseball, McGwire invoked his Fifth Amendment rights against self-incrimination, repeatedly saying "I'm not here to talk about the past." In a prepared statement, while fighting back tears he said "Asking me or any other player to answer questions about who took steroids in front of television cameras will not solve the problem. If a player answers no, he will simply not be believed. If he answers yes, he risks public scorn and endless government investigations."[15]

Five years after those hearings McGwire finally came clean, admitting that he used steroids during his career, specifically during the 1998 assault on the home run record. "I wish I had never touched steroids. It was foolish and it was a mistake. I truly apologize. Looking back, I wish I had never played during the steroid era."

Mark McGwire

73. Mark McGwire is one of only four ballplayers to hit at least 200 home runs with two different teams. Who are the other three?

French

1B	Jim Beauchamp	P	Tom Glavine
2B	Nap Lajoie	P	Ron Guidry
3B	Rabbit Maranville	P	Lew Burdette
SS	Lou Boudreau	P	Andy Pettitte
OF	Dante Bichette	RP	Eric Gagne
OF	Ginger Beaumont		
OF	Edd Roush		
C	Bruce Bochy		
DH	Andrew Ethier		

Louisiana Lightning

"I always thought I could be a better center fielder than a pitcher, but somebody had another idea."
Ron Guidry

I n the fall of 1976, Ron Guidry was almost left unprotected in the expansion draft that staffed the Seattle Mariners and Toronto Blue Jays franchises from the existing clubs. After spending six years in the Yankee farm system, he finally reached the big league club, but showed little to prove that he deserved to be in the same rotation as Catfish Hunter, Ed Figueroa, and Dock Ellis. Many, including Yankee manager Billy Martin, were ready to give up on the skinny, bow-legged, 160 pound southpaw.

In April, 1977 just as Martin was about to send Guidry packing, he needed a lefthander to pitch to the dangerous George Brett with a runner on second in the seventh inning of a 3-3 game against the Kansas City Royals. Guidry was warned that this was his chance to prove what he was made of. Brett lined a single to center, but Frank White hesitated just long enough for Yankee center fielder Mickey Rivers to throw him out at home. Guidry retired the side in order in the eighth and ninth, and the Yankees scored a run in each inning to give him his first major league victory.

Rivers may or may not have saved Guidry's career in 1977, but the following year, Guidry required help from no one. His 1978 season was one of the most outstanding years for a pitcher ever. He went 25-3 with a 1.74 ERA. He threw nine shutouts, while limiting opposing hitters to a paltry .193 batting average. He was the unanimous choice for the Cy Young Award and just missed winning the Most Valuable Player Award, losing to Boston's Jim Rice.

That same year, the Yankees came from 14 games back on July 19 to tie the Boston Red Sox for the Eastern Division Championship, forcing a one-game playoff. There was no question who would start the game for the Yankees; Guidry held the Red Sox to two runs over 6-1/3 innings and got the victory when Bucky Dent crushed Boston's hopes with a three-run homer. The Yankees then easily defeated the Royals in the ALCS and the Los Angeles Dodgers in the World Series.

Guidry never had another year to rival his 1978 masterpiece, but he was a stalwart of the Yankees rotation for another 10 years, spending his entire career with them. Ron Guidry is, in my opinion, just a step below a Hall of Fame candidate. By some measures his record is similar to Sandy Koufax's, although Sandy had six dominant years, while Guidry really only had the one. Then again, Guidry retired with a 170-90 record, an astounding 80 games over .500. By comparison, Gaylord Perry, who is deservedly in the Hall, had a 314-265 record, 49 games over .500.

Guidry played in four All-Star games, was on two World Series championship teams, and won five Gold Gloves. He loved playing defense, as evidenced by the quote at the top of this section. But because he got to the major leagues so late in his career, and because he did not dominate for long enough, he falls a notch below serious Hall of Fame consideration.

Ron Guidry

74. From 2002-04 Eric Gagne set a record for consecutive successful save opportunities. How many did he save?

1B	Lou Gehrig	P	Warren Spahn
2B	Charlie Gehringer	P	Carl Hubbell
3B	Mike Schmidt	P	Eddie Plank
SS	Honus Wagner	P	Orel Hershiser
OF	Mel Ott	RP	Hoyt Wilhelm
OF	Harry Heilman		
OF	Babe Ruth		
C	Joe Mauer		
DH	Cal Ripken		

Warren Spahn

" Well, there was the Battle of the Bulge."
Warren Spahn, when asked if he had ever felt more pressure than he had
when pitching in a World Series

When I put these teams together I had no preconceived notions as to which teams would have the best players. I knew that the African-American and Hispanic teams would be great, but I didn't realize just how good the German team was until I assembled it. One could argue that it boasts the best player ever at several positions: Gehrig at 1B, Schmidt at 3B, Wagner at SS, Ruth in RF, and Spahn at LHP.

Warren Spahn was born on April 23, 1921 in Buffalo, N.Y. His father was a semi-pro ballplayer who, like Bob Feller's father, built his son a practice pitching mound and taught young Warren how to pitch through constant and relentless practice. One could argue that Spahn's 21-year career can be attributed in large part to his father's lessons on how to throw and follow through with minimal strain on his arm and shoulder.

Spahn actually wanted to be a first baseman, but when he tried out for his high school baseball team he discovered to his dismay that first base was taken, so he reluctantly agreed to join the pitching corps. He excelled at his second choice and was drafted by the Boston Braves, making his major league debut on April 19, 1942. Spahn showed some promise in the minor leagues, but struggled in spring training of 1942 and appeared in just four games that season. His doubts about making it in the big leagues were exacerbated when, during spring training, he was warming up with catching legend Ernie Lombardi. The big catcher called for a fastball and was so unimpressed with it that he caught it bare-handed and threw it back to Spahn even faster than he had received it.

Once the season started, Spahn found himself on the receiving end of manager Casey Stengel's temper. On one occasion, Stengel ordered Spahn to throw at Pee Wee Reese. When Spahn failed to plunk Reese, Stengel took the ball away from him, shouted that he had no guts, and ordered him to report to Hartford. He did, and pitched well, returning to the Braves to finish out the season.

After the 1942 season Spahn had more than National League batters or an irascible manager to worry about. He had been drafted and was sent to France as part of an engineering unit of the Ninth Armored Division bound for Germany. Their task was to hold the bridge at Remagen. The setting was the infamous Battle of the Bulge.

Spahn's heroism in the war forced Stengel to retract his earlier comment about Warren lacking guts. He was nicked by bullets in the head and stomach, and more seriously, took shrapnel in his left foot while holding the bridge along with his fellow GI's. He earned a Purple Heart, a battlefield promotion, and a Presidential citation. Upon his return to Major League Baseball in 1946, he said, "After what I went through overseas, I never thought of anything I was told in baseball as hard work. You get over feeling like that when you spend days on end sleeping in frozen tank tracks in enemy-threatened territory. The Army taught me what's important and what isn't."[16]

The 1947 season was Spahn's first full year as a major league pitcher. So what did the war hero do? He simply led the league in ERA (2.33), innings pitched (290), and shutouts (7). He also notched 21 wins.

233

A year later, the superb pitching of Spahn and Johnny Sain powered the Boston Braves to the pennant. Even though the rest of the pitching staff was not as bad as some claim, a famous saying was heard throughout New England as the fall classic approached: "Spahn and Sain and pray for rain." Unfortunately for Boston, it didn't rain, and the Cleveland Indians' equally talented duo of Bob Feller and Bob Lemon outdueled the Braves aces to win the World Series

From 1947-61, Spahn led or tied for the National League lead in wins eight times, complete games nine times, shutouts and innings pitched four times each, strikeouts four times, and ERA three times. He played most of his career before the Cy Young Award was introduced in 1956, though he won it in 1957, when there was only one award for the entire major leagues. He surely would have won it more often had it been in place earlier in his career.

Spahn had a stellar 1951 season, leading the league in complete games, shutouts, and strikeouts. His numbers were almost identical in 1952, and in some cases better, but he went 14-19 for a Braves team that lost 89 games. Before the 1953 season, Braves owner Lou Perini tried to cut Warren's salary from $25,000 to $20,000. Spahn refused to sign the contract, so Perini countered with a deal that would pay his pitcher 10 cents for every admission to the Braves home games. Spahn refused that deal as well. Finally, Perini relented and paid Spahn the original $25,000. Ironically, the Braves moved from Boston to Milwaukee for the 1953 season. The Milwaukee fans wildly greeted their new ball club and filled the stadium. If Spahn had accepted Perini's offer, he would have earned $150,000!

Spahn certainly had some spectacular seasons, but I think it was his longevity that epitomized his marvelous career. He pitched for 21 years in the major leagues, all but one year with the Braves. And he lost three years in his prime to military service. He kept himself in shape throughout the year. This, combined with his smooth, seemingly effortless pitching motion were the keys to his longevity. It seemed that he got better with age. He won 20 or more games seven times, 180 in all, after turning 35 years of age. He threw his first no-hitter at age 39 and his second at age 40. He's the oldest pitcher to win 20 games: he went 23-7 (including seven shutouts) at age 42. One reason for his success in his later years was that after his fastball faded, he learned to throw a devastating screwball.

Perhaps the greatest example of Spahn's enduring talent in his "dotage" came in 1963 when he faced off against Juan Marichal, the San Francisco Giants' ace. The game went into the 16th inning before the Giants finally scored a run to win it. Both pitchers went the distance!

When at one point Giants manager Alvin Dark approached the mound to relieve Marichal, the Giants ace retorted, "Do you see that man pitching for the other side? Do you know that man is 42 years old? I'm only 25. If that man is on the mound, nobody is going to take me out of here." In attendance at the park that day was Carl Hubbell, the Giants pitching Hall of Fame legend. Upon witnessing the spectacle performed by the 42 year old Spahn, Hubbell quipped, "He ought to will his body to medical science." Regarding his longevity, the great Cardinals hitter Stan Musial said, "Spahn will never get into the Hall of Fame. He won't stop pitching."

Spahn retired with 363 wins, the most ever for a southpaw, and fifth-best overall. The players ahead of him on the list all began their careers before World War I. Spahn's pitching strategy was simple: "Hitting is timing. Pitching is upsetting timing." Would he have won more than 400 games if he had pitched for a better hitting team and if he had not lost three years to military service? We'll never know.

Spahn was also a decent hitter. He accumulated 363 career hits, the same number as his pitching victories. He also hit 35 home runs in his career, still the National League record for a pitcher. He played in 17 All-Star games, won one World Series, a Cy Young Award, and was voted to the All-Century team. He was voted to the Hall of Fame in 1973. The Warren Spahn Award is given annually to the best left-handed pitcher in the game. There is a wonderful statue of Warren showcasing his signature high leg kick outside of Atlanta's Turner Field.

Warren Spahn

75. What player listed above on the German team, besides Warren Spahn, also won a Purple Heart while serving in WWII?

1B	Albert Pujols	P	Juan Marichal
2B	Rod Carew	P	Pedro Martinez
3B	Miguel Cabrera	P	Luis Tiant
SS	Alex Rodriguez	P	Fernando Valenzuela
OF	Ted Williams	RP	Mariano Rivera
OF	Tony Oliva		
OF	Roberto Clemente		
C	Ivan Rodriguez		
DH	David Ortiz		

The Dominican Academies

"San Pedro de Macoris, Dominican Republic
is to middle infielders what Saudi Arabia is to oil."
George Will

They've been playing baseball in Latin America for a very long time, and that part of the world has had many outstanding ballplayers over the years. These include several, like those who were restricted to the Negro Leagues, who never got the chance to play in the majors.

Martin Dihigo was one such player. He played during the 1920s for the Cuban Stars before starring in the Negro Leagues. John McGraw, while managing the New York Giants, lamented that he could not hire Dihigo for his team. He called Dihigo the greatest natural ballplayer he had ever seen. Buck Leonard, the great Negro Leagues star, said of Dihigo, "He is the greatest all-around player I know."

After Jackie Robinson broke the color line for African-Americans, Hispanic players also started to populate major league rosters. Players like the ageless Minnie Minoso, Chico Carrasquel, and Pedro Ramos paved the way. Soon stars like Luis Aparicio, Juan Marichal, Tony Oliva, Orlando Cepeda, and the greatest of them all, Roberto Clemente, soon followed. The floodgates were about to open for Hispanic players to join Major League Baseball in significant numbers.

Once the lords of baseball realized that there were players like Clemente in Puerto Rico, Aparicio in Venezuela, and Marichal in the Dominican Republic, they sent scouts down in earnest to harvest the crop of ballplayers. The benefit of recruiting Latin American players was two-fold. First, the available talent was seemingly inexhaustible, and second, a top prospect could be bought for a fraction of what it would cost to land an American prospect of equal quality. For example, in 1986, the Texas Rangers signed Sammy Sosa from the Dominican Republic for $3,500 while the same year they signed pitcher Kevin Brown in the amateur agent draft for $174,500.

The Dominican Republic soon fielded more major leaguers than any other Latin American nation. The big league clubs were well into recruiting Dominican players when in 1976 Epy Guerrero, an ex- major leaguer, and Pat Gillick, a scouting director for the Houston Astros, formed a partnership with the goal to formalize the Dominican/Major League Baseball connection.

The American League was expanding in 1977 to include two new teams, the Toronto Blue Jays and the Seattle Mariners. The Blue Jays concluded that they needed an economical talent pool to field a team. Working with Guerrero and Gillick, they established the first baseball academy in the Dominican Republic.

The Los Angeles Dodgers were quick to follow their lead. The low cost of signing Dominican recruits early justified the expenditure required to build these academies, replete with dorms, dining halls, and classrooms, as well as baseball training facilities. Eventually, the academies even taught the recruits English, media relations, and U.S. culture. As of 2014 every major league team either has a contract with a Dominican academy or has built one of their own.

When Juan Marichal was elected to the Hall of Fame in 1983, Commissioner Bowie Kuhn spoke during his induction ceremony. He said: "I doubt that any country in the world has produced as many ballplayers per capita as your homeland." Some of the most common names in the major leagues today are: Martinez, Perez, Rodriguez, Ramirez, and Gonzalez. In 2014, there were approximately 475 players from the Dominican Republic playing on either a major league team or one of their AAA teams.

Juan Marichal

76. What was Rod Carew's highest seasonal batting average, and in what year did he achieve it?

1B	Joey Votto	P	Sal Maglie
2B	Craig Biggio	P	Vic Raschi
3B	Ron Santo	P	Johnny Antonelli
SS	Phil Rizzuto	P	Barry Zito
OF	Carl Furillo	RP	John Franco
OF	Joe DiMaggio		
OF	Rocky Colavito		
C	Yogi Berra		
DH	Mike Piazza		

Ron Santo

"Ronnie will forever be the heart and soul of Cubs fans."
Chicago Cubs Chairman Tom Ricketts

From Major League Baseball's beginnings to the 1920s, players were mostly of Anglo-Saxon, German, or Irish stock. As the children of immigrants from central Europe came of age, teams started to sign players of Italian, Polish, and Jewish heritage as well. As Benjamin Rader notes in "Baseball, A History of America's Game," The Sporting News boasted in 1923 that "Except the Ethiopian (black), the Mick, the Sheeney, the Wop, the Dutch, and the Chink, the Cuban, the Indian, the Jap or the so-called Anglo-Saxon, his nationality is never a matter of moment if he can hit, or pitch, or field."[17]

It's interesting to note that in 1923 a national publication like The Sporting News can "boast" of Major League Baseball's progressiveness while ignoring the fact that it still would not allow black players within its ranks. Of course, it's also instructive of the times that the article uses so many ethnic slurs with abandon. The door may have been open for the immigrant sons, but their path was not a smooth one. Jews were called "Christ killers" and Italians were called "Wops" or "Dagos", not only from opposing dugouts, but from the mainstream press as well. (And sometimes from their own mangers: see the earlier chapter on the New York Yankees, where Casey Stengel refers to the great

DiMaggio as "Dago.") However, players like DiMaggio, Hank Greenberg, and Stan Musial quickly gained respect for their respective Italian, Jewish, and Polish ethnic groups.

Ron Santo was born on February 25, 1940 in Seattle, not the "typical" background for most Italian Americans. He excelled at baseball, football, and basketball in high school, but baseball was his passion. He was offered more money from other teams, but due to his loyalty to the scout who discovered him, he signed with the Chicago Cubs.

His first real test to determine whether he could make it to the major leagues or not, came in rookie camp in 1959. He and future teammate Billy Williams were both trying to earn a spot on the major league roster. Toward the end of their tenure at the camp, the great Rogers Hornsby, who was the batting coach, sat his charges down on a bench and one-by-one evaluated each prospect's chances of moving up to the majors. Santo and Williams were sitting at the end of the bench. The two nervous ballplayers listened as Hornsby told each player to learn how to shine shoes, because they would not hit major league pitching. Santo whispered to Williams, "If he tells me that I'm going to cry." When Rogers got to Billy Williams, he said, "You can hit in the majors right now." Then, he turned to Santo, whose sphincter muscle was tightening, stared at him for a while and said, "So can you."[18]

Santo went on to become one of the mainstays of the Chicago Cubs for 14 years. He, along with Williams and Ernie Banks, formed one of the most potent offenses in the National League during the 1960s. Santo was a multi-tool third baseman throughout his career. He could hit for average and for power; he was an outstanding defensive third baseman, and had a strong and accurate arm; and his league-leading 13 triples in 1964 attests to his speed. He was a patient hitter, leading the league in walks four times. He was the only third baseman to have eight consecutive seasons with at least 90 RBIs.

Santo was also involved in two unusual firsts. He was the first player to wear a helmet with protective ear flaps. After being beaned by Mets pitcher Jack Fisher, he fractured his cheekbone. He donned the new helmet upon his return. His other first was to veto a trade based on a new rule that granted players that right if they had at least 10 years in the majors and at least five years with one club. The Cubs wanted to trade him to the California Angels, but Santo wanted to stay in Chicago. He finally agreed to a trade to the Chicago White Sox for the 1974 season. The Sox used him primarily as a designated hitter, which he despised. He had a terrible year and quit at the end of the 1974 campaign.

Santo finished his career with a career .277 average, 2,254 hits, 342 home runs, and 1,331 RBIs. He played in nine All-Star games, and won five consecutive Gold Gloves. Throughout his career, Santo played with a serious case of diabetes, something he rarely mentioned to anyone during his playing days. His accomplishments are all the more significant given his disease. Eventually, he lost the lower half of both legs due to diabetes, and it contributed to his death at age 70 in 2010.

The Baseball Writers Association of America (BBWAA) failed to elect Santo into the Hall of Fame, and his eligibility expired in 1999, 15 years after the end of his career. His former teammate Williams began a long and vigorous campaign to right what he perceived as an oversight, and in 2012, the Veterans Committee finally got it right. But not while Santo was alive to enjoy it; he had died two years earlier of bladder cancer.

Perhaps, if Santo had played shortstop, second base, or catcher, he would have been elected to the Hall right away. His offensive statistics would have placed him high on the list for those positions. Then again, those same offensive statistics may have suffered if he had spent 14 years at more demanding defensive positions. One argument that many of the voters used to justify excluding Santo during his 15 years of eligibility was the fact that he played in Wrigley Field, the most notorious hitter's park in the major leagues. When visiting Wrigley Field today, you can see a statue of Santo, set to throw a bullet to first base.

Ron Santo

77. When Santo was traded to the Chicago White Sox in 1974, he did not become their starting third baseman. Who was their starting third baseman?

1B	Hank Greenberg	P	Sandy Koufax
2B	Ian Kinsler	P	Steve Stone
3B	Al Rosen	P	Ken Holtzman
SS	Andy Cohen	P	Joel Horlen
OF	Ryan Braun	RP	Larry Sherry
OF	Sid Gordon		
OF	Shawn Green		
C	Moe Berg		
DH	Mike Epstein		

Thinker, Catcher, Scholar, Spy

"He can speak seven languages, but he can't hit in any of them."
Dave Harris, teammate of Moe Berg

Major League Baseball opened its doors to Jewish players fairly early in its history, but they didn't make things easy for them. Neither did the press or the fans. Almost every Jewish player had to suffer the taunts of "Christ killer" or "sheeney" from opposing players, including those players who had Jewish teammates! At one point Hank Greenberg, the muscular first baseman for the Detroit Tigers, had enough. He charged into the opposing team's locker room and challenged anyone to say the offending names to his face. Silence followed. Ballplayers from the beginning through the 1950s were a rough and vulgar bunch. One could almost excuse the abuse from them. However, what was particularly appalling was way the mainstream press treated Jews, blacks, and other ethnic groups.

In one incident in 1898, Baltimore Orioles outfielder Ducky Holmes was bantering back and forth with players from his former team, the New York Giants, which was owned by Andrew Freedman, who was Jewish. When the bantering increased, Holmes fired back, "Well I'm glad I'm not working for a sheeney anymore." Freedman demanded that Holmes be thrown out of the game, but the umpire refused, at which point Freedman pulled his team from the field and forfeited the game. The league fined Freedman and suspended Holmes for the duration of the season. As Benjamin Rader tells it in *Baseball, A History of America's Game*, the players, the newspapers, and most of the owners sided with Holmes. Sporting Life magazine reflected the casual anti-Semitism of the day when it declared that the suspension of Holmes for the "trifling offense" of "insulting the Hebrew race" was a perversion of justice." Only 10 days after the incident, the league reinstated Holmes.[19]

Years ago, my wife and I visited the CIA headquarters in Washington D.C. I was struck by a piece of paraphernalia in one of the displays that seemed out of place. It was Moe Berg's baseball card. If Moe Berg's baseball card seemed out of place in the CIA headquarters building, then Berg himself would have seemed even more out of place in Tokyo in 1934. He was there as part of a U.S. All-Star team.

A casual observer might well have asked, "Why is a third-string catcher playing on an All-Star team with the likes of Babe Ruth and Lou Gehrig?" Berg was added to the team by the U.S. government to spy on the Japanese. He was a good choice for the job for multiple reasons, not least of which was that he spoke fluent Japanese. In fact, he delivered the welcoming speech in Japanese, and met with the Japanese legislature as well.

One day, feigning sickness, he excused himself from the ball field, and as his biographer Nicholas Dawidoff describes it, "Moe bluffs his way up on to the roof of the hospital, the tallest building in Tokyo at the time. And from underneath his kimono he pulls out a movie camera. He proceeds to take a series of photos panning the whole setting before him, which includes the harbor, the industrial sections of Tokyo, possible munitions factories and things like that. Then, he puts the camera back under his kimono and leaves the hospital with these films." Those films were later used by General Jimmy Doolittle in 1942 in his bombing raids on Tokyo.

Moe Berg was born in a cold water flat in New York City on March 3, 1902. When he was nine months of age his family moved to Newark, New Jersey. Ironically, one reason given for the move by Moe's father was to get away from the Jews in New York. Once established in New Jersey, Berg played for a Methodist Church team at age seven. Being Jewish was a liability in his new setting, so he temporarily changed his name to Runt Wolfe.

Berg went on to gain a degree from Princeton University and a law degree from Columbia Law School before signing with the Brooklyn Robins of the National League on June 27, 1923. But he couldn't hit a lick, and was back in the minors after just 49 games. In 1927, however, the Chicago White Sox lost their two top catchers to injuries, and suddenly Berg was thrust into the role of starter.

Pitcher Ted Lyons, who eventually went to the Hall of Fame, credits Berg for helping him to hone his pitching skills. As a player Moe Berg lacked the skills of almost every other player portrayed in this book. But, he certainly did not lack pizzazz or notoriety. Casey Stengel called him "the strangest man ever to play baseball." Many others said he was the smartest man ever to play baseball.

Upon retirement in 1939 he joined the Office of Strategic Services (OSS), working for the legendary Wild Bill Donovan. The OSS would eventually become the CIA. One of his assignments was to find out how German scientists were progressing with their nuclear weapons program. If he ascertained that their nuclear program was on the verge of being ready for deployment, he was to assassinate the scientist in charge, one Werner Heisenberg.

It is ironic that the "smartest man in baseball" donned "the tools of ignorance," the equipment of a major league catcher. Berg's intelligence served him not only in his role as a secret agent, but also in civilian life. He made a fortune on a game show called "Information Please." After his adventures on the baseball diamond and his forays into foreign countries came to a close, he finally put his law degree to good use.

When asked why he would "waste" his law degree and superior intellect playing baseball rather than go directly into law after graduating from Columbia Law School, he replied, "I'd rather be a ballplayer than a Supreme Court justice." He died on May 29, 1972 in Belleville, New Jersey at the age of 70.

Moe Berg

78. What egotistical slugger wanted to be known as "SuperJew"?

Polish

1B	Ted Kluszewski	P	Phil Niekro
2B	Bill Mazeroski	P	Stan Coveleski
3B	Alan Trammell	P	Joe Niekro
SS	Troy Tulowitzki	P	Frank Tanana
OF	Carl Yastrzemski	RP	Ron Perranoski
OF	Al Simmons		
OF	Stan Musial		
C	A.J. Pierzynski		
DH	Greg Luzinski		

The Man

"No man has ever been a perfect ballplayer. Stan Musial, however, is the closest thing to perfection in the game today."
Ty Cobb

Like so many ballplayers before and of his time, Stanley Frank Musial was born into a rough and tumble existence. His father, Lukasz, immigrated to the United States from Poland, and worked in the steel and zinc mills of Donora, Pennsylvania. His son Stan worked in the mines just long enough to realize that he wanted a better life.

Musial was an outstanding high school basketball player and turned down a basketball scholarship to the University of Pennsylvania in order to play baseball. He showed so much promise as a young ballplayer that he went from Class C to AAA to the majors in one season. He started his career as a pitcher, but hurt his shoulder in the minors. He continued to pitch after the injury. But in 1941, he hit a 450-foot home run, whereupon Burt Shotten, his manager, said, "From now on, you're not going to be a pitcher."

Musial made his major league debut with the Cardinals on September 17, 1941, where he hit a sizzling .426 over 12 games and 47 at bats. He played in four World Series in his first five years, winning three of them. The 1946 series, his last, pitted Musial against the best hitter in the American League, Ted Williams. Unfortunately for the fans, neither man hit very well. Musial batted .222 and Williams .200.

Musial picked up his nickname in 1946, not from his home fans, but from those in Brooklyn. He was murder on Dodger pitchers at cozy Ebbets Field, where he compiled a .359 lifetime batting average and relentlessly peppered the outfield walls with doubles. Whenever Musial approached the plate, he heard fans chanting "Here comes that man again." A sportswriter retold the story, and a nickname was born.

After winning his second MVP Award in 1946, Musial had what he called "that lousy year" in 1947. He suffered the double whammy of appendicitis and tonsillitis, yet still managed to bat .312. If there were any lingering doubts about Musial's ability at the outset of the 1948 season, he quickly put them to rest. He simply had one of the most outstanding years of any hitter in major league history. He led the league in every significant offensive category except home runs: his total of 39 was one short of the pace set by Ralph Kiner and Johnny Mize. Musial did actually hit 40 home runs that year, but one was nullified because a game in which he had hit one was rained out before the end of the fifth inning. If not for that cancellation, he would have led or shared the lead in *every* significant offensive category. No batter has ever done that.

Musial was a legitimate five-tool player. The "Donora Greyhound" could certainly hit, hit with power, run, and field. And even with his injured shoulder, he had an accurate arm with enough juice on the ball. Some baseball historians believe that Musial would have won several Gold Gloves if Rawlings had started awarding them before 1957, when Musial was 36 years old. He led the league in fielding three times.

People who knew Musial usually accentuate two aspects about the man. The first is obviously his excellence on the ball field. The second is a unanimous opinion of Musial as a gentleman and family man, who always went out of his way to sign autographs and treat people with respect. Bob Gibson called him the "nicest man I ever met in baseball."

Musial was never involved in a scandal, and he was never ejected from a game. Unlike his peers, DiMaggio and Williams, he was accessible and friendly. He had no ego or sense of self-importance. When asked why he was always smiling, he replied, "Well, if you were me, wouldn't you be smiling?" He was the antithesis of today's super stars. He never drank to excess, never took drugs, committed no criminal acts, was never vulgar, and was never unfaithful to his wife. Before the 1960 season, Musial asked for a 20% pay cut! He went from $100,000 to $80,000 because he did not think he deserved the bigger salary since he did not have a good year in 1959. (The Cardinals obliged.) Can you imagine today's players doing that?

There is so much to write about Musial's exploits that I thought I would simply list some of them.

- Bill James picked Musial as the best player in the majors for five different seasons: 1944, 1948, 1949, 1951, and 1952

- In 1956 Musial was named as the "Player of the Decade" for the years starting after the end of World War II. DiMaggio and Williams finished second and third respectively.

- Musial had a perfectly balanced 1,815 hits at home and 1,815 hits on the road. He didn't care where he played. He just flat out hit bullet line drives.

- He led the league in doubles eight times and triples five times. He never struck out more than 46 times in a season, and averaged fewer than 35 strikeouts per year.

- Illinois statistician Ron Skrabacz published a Relative Performance Measurement (RPM) that has gained credibility with baseball historians. It is meant to realistically compare offensive dominance of major league ballplayers from different eras. Ty Cobb is ranked first. Stan Musial is second.

- Musial exceeds all but Barry Bonds in the total number of MVP votes.

- He played in 895 consecutive games, a National League record at the time.

- He is the only player ever to finish his career in the top 25 of career batting average, on base percentage, slugging average, hits, doubles, triples, home runs, and RBIs.

Musial's peers offer a plethora of praise:

- Preacher Roe: "I throw him four wide ones, and then I try to pick him off first."

- Carl Erskine: "I throw him my best stuff, then run over to back up third base."

- Warren Spahn: "He was the only batter that I intentionally walked with the bases loaded." Spahn also said, "Once Musial timed your fastball, your infielders were in jeopardy."

- Bob Costas: "All Musial represents is more than two decades of sustained excellence and complete decency as a human being."

- Vin Scully: "How good was Stan Musial? He was good enough to take your breath away."

- Joe Garagiola: "Musial could have hit .300 with a fountain pen."

- Yogi Berra, to his pitchers at an All-Star game: "You guys are trying to stop Musial in 15 minutes when the National League ain't stopped him in 15 years."

When Musial finally retired from Major League Baseball, he had a .331 batting average, 3,630 hits, 475 home runs, and 1,951 RBIs. He played in 24 All-Star games (20 years) and won three World Series titles. He won three MVP Awards, seven batting titles, and two RBI titles. He was voted to the All-Century team, and The Sporting News voted him the 10th-best player of all time. He was voted into the Hall of Fame in 1969 on the first ballot.

Outside of Busch Stadium in St. Louis stands a bronze statue of Stan Musial at bat. The inscription reads: "Here stands baseball's perfect warrior. Here stands baseball's perfect knight."

Stan Musial

79. Stan Musial retired in 1963 with a .331 career batting average. Only one player since has retired with a higher average. Who is he?

Seventh Inning

Decades

In this section I've selected the best team from each decade starting with the 1800s up to the 2010s. I've lumped every decade of the 1800s into one team. Some players, like Stan Musial and Honus Wagner were great for two decades, and are represented on two teams. Some were great for only half a decade, like Sandy Koufax and Jackie Robinson, but their greatness was such that they made the team. Other players, like Mickey Cochrane and Ralph Kiner, were great for the latter half of one decade and the first half of the succeeding one, so they make neither. Dale Murphy, on the other hand, played against several players who were ultimately superior outfielders; however in the 1980s, nobody was better. Finally, as I write this in December of 2015, the team of the 2010s is based on actual performance as well as my best guess as to their future performance.

1B	Cap Anson	P	Old Hoss Radbourn
2B	Kid Gleason	P	Mickey Welch
3B	Jerry Denny	P	Tim Keefe
SS	Montgomery Ward	P	Rube Waddell
OF	King Kelly	RP	Pud Galvin
OF	Hugh Duffy		
OF	Ed Delahanty		
C	Buck Ewing		
DH	Dan Brouthers		

Genesis

"I see great things in baseball. It's our game –
the American game."
Walt Whitman, 1889

The origins of Major League Baseball are lost in the mist of time. Certainly cricket and a game called rounders went into the mix. Soldiers playing with a ball, a stick, and bases are cited in memoirs as far back as the harsh winter of 1777-78 in Valley Forge. Jane Austen mentions a tomboy playing cricket *and* baseball in her 1817 work, "Northanger Abbey," which she wrote in 1798.

There is even disagreement over who the father of modern American baseball is, though to me, it is unquestionably Alexander Cartwright, a bank clerk, who cobbled together a "team" of like-minded men to form a club called the New York Knickerbockers. Cartwright created a set of rules to give more structure to the haphazard pastime that was becoming popular among towns and cities along the east coast. He mandated that each team should field nine players, a game should consist of nine innings, and each inning should consist of three outs.

A fielder had to throw to a base in order to score an out rather than hit the runner with the ball. Pitchers still threw underhanded and batters could demand where they wanted the ball to be pitched high, low, inside, outside, or over the middle of the plate. Those rules were changed soon enough to conform to the modern game. One rule that Cartwright kept was that bases should be 90 feet apart, which is an absolutely perfect distance. To this day, a distance of either 89 or 91 feet would alter the game dramatically. If, for example, bases were 89 feet apart, .400 hitters would be commonplace due to the dramatic increase in "leg hits," stolen base leaders could conceivably pilfer 200 bases per year, and scores would be completely outside of the realm of today's statistics. Conversely, 91 foot distances between the bases would ensure a plethora of low-scoring games, anemic batting averages, and few stolen bases. Surely, divine inspiration had a hand in this particular rule.

Cartwright presided over the first "official" baseball game played in America on June 19, 1846. It was a contest between the New York Knickerbockers and the New York Nine and was played on a diamond in Newark, New Jersey with the magical name of the Elysian Fields. Once Cartwright's "Knickerbocker Rules" were in place and organizational structure was added, the game rapidly gained in popularity.

Another baseball pioneer, Henry Chadwick, further added to the allure of the game by inventing the box score, thus making it easy for fans to follow their teams and the players. In fact, employers of clerks and carpenters lamented the time taken by their employees to play ball, as is evidenced in the following ditty of the day:

Our merchants have to close their stores
Their clerks away are staying
Contractors too, can do no work
Their hands are all out playing[20]

In 1862, William Cammeyer built the first enclosed field by filling in his pond and charging a fee for all those fans who ventured within the enclosure. Thus, fans, or kranks as they were called, because when their team lost, they became cranky, were now financing the new teams rather than expenses being paid from membership dues. This "enclosure movement" meant that teams had to play more games, against more teams, necessitating an organized league. Owners of teams tried to squeeze as many fans into the enclosures, but many fans found ways to get around paying the fees. The phrase "knot hole gang" for example comes from the practice of those fans who would peek through knot holes in the plywood that constituted the boundary of some enclosures. Other fans could buy cheap seats, but get bleached in the sun, hence the term, bleachers. Gross receipts from these early franchises were modest indeed. They might equal those of the dry cleaner or delicatessen next door. Pitchers might only be paid on the day that they pitched and other players might only be paid a portion of the gate after expenses.

It soon became obvious that those teams that paid some of their players performed better on the field. They attracted more fans, which led to more revenue. In 1869 the Cincinnati Red Stockings established the first all-professional team. As predicted, they routed their opponents. The Boston Red Stockings (the forerunner of the Braves, not the Red Sox) took notice of Cincinnati's success, and under the tutelage of player-manager Harry Wright, dominated the league for a decade, led by players such as George Wright (Harry's brother), Ross Barnes, Deacon White, and ace pitcher Albert Goodwill Spalding.

After he was finished frustrating batters with his fastball, Spalding went on to become a successful entrepreneur. His Spalding sporting goods company is still a giant in the field. The Chicago White Stockings (a franchise that went on to become the Cubs, rather than the White Sox) were not to be denied by either Boston or Cincinnati. They bought the contracts of the two biggest stars of the day, Adrian "Cap" Anson and Mike "King" Kelly. Like Boston before them, they dominated professional baseball through the 1880s.

In 1876, William Ambrose Hulbert, President of the White Stockings, joined with several other owners to create the National League. It consisted of eight franchises: Boston, Cincinnati, St. Louis, Hartford, New York, Philadelphia, Louisville, and Chicago. It added to existing rules by stipulating that no player could leave his team for another (the reserve clause), umpires would be paid, and gambling, which was rampant, would be outlawed and perpetrators severely punished. In the spring of that year, while George Armstrong Custer was facing Crazy Horse, the Cincinnati Red Stockings were facing the Chicago White Stockings in the National League's opening year.

Many teams came and went. Only Boston and Chicago fielded the same teams from 1876-90. The newly established National League was significantly challenged by a players' revolt in the 1890s. At issue was the hated reserve clause. Players demanded the right to join another club if they felt they were being underpaid or misused by their own club. Multiple leagues were formed to accommodate those players who desired to defect, only to be dissolved soon thereafter. The revolt was squashed by the hard-nosed owners, the reserve clause stayed, and the National League enjoyed a monopoly on professional baseball, at least for a little while.

Adrian "Cap" Anson

80. What flamboyant star of the 1880s is thought to be the inspiration of the iconic poem, "Casey at the Bat"?

1B	Frank Chance	P	Christy Mathewson
2B	Nap Lajoie	P	Cy Young
3B	Jimmy Collins	P	Eddie Plank
SS	Honus Wagner	P	Mordecai Brown
OF	Fred Clarke	RP	Ed Walsh
OF	Elmer Flick		
OF	Sam Crawford		
C	Roger Bresnahan		
DH	Willie Keeler		

The Emergence of the American League

"All umpires ought to tip their hats whenever
Ban Johnson's name is mentioned."
Clarence "Pants" Rowland

The turn of the century witnessed an uptick in the public's interest in their national pastime. "Take me out to the ballgame," written by Jack Norworth and Albert von Tilzer in 1908, became a hit song at ballparks across the country. Attendance soared as owners built new concrete and steel parks. Shibe Park in Philadelphia could seat 30,000 spectators and Forbes Field in Pittsburgh welcomed 25,000.

The fundamentals of the game changed as new rules and new equipment were introduced. Foul balls now counted as strikes and the infield fly rule prevented infielders from turning two quick outs on a lazy popup. New York Giants catcher Roger Bresnahan invented the catcher's mask and shin guards, thus, not only protecting himself from bodily harm, but also enabling him to crouch closer behind the plate, thus, getting a better jump on would be base stealers. After initially ridiculing Bresnahan, the rest of the catchers in the league quickly adopted the new equipment as well. Defenses improved dramatically as bigger gloves and better maintained fields were introduced.

In spite of the increased popularity and attendance, the National League owners still refused to eliminate the hated reserve clause and

$2,400 salary cap. Stars like Jimmy Collins, Ed Delahanty, and Amos Rusie were disgruntled by the artificial ceiling on their earnings, and were constantly threatening to hold out or jump to another league. Rusie's fastball was so fast that it was a major factor in the decision to move the mound to 60 feet six inches from 50 feet.

There was demand for adding franchises in new cities, as well as for second teams in cities that already had teams, like Chicago, New York, Philadelphia, Boston, and St. Louis. The time was ripe for forming a new league, and in 1900 Ban Johnson, a Cincinnati sportswriter, and Charles Comiskey, owner of the Sioux City franchise, assembled several other baseball men and created a new league from the minor league Western League. They called it the American League.

The new league set three rules that differentiated it from the established National League. The first was that no liquor would be sold in the parks. This had the effect of curbing the rowdiness of the fans and thus, made it more attractive for families and women to attend the games. The second rule was that umpires were given total authority. This gave the game more structure and discipline, and helped to speed the game along. The third rule was the elimination of the $2,400 salary cap.

Even with this solid beginning, the new league was not a sure bet. One of Ban Johnson's most fortuitous moves was to lure Clark Griffith, a National League star pitcher, to leave the Cubs for the upstart White Sox. Griffith added much needed credibility to the fledgling enterprise, which convinced other National League stars to join the new league.

The National League was forced to recognize the American League as a legitimate equal after 100 players, including stars like Jesse Burkett, Willie Keeler, Bobby Wallace, Ed Delahanty, Jimmy Collins, and the biggest star of all, Nap Lajoie, had switched their allegiances to the upstart league. Thus, the American League attained almost instant parity with the senior circuit. And, with the recruitment of players like Ty Cobb and Tris Speaker, it attained superiority.

The Pittsburgh Pirates emerged as the dominant team of the decade, and their shortstop, Honus Wagner, was the best player in the National League and every bit as good as his American League counterpart, Cobb. It was the pitchers however, who dominated. Making judicious use of the spitball, which was legal until 1920, pitchers like Cy Young, Jack Chesbro, and the enigmatic Rube Waddell epitomized the new style of pitching. Helping the pitcher's cause was the new practice of managers using a three-or four-man rotation instead of two, thus giving starting pitchers more rest. Batting averages fell, so teams relied on the stolen base as their major offensive weapon. One of the best pitchers of all time made his major league debut on July 17, 1900 for the New York Giants. His name was Christy Mathewson.

In 1903, the year that John McGraw took the helm as manager of the New York Giants, his two aces, Mathewson and "Iron Man" Joe McGinnity, won a combined 61 games. The following year, even with a four-man rotation, Jack Chesbro won 41 games for the New York Highlanders while compiling a 1.82 ERA. He made 51 starts that year, and completed 48 of them. His victories accounted for 45% of the team's total. Rube Waddell struck out 349 with his devastating fastball, and Cy Young pitched the American League's first perfect game.

After initiating a World Series in 1903, the two league champions decided not to square off against each other in 1904. They resumed the tradition in 1905, with two pitching powerhouses meeting in the fall classic. Every game was a shutout, as Mathewson and McGinnity outdueled Chief Bender and Eddie Plank of the Philadelphia Athletics. The Giants gave up just three runs in the series, all of them unearned, while the Athletics posted a 1.67 ERA for the series. Mathewson had three shutout victories.

Mordecai "Three Finger" Brown continued the pitching dominance in 1906 by posting a 26-6 record for the Chicago Cubs to go along with his 1.04 ERA. His cross town rivals, the White Sox, called the "hitless wonders," won 19 straight games, then went on to beat the Cubs in an all-Chicago World Series.

Ban Johnson

81. In 1898 "Wee" Willie Keeler hit 206 singles, a record that stood for over 100 years. Who broke his record?

1B	Stuffy McInnis	P	Walter Johnson
2B	Eddie Collins	P	Grover Alexander
3B	Frank Baker	P	Rube Marquard
SS	Honus Wagner	P	Stan Coveleski
OF	Joe Jackson	RP	Chief Bender
OF	Tris Speaker		
OF	Ty Cobb		
C	Ray Schalk		
DH	Zack Wheat		

Dead Balls and Live Arms

"Pitching is 75% of baseball."
Connie Mack

Ty Cobb hit .387 for the 1910s decade. Honus Wagner, Tris Speaker, "Shoeless" Joe Jackson, and Eddie Collins were right behind him. However, as was the case in the first decade of the 20th century, pitchers dominated in the second decade as well. The "dead" ball used during this decade was one of several factors contributing to the dominance of the pitchers. A pitcher could ease up during a grueling game, even with a runner on base, because he was safe in the presumption that the batter would not likely hit one out of the park.

Two teams were prominent during this decade: John McGraw's New York Giants, and Connie Mack's Philadelphia Athletics. McGraw was a genius at playing for one run at a time, a true dead ball strategist. Both McGraw and Mack sought out great pitchers to complement their "small ball" style of play. McGraw had Christy Mathewson, Joe McGinnity, and Rube Marquard, while Mack utilized Eddie Plank, Chief Bender, and Rube Waddell. All six are in the Hall of Fame. Of Chief Bender, Connie said; "If I had all the pitchers that I ever handled, with one game coming up that I simply had to win, I would call on the Chief. He was my greatest money pitcher."[21] Mathewson, Cy Young, and Mordecai "Three Finger" Brown, were the mound aces of the 20th century's first decade. The pitching stars of the 1910s: Walter Johnson, Grover Cleveland Alexander, and Babe Ruth may have been even better.

The decade of the pitcher started off with a bang as evidenced by the 1910 highlights. Significant seasonal highlights were:

1910   •   Jack Combs of the A's won 31 games, 13 of them shutouts, an American League record that still stands.

     •   Cy Young won his 500th game.

1911   •   The New York Giants won 20 of their last 24 games to take the National League pennant.

     •   Ty Cobb won the batting title with an astronomical .420 average.

     •   Grover Cleveland Alexander won 28 games as a rookie, another record that still stands. In a changing of the guard, he out- dueled an aging Cy Young, 1-0.

1912   •   Smokey Joe Wood went 34-5 for the Boston Red Sox. Walter Johnson, considered to be the fastest pitcher ever, said: "No man alive throws faster than Smokey Joe Wood."

     •   Rube Marquard won 19 straight games for the Giants.

1913   •   Walter Johnson won pitching's triple crown with 36 wins, 243 strikeouts, and a 1.14 ERA

1914   •   The Boston Braves came from nowhere to win the National League pennant and sweep the A's in the World Series.

     •   Babe Ruth made his major league debut with Boston on July 11.

     •   The Federal League was established and poached many players from major league rosters.

     •   Honus Wagner and Nap Lajoie each got their 3,000th hit.

     •   Dutch Leonard of the Red Sox posted a 0.96 ERA, second-lowest ever.

1915   •   Ty Cobb stole 96 bases, a record that stood for 47 years, until Maury Wills broke it with 104 in 1962.

- The Federal League folded after just one season.

1916
- Grover Cleveland Alexander won 33 games, pitched 38 complete games, compiled a 1.55 ERA, struck out 167, and threw 16 shutouts (a record that still stands).
- Sam Crawford of the Detroit Tigers hit his 312th triple, another record that still stands.

1917
- Cincinnati's Fred Toney and Chicago's Hippo Vaughn threw no-hitters against each other on May 2.

1918
- The season ended on Labor Day, as World War I claimed dozens of players.
- Walter Johnson's ERA of 1.27 was .47 lower than that of second-place finisher Hippo Vaughn.

1919
- The heavily favored Chicago White Sox threw the World Series to the underdog Cincinnati Reds in what became known as the infamous Black Sox scandal.

Grover Cleveland Alexander

82. What three players on my all-1910s team played for the Chicago White Sox in the 1919 World Series?

1B	George Sisler	P	Dazzy Vance
2B	Rogers Hornsby	P	Red Faber
3B	Pie Traynor	P	Waite Hoyt
SS	Dave Bancroft	P	Burleigh Grimes
OF	Ty Cobb	RP	Herb Pennock
OF	Tris Speaker		
OF	Babe Ruth		
C	Gabby Hartnett		
DH	Harry Heilmann		

Live Balls, Live Bats

"Ruth could knock your brains out, but Cobb would drive you crazy."
Tris Speaker

As Major League Baseball entered the new decade in 1920, it was beset with problems. The notorious Black Sox scandal of the previous year had done much damage to its image and attendance was down as fans contemplated other options that might be more deserving of their loyalties and support.

Two men stepped forward to save the game from itself. The first was Judge Kenesaw Mountain Landis, who banned not only the players implicated in the Black Sox scandal, but several more that were involved in betting on the game. The result was a restored integrity to the game.

The second man was the "Paul Bunyan" of baseball, a man who to this day is the most revered name to ever play the game. His name was Babe Ruth. The Babe's exploits with his bat had fans coming back to the stadiums in large numbers. He not only saved baseball, he redefined the game with his prodigious home runs. Ruth was the prime factor in the 40% increase in American League attendance over the previous decade, from an average of 5.6 million per year to 9.3 million. The advent of radio broadcasts also helped to increase fan support.

The balance of power shifted from pitching to hitting. Aside from Ruth's influence on the way the game was played, there were three other reasons for this shift: 1) Some baseball historians claim that the ball was "juiced up" at the beginning of the decade (however, just as many deny this theory); 2) More fresh balls were used per game. Up to this point, balls were used until they were lost, or so badly beat up that they simply could not be put in play any longer. Edd Roush, star center fielder for the Cincinnati Reds, would complain prior to 1920 that ground balls coming his way in center field would bounce around like jumping beans because they were so lopsided; 3) The spitball, and other illegal pitches were banned. This made hitting the ball infinitely easier.

Despite these changes, it's impossible to overstate the effect that Ruth had on the resurgence of offense. When other players noticed the impact his uppercut swing had, they started to emulate it. Soon, many other hitters in both leagues were thumping the ball to all parts of the diamond. Even the great Rogers Hornsby altered his swing to gain more power. Home runs increased dramatically and stolen bases and sacrifices decreased.

In the 1910s the major league batting average was .250; in the 1920s it was .280. Batters hit .400 or better an amazing seven times during the 1920s. Perhaps, the greatest endorsement of the new style of hitting came from the two most respected managers of the day, John McGraw and Connie Mack. These two men had perfected the strategy of the hit and run, stolen base, pitching, and defense, but in the 1920s, they too preached slugging.

There were subtle and dramatic changes to the game during the decade. Players shifted to thick-barreled bats with thin handles for better home run production. They sported bigger and better-padded gloves, improving defense. The size of the field changed too, as many owners changed their stadium dimensions to generate more home runs. Branch Rickey developed the farm system in St. Louis, a creation that soon became universal across both leagues. It was a golden age of baseball. More than 30% of today's Hall-of-Famers played in the 1920s.

A year-by-year examination of the 1920s includes the following highlights:

1920
- On August 16, Ray Chapman, shortstop for the Cleveland Indians, was hit on the head by Carl Mays. He died the next day.
- Babe Ruth was sold to the Yankees for $100,000. He hit 54 home runs, scored 158 runs, and had an .847 slugging average.
- Judge Kenesaw Mountain Landis banned eight members of the 1919 Chicago Black Sox for life.
- Walter Johnson won his 300th game.
- George Sisler won the American League batting title with a .407 average. His 257 hits were a record that stood for 64 years until Ichiro Suzuki got 262 hits in 2004.
- The spitball was banned, but players who used it up to this point were grandfathered through the end of their careers.

1921
- Baseball had its first subway series, between New York's Giants and Yankees. The Giants won five games to two.
- Ruth hit 59 home runs, with 171 RBIs, and 457 total bases, and scored 177 runs.
- Stuffy McInnis registered a .999 fielding average, making just one error in 1,653 chances.
- Ty Cobb got his 3,000th hit

1922
- Sisler batted .420: Ty Cobb was a distant second at .401. Sisler's 41-game hit streak also bested Rogers Hornsby's streak of 33 games.
- Rogers Hornsby led all National League hitters with a .401 average, 42 home runs, 152 RBIs, 250 hits, and a .722 slugging average.

1923
- Harry Heilmann hit .403
- Tris Speaker set a modern day record with 59 doubles.
- Yankee Stadium opened. Ruth christened it with a home run,

and the Yankees won their first World Series.

1924 • Walter Johnson set a record by leading the league in strikeouts for the 12th time.

• Hornsby hit an astounding .424, a post-1900 record

• Firpo Mayberry of the Washington Senators became the first relief specialist.

1925 • Hornsby hit .403 and won the Triple Crown.

• Eddie Collins and Tris Speaker each collected their 3,000th hit.

1926 • Ruth hit 47 home runs, 26 more than anyone else.

• On August 28, Dutch Levsen of the Indians won two complete games in one day.

1927 • The Yankees compiled a .307 team batting average and utterly dominated all opposition. Many baseball historians consider this "Murderer's Row" team to be the best ever. Ruth hit 60 home runs, more than any other team in the American League (the Athletics were second with 56). Lou Gehrig drove in 175 runs and won the MVP.

• Ty Cobb got his 4,000th hit.

• Walter Johnson retired with 110 shutouts, a major league record.

1928 • Cobb retired, holding records in: batting (.367); runs (2,246); hits (4,191); stolen bases (892); and RBIs (1,938). His batting average record still stands.

• Tris Speaker retired with two records that still stand: career doubles (792); and assists by an outfielder (449).

• Eddie Collins retired with a record 2,650 games played at second base.

1929 • Lefty O'Doul of the Phillies batted .398 and set the all-time National League record of 254 hits (tied the following year by Bill Terry).

George Sisler

83. What Hall-of-Famer was the second baseman for the New York Yankees "Murderers Row" of 1927?

1B	Lou Gehrig	P	Lefty Grove
2B	Charley Gehringer	P	Carl Hubbell
3B	Jimmie Foxx	P	Dizzy Dean
SS	Arky Vaughn	P	Lefty Gomez
OF	Joe Medwick	RP	Ted Lyons
OF	Paul Waner		
OF	Mel Ott		
C	Bill Dickey		
DH	Hank Greenberg		

1930-A Most Unusual Year

"The screwball's an unnatural pitch. Nature never intended a man to turn his hand like that throwing rocks at a bear."

Carl Hubbell

In 1930, in the National League, Babe Herman batted .393. Chuck Klein had 250 hits, 40 home runs, 170 RBIs, and a .687 slugging average. Kiki Cuyler hit 50 doubles and scored 155 runs, and Hack Wilson had 423 total bases. In the American League, Lou Gehrig batted .379, hit 41 home runs, had 220 hits and had a .721 slugging average. Al Simmons had 165 RBIs and 392 total bases. Heine Manush hit 49 doubles and Babe Ruth scored 150 runs. Very impressive statistics; however, *all* of them were second place finishers!

Offensive records were set in 1930 that stood for decades, including one that may never be broken: Hack Wilson's 190 RBIs. Other notable offensive achievements that year include: Bill Terry's .401 batting average (still the last man in the NL to break .400); Chuck Klein's 158 runs scored; Wilson's 56 home runs; Terry's 254 hits; Lou Gehrig's 174 RBIs; and Al Simmons' 152 runs scored. The National League combined batting average was an astounding .303! By the way, another impressive achievement was Dazzy Vance's 2.61 ERA in the greatest of hitters' years. It was 1.16 lower than that of second -place finisher Carl Hubbell's.

The Great Depression had a devastating economic impact on every American. Every facet of the country suffered, including Major League Baseball. Attendance dropped dramatically, especially in smaller cities and for teams with losing records. To create more offense, and thus, attract more paying customers to the ballparks, the owners decided to "juice up" the baseball. They injected Australian wool into the core of the balls to make them fly like golf balls. They also flattened the seams so pitchers couldn't grip their curve balls. The owners got more offense than they bargained for, and the experiment only lasted only one year.

The A's of Jimmie Foxx, Lefty Grove, Al Simmons, and Mickey Cochrane dominated the beginning of the decade in the AL, but they were overtaken by the Yankees of Gehrig, Lefty Gomez, Joe DiMaggio, and Red Ruffing in the second half. The Tigers and Senators also won pennants in the decade. The National League witnessed the Giants, Cardinals, and Cubs winning all but one year, when the Reds captured the flag in 1939.

When the ball was deadened after 1930, attendance again dropped. The mighty A's only attracted 400,000 fans in 1932, and by 1936 Connie Mack had sold all four of his Hall-of-Fame super stars for much-needed funds. The A's finished no higher than fourth until 1969. Attendance was even worse in St. Louis, where the Cardinals drew just 335,000 fans despite winning the World Series. The following year the Browns drew an abysmal 81,000.

The 1930s are called the "golden age" of Major League Baseball. Many of the game's greatest players starred during the decade.

1931: Lefty

Lefty Grove dominated American League batters in 1931. Not even Ruth and Gehrig could hit him. He won the pitching triple crown with 31 victories, 175 strikeouts, and a 2.06 ERA. He threw 27 complete games en route to winning the AL MVP award.

Grove also had a combustible temper to go along with his blazing fastball. In August of the 1931 season, Grove was riding a 16-game winning streak. When he took the mound in hopes of matching Walter Johnson's record of 17 straight wins. Al Simmons got the day off and rookie Jimmy Moore played in his place. Unfortunately for the hapless Moore, he misjudged a fly ball that cost the Athletics a run and Grove lost the game 1-0. Moore made himself invisible as the enraged Grove tore up the locker room and refused to talk to his teammates for days. Grove bounced back however, and went on to win his next six games. His record for the 1930-31 seasons was 59-9.

Other notable events in 1931 included Lou Gehrig's offensive season. The Iron Horse had 46 home runs, 184 RBIs, 211 hits, and 410 total bases. His Yankees scored a record 1,067 runs. Red Sox outfielder Earl Webb banged out 67 doubles, despite never hitting more than 30 before or after. In a significant rule change, balls bouncing over or through a fence were now counted as doubles instead of home runs.

1932: The Beast

Lefty Gomez once quipped that, "Jimmie Foxx wasn't scouted, he was trapped." Indeed, American League pitchers must have thought that they were pitching to another species when facing the muscle-bound Foxx. When he retired, Foxx was second only to Babe Ruth in home runs with 534. In 1932 he hit 58 out of the park. He should have had more. Five of his blasts were lost to newly erected screens in Cleveland and St. Louis. These screens were not present in 1927 when Ruth hit 60 home runs. The "right handed Babe Ruth" led the league in home runs and RBIs in 1932 but missed the batting title, and, therefore the Triple Crown, by three points. He also led the league in fielding.

The 1932 season also saw Lou Gehrig hit four home runs in one game and Johnny Burnett of Cleveland get nine hits in an 18-inning game.

1933: The Boy Manager

In 1933 the Washington Senators named Joe Cronin, their 26-year old star shortstop, the team's manager. To everyone's surprise, the Senators, under Cronin's tutelage and stellar play, won the pennant. Despite this success, Senators, owner Clark Griffith, who was also Cronin's father-in-law, sold him to the Boston Red Sox in 1935 for $250,000, the greatest amount paid for any player up to that time.

The 1933 season saw a Triple Crown winner in both leagues, Jimmie Foxx in the American and Chuck Klein in the National, an event that has never been duplicated. In spite of Klein's performance at the plate, the NL MVP Award went to pitcher Carl Hubbell of the New York Giants, who posted a stingy 1.66 ERA. The American League won the first All-Star game, which was conceived as a one-time event to raise money for retired players. But, it was such a smash hit with the fans that it remains a fixture of the season to this day.

1934: Dizzy

Jay Hanna Dean was a product of rural Arkansas who never got past fourth grade. In 1934 he was the best pitcher in baseball. Pitching for the St. Louis Cardinals' "Gashouse Gang," Dean won 30 games and was named the NL MVP. He was known not only for boasting about his exploits on the diamond, but for fulfilling his predictions. As he once said, " It ain't bragging if you can back it up." A typical Dean prediction occurred before a game against the Boston Braves. He poked his head inside their dugout and said, "No curves today fellas, just hard ones."[22] He shut them out on three hits even though they knew what he was going to throw all game.

The Tigers took the American League flag, but it was a banner year for three great Yankee players. Ruth hit his 700th home run, Gehrig won the Triple Crown, and Gomez won 26 games, led the league in strikeouts with 158, tossed six shutouts, and threw 25 complete games. Hubbell made history by striking out future Hall-of-Famers Ruth,

Gehrig, Foxx, Simmons, and Cronin consecutively in the All-Star game.

1935: The Original Hammerin' Hank

Hank Greenberg won the AL MVP Award in the American League on the strength of his 170 RBIs, 50 more than runner-up Lou Gehrig! The Yankees courted Greenberg, a New York native who ordinarily would have been a perfect fit. However, Greenberg was very much aware that the Yankees already had a first baseman, a gentleman named Lou Gehrig, so he rejected the offer and signed with the Detroit Tigers. His ratio of 0.92 RBIs per game ties him with Gehrig and Sam Thompson for the best ratio ever. He lost three years to WWII and three more to injuries, otherwise his career statistics would be even more impressive. His .605 slugging average was sixth-best ever as of 2015.

The first night game took place on May 24 at Crosley Field in Cincinnati. Babe Ruth retired with major league career records in home runs (714), slugging average (.690), walks (2,056), RBIs (2,213), on-base-percentage (.474), and extra base hits (1,356). All of those records have since been surpassed except for his career slugging average.

1936: The Meal Ticket

Carl Hubbell won his second Most Valuable Player Award in 1936. During a span in 1936-37, he won 24 straight games! His signature pitch was the screwball, a pitch perfected by very few major league hurlers. The screwball, combined with pinpoint control, fueled his Hall of-Fame career. In 1933, he beat the Cardinals in an 18-inning game, 1-0, essentially throwing two shutouts in one game. He also threw 46-1/3 consecutive scoreless innings in that same year.

In 1936 the Yankees were at it again, collecting 2,703 total bases and 997 RBIs, both major league records. Joe Medwick of the Cardinals set a record by rapping out 64 doubles, and Luke Appling, of the Chicago White Sox won the batting title with a .388 average, the highest by a shortstop in the modern era. Joe DiMaggio and Bob Feller made their debuts, and the Hall of Fame was created, admitting Ty Cobb, Babe Ruth, Honus Wagner, Walter Johnson, and Christy Mathewson as charter members.

1937: Muscles

The St. Louis Cardinals' "Gashouse Gang" counted several characters among its ranks, one of which was Joe "Ducky" Medwick. He won the National League Most Valuable Player Award in 1937, as well as the Triple Crown with a .374 batting average, 31 home runs, and 154 RBIs. In fact, he led the National League in every significant offensive category except triples. He was also a very good defensive outfielder. Medwick grew up as a tough kid in New Jersey and was known as a brawler, even with his own teammates. Dizzy Dean said of him. "You argue with him and before you can say a doggone word, he bops you."[23]

A near tragic event occurred in 1937. Tiger catcher Mickey Cochrane was beaned by Yankee pitcher Bump Hadley and almost died as a result. He lived, but it ended his illustrious career.

1938: Two no-no's

Some baseball records will never be broken, Cy Young's 511 victories and Cal Ripken's 2,632 consecutive game streak come to mind. Another such record is Johnny Vander Meer's consecutive no-hit games in 1938. The thought of even a great pitcher pitching three consecutive no-hit games is unfathomable.

While we're talking about streaks, Pinky Higgins of the Red Sox got 12 hits in 12 consecutive at bats in 1938, a record. Home runs made the news that year as Hank Greenberg belted 58 and Lou Gehrig hit his record 23rd grand slam.

1939: Bucky

In 1939 the Cincinnati Reds surprised the baseball world by

capturing the National League pennant. They did it primarily on the backs of their two ace pitchers: Bucky Walters and Paul Derringer. Walters won 27 games and Derringer won 25. From the last half of the 1930s to the first half of the 1940s, Bucky Walters was arguably the best pitcher in the National League. From 1939 to 1946 he led both leagues in wins (141), innings pitched (2,030), and complete games (178). Besides being a great pitcher, he was also a very good hitter, fielder, and base runner. He hit .325 in 1939, and won the National League Most Valuable Player Award.

The Reds lost to the Yankees in the World Series, which made it four championships in a row for the Bronx Bombers. The first televised game was played on August 26, at Ebbets Field. Lefty Grove led the league in ERA (2.54) for a record-breaking ninth time. Lou Gehrig retired, giving the most memorable speech in baseball history, and Ted Williams debuted, winning the RBI title with 145, the most ever by a rookie.

Stars of the 1930s Jimmie Foxx, Babe Ruth, Lou Gehrig, Al Simmons

84. What brother combo from the 1930s and 1940s
is in the Hall of Fame?

276

1B	Johnny Mize	P	Bob Feller
2B	Bobby Doerr	P	Hal Newhouser
3B	Bob Elliott	P	Rip Sewell
SS	Lou Boudreau	P	Bucky Walters
OF	Stan Musial	RP	Joe Paige
OF	Joe DiMaggio		
OF	Enos Slaughter		
C	Walker Cooper		
DH	Ted Williams		

The Mahatma

"No man in baseball in the last quarter century, with the possible exception of Judge Landis and Babe Ruth, has left so deep an impress on the game as Branch Rickey."

Sportswriter Fred Lieb 1945

During the 1940s fans were treated to eight down-to-the-wire pennant races that were decided by two games or less. The Depression was over and fans started flocking back to the ballpark. It wasn't just the major leagues that enjoyed a resurgence in attendance either: 500 minor league teams were in place during the decade. These teams drew 35 million fans in 1940 alone. Four new themes dominated the game in the 1940s: night games became widespread, television coverage became commonplace, World War II disrupted play by taking away many players away, and the game was finally integrated. A third league, the Mexican League, had a short life, but added to the chaos of 1940s Major League Baseball.

Other than player strikes, World War II caused the biggest disruption to Major League Baseball ever. So many players, including some of the game's biggest stars, were drafted or enlisted that by the time they returned to their teams in 1946, only about a third of the regulars remained from the 1945 rosters. Players were drafted or enlisted as early as 1942, including such luminaries as Bob Feller, Hank Greenberg, and Cecil Travis. They stayed in the army longer than most of their counterparts who were drafted later. Travis was an All-Star shortstop for the Senators and a potential Hall-of-Famer when he was sent to fight at the Battle of the Bulge. His feet were so badly frozen in that episode that he was never the same player he was before the war.

There was talk of cancelling the games during the war, but President Franklin Roosevelt declared that the season should continue. Teams were so desperate for talent that retired players such as Paul and Lloyd Waner and Pepper Martin were called back into service. The Reds signed Joe Nuxhall, a 15-year-old, though he appeared in just one game. In two extreme cases, one-legged Bert Shepard and one-armed Pete Gray were called into action. Shepard only pitched in one game, but Gray played outfield for the St. Louis Browns for the entire 1945 season. The Browns won the pennant for their first and only time in 1944, and played the Cardinals for the only all-St. Louis World Series. In fact, the entire series was played in Sportsman's Park, which both teams called home.

Individual milestones abounded during the decade. Bob Feller pitched a no-hitter on Opening Day in 1940, won 27 games the same year, and struck out 348 batters in 1946. The three best hitters of the era also had significant accomplishments. Joe DiMaggio had his incredible 56-consecutive-game hitting streak, and became the first player to receive a $100,000 salary. That same year, Ted Williams hit .406 on his way to the Triple Crown, the first of two occasions when he won the Triple Crown but lost the MVP Award to DiMaggio. Williams finished in the top three of MVP voting every year from 1941-49 (excluding the three years he spent in the military), and won the award in 1946 and 1949.

The third great hitter of the era, Stan Musial, had a magnificent decade, including one of the greatest years ever for a hitter in 1948 when he won the Triple Crown to go along with his astounding 429 total bases. The New York Giants set a significant team record by mashing 221 home runs in 1947, obliterating the previous record of 182.

Lefty Grove won his 300th game, and Paul Waner collected his 3,000th hit. Pete Reiser of the Brooklyn Dodgers became the youngest player to win a batting title in 1941, and set a record in 1946 for stealing home seven times. Ralph Kiner became the first rookie to win a home run title. Detroit's Hal Newhouser won consecutive MVP Awards in 1944-45. In 1944, he and teammate Dizzy Trout won 29 and 27 games respectively, a post dead-ball era record. But the Tigers still finished second to the surprising Browns.

Jackie Robinson set Major League Baseball on its ear by integrating the game in April of 1947. Larry Doby did the same for the American League when he joined the Cleveland Indians in July. Robinson won Rookie of the Year, and two years later captured the MVP Award. One of the unfortunate unintended consequences of integration was the collapse of the Negro Leagues during the decade, as its stars all migrated to the major leagues.

Pitcher Spud Chandler of the Yankees retired with a won-lost record of .717, the highest winning percentage of any pitcher with over 100 wins. Three giants of the game died during the 1940s: Commissioner Kenesaw Mountain Landis, Babe Ruth, and Lou Gehrig.

Wesley Branch Rickey was one of the greatest innovators in the history of baseball. In a previous section of this book, I quoted Red Barber as saying that Jackie Robinson, Babe Ruth, and Marvin Miller were three of the most significant contributors to the game. I should add Branch Rickey, Judge Landis, and Alexander Cartwright, to that august list.

Rickey is best remembered for bringing Jackie Robinson, and thus integration, to Major League Baseball. That feat alone would place Rickey in the pantheon of baseball's immortals, but he was the driving force behind two other major changes to the game, namely the establishment of the farm system, and expansion in the 1960s.

Branch Rickey was a mediocre catcher for the St. Louis Browns in 1905, but his real forte was as a baseball executive and visionary. After realizing that he was not going to be the next Buck Ewing, he dropped out of the game in order to get his law degree from the University of

Michigan. While there, he discovered George Sisler, and brought him to the St. Louis Browns. In 1920 Rickey became President/Manager of the Cardinals, where his true talents became apparent. The franchise was always strapped for cash, so they could not compete with the richer teams like the Yankees, Giants, and A's for talented players. He established a farm system for the Cardinals that enabled the team to find and hold young players, mainly across the south and west, at bargain rates. He would even buy whole teams, not just players, to add to the ever-expanding farm system, which came to be called the "Rickey Plantation." By 1936, the Cardinal farm system boasted 28 teams. Such stars as Rogers Hornsby, Stan Musial, Dizzy Dean, Joe Medwick, Pepper Martin, and Jim Bottomley were obtained this way, enabling the Cardinals to have a winning record second only to the Yankees.

Rickey was the coach of the Ohio Wesleyan University baseball team in 1903. The team had one black player, Charley Thomas. When the team checked into the Hotel Oliver in South Bend, Indiana for a game against Notre Dame, Thomas was denied a room because of his race. Rickey managed to convince the hotel management to allow Thomas to sleep on a cot in his room. When Rickey returned to the room he found Thomas sobbing and trying to claw his skin off, saying "It's my skin Mr. Rickey, if only I could make it white."[24]

From that day forward, Rickey vowed to make things right for black players who deserved to play. But to convince the baseball establishment to allow Robinson to play, he had to be both tough and shrewd. Two examples of this shrewdness were waiting for Judge Landis to die, and assigning Jackie to Montreal for his minor league experience. Landis opposed integrating Major League Baseball, and Rickey knew that he would have a hard time prevailing against the powerful commissioner. Landis died in 1944 and was succeeded by "Happy" Chandler, who was sympathetic to integration.

When integration finally looked like it could become a reality, Rickey assigned Robinson to Montreal because he knew it had a more tolerant racial climate than most American cities. When several of Robinson's Dodger teammates threatened a boycott, Rickey was tough enough to tell them he would trade them, even if he could not get equal value in return. Thus an argument can be made that Branch Rickey played a more significant role in integrating Major League Baseball than Robinson. The impact on American society as a result of Jackie breaking the color line in baseball cannot be underestimated. American citizens started to realize that if the two races could play on the same team, then why couldn't they work together, go to school together, and live together?

Rickey was an energetic supporter of expanding Major League Baseball, not just within the boundaries of the United States, but indeed around the world. He thought it just might be an instrument of international stability. In 1959, he and Bill Shea, among others, presented a case to the two leagues for expansion. When they met opposition from the owners, Rickey, in his typical bulldog fashion, threatened to form a third league, called the Continental League, with him as its president unless they agreed. The owners capitulated and in 1960, the National League agreed to add two expansion teams.

Branch Rickey

85. What was Branch Rickey's response to Jackie Robinson's question; "Do you want a player with guts enough to fight back"?

1B	Stan Musial	P	Warren Spahn
2B	Jackie Robinson	P	Early Wynn
3B	Eddie Mathews	P	Whitey Ford
SS	Ernie Banks	P	Robin Roberts
OF	Duke Snider	RP	Bob Lemon
OF	Willie Mays		
OF	Mickey Mantle		
C	Yogi Berra		
DH	Ted Williams		

Willie, Mickey, and the Duke

"Snider, Mantle, and Mays; you could get a fat lip in any saloon in New York by starting an argument as to which was best."
Red Smith

I was born in 1945 in Garden City, New York, about 25 miles east of the Big Apple. A baseball fan could not have come into this world at a better time or in a better place than yours truly. I was five years old when the 1950s began, just the right age to give my full attention to the game and to a team. My team was the New York Giants, which meant that I not only loved the Giants, but I was duty-bound to hate both the Dodgers and Yankees.

The playground arguments about who was the best team of the three were hot, but the arguments over who was the best center fielder were furious. Willie Mays of the Giants, Mickey Mantle of the Yankees, and Duke Snider of the Dodgers came into greatness right in my backyard. Mantle by the way, had just taken over from another pretty good center fielder, a guy named Joe DiMaggio. The refrain, "Willie, Mickey, and the Duke," (set to music in the 1981 Terry Cashman song "Talkin' Baseball") has a certain ring to it that still puts a smile on my face.

My vote of course, goes to Willie Mays, who I think is the best ballplayer of all-time. Mickey Mantle was almost as good, and indeed may have been better if not for debilitating injuries and a carousing lifestyle. To my mind, the "Duke of Flatbush" doesn't really compare with the other two, even though he out-homered them during the four full years that all three played in New York. In fact, Snider out-hit both Willie and Mickey for the entire decade. He had 1,605 hits, 326 home runs, and 1,031 RBIs to Mickey's 1,392, 280, and 841, and Willie's 1,111, 250, and 709 respectively. Of course, Snider played all 10 years during the decade whereas Mickey played nine, and Willie only 7.5. Nevertheless, all three were outstanding five-tool stars, and all are enshrined in the Hall of Fame.

As a Giants fan, I could only argue about who was the best center fielder. My Dodger and Yankee buddies spent as much energy arguing about their team's shortstops and catchers as they did their center fielders. Who was the better catcher, Yogi Berra or Roy Campanella? Each won three Most Valuable Player Awards during the '50s and each is in the Hall of Fame. As to the best shortstop, Dodger Pee Wee Reese and Yankee Phil Rizzuto were also hotly argued over. I would argue that Giant shortstop Alvin Dark was only a notch below them.

The greatest home run, the greatest catch, and the greatest World Series pitching performance all happened in the 1950s in New York. I refer to Bobby Thompson's home run in 1951 to wrest the pennant from the Dodgers, Mays's over-the-shoulder catch of Vic Wertz's long fly ball in the 1954 World Series, and Don Larsen's perfect game in the 1956 World Series. As good as the Dodgers and Giants were, the 1950s belonged to the Yankees. The three New York teams won 14 out of 20 pennants during the decade; the Yankees won eight of them. The same teams won 11 of the 20 MVP Awards; the Yankees won six. All three teams, especially the Dodgers, were loaded with talent on the field. Perhaps the difference maker for the Yankees was their manager, Casey Stengel.

Television made an impact on Major League Baseball during the 1940s, but it really took off in the 50s. The geographic landscape of the major leagues also changed dramatically. In 1953, the Boston Braves, who shared what was already a small market with the Red Sox, moved the franchise to Milwaukee. The St. Louis Browns, weary of sharing their city with the Cardinals, became the Baltimore Orioles in 1954. And in 1955, the Philadelphia A's decided that they also did not want to share a city with another team, and moved to Kansas City.

These moves however, were merely tremors. The earthquake occurred after the 1957 season when the Brooklyn Dodgers and New York Giants moved as far away from home as possible; the Dodgers going to Los Angeles and the Giants going to San Francisco. Brooklyn fans to this day put Dodger owner Walter O'Malley second only to Adolph Hitler on their most hated persons list.

Notable achievements and events for the decade include:

- Connie Mack retired after 50 years in the game.
- The Yankees won five consecutive World Series championships.
- Bobo Holloman, a 30-year-old rookie for the Browns pitched a no-hitter in his first major league start. He won just two more games that season and never pitched again in the major leagues.
- Mickey Mantle hit the longest home run ever (565 feet).
- The Cleveland Indians won 111 games to take the American League pennant in 1954.
- On May 2, 1954, Stan Musial hit five home runs in a double header. He became the first National Leaguer to earn $100,000. He got his 3,000th hit in 1958.
- Al Kaline, 20, became the youngest player to win the batting title.
- Ernie Banks hit a record five grand slams in 1955.
- The Reds hit 221 home runs in 1956.
- Dale Long of the Pirates set a record by hitting a home run in

eight consecutive games.

- Ted Williams reached base in 16 consecutive plate appearances.
- Lew Burdette of the Braves pitched three complete game victories over the Yankees in the 1957 World Series.
- Jackie Robinson retired after the 1957 season: that same off-season, Roy Campanella was paralyzed in a car accident.
- Roy Face of the Pirates won 17 straight games in relief and ended the 1959 season with an 18-1 record.
- Larry Sherry won two games and saved two others in the Dodgers' victory over the White Sox in the 1959 World Series
- The Red Sox acquired Pumpsie Green, becoming the last team in baseball to integrate its roster.
- On May 26, 1959, Harvey Haddix of the Pirates pitched 12 perfect innings against the Braves, but lost the game 1-0 after giving up an unearned run in the 13th inning.

Willie   Mickey   The Duke

86. The last home run in the Polo Grounds was hit in 1963. Who hit it and what team did he play for?

1B	Willie McCovey	P	Bob Gibson
2B	Bill Mazeroski	P	Juan Marichal
3B	Brooks Robinson	P	Don Drysdale
SS	Ernie Banks	P	Sandy Koufax
OF	Frank Robinson	RP	Hoyt Wilhelm
OF	Willie Mays		
OF	Roberto Clemente		
C	Joe Torre		
DH	Hank Aaron		

Jackie's Legacy

*"Robinson is a good player. There may even be
three or four other blacks in the country who can play
well enough to get a chance in the big leagues."*
Sam Breadon, President, St. Louis Cardinals

The 1960s saw several major changes to Major League Baseball. Eight new teams were added, increasing the size of the league by 50%. Revenue increased dramatically for most clubs, with television revenue in particular increasing tenfold. Marvin Miller was named as Executive Director of the Players Association and, together with Curt Flood challenged the reserve clause. Pitching once again assumed a dominant role. A free agent draft was adopted. The Yankee dynasty collapsed. And black players rose to excellence, especially in the National League.

Every year of the decade witnessed a thrilling or historic event. In 1960 it was Bill Mazeroski's walk-off home run in the seventh game of the World Series to beat the Yankees. In 1961, it was the dramatic home run race between the Yankee M&M boys, Roger Maris and Mickey Mantle, with Maris besting Babe Ruth's single season record set in 1927 by blasting 61 home runs. Maury Wills of the Dodgers shattered Ty Cobb's stolen base record by stealing 104 in 1962. In 1963, Warren Spahn, at 42 years of age became the oldest pitcher ever to win 20 games. The Philadelphia Phillies experienced the greatest collapse of any pennant contender in history in 1964.

The opening of the Astrodome brought baseball indoors for the first time in 1965. The Yankees finished in last place in 1966, and the Red Sox overcame Las Vegas odds of 100-1 to win the pennant in what was the greatest pennant race ever in 1967. Pitchers completely overwhelmed hitters in 1968, the "year of the pitcher", and in 1969 the truly unthinkable happened: the New York Mets, who won 40 and lost 120 games in 1962, won the World Series.

A plethora of records were set during the 1960s. Relief pitching became a specialty, and almost every year a relief pitcher set a new save record. Lindy McDaniel of the Cardinals started the trend in 1960 with a National League record 26 saves, and Luis Arroyo saved 24 for the Yankees in 1961. McDaniel's record lasted all of two years when Roy Face of the Pirates racked up 28 saves in 1962; that, too, was bested in 1965 by Ted Abernathy's 31 saves for the Cubs. Jack Aker of the Royals broke Arroyo's record in 1966 with 32 saves.

Maris and Wills weren't the only two to register significant achievements during the decade. Tony Oliva of the Twins became the only player ever to win the batting title in his first two years in the majors, Eddie Mathews set a National League record with his ninth consecutive year hitting 30 or more home runs, Sandy Koufax set a modern National League record by striking out 306 batters in 1963, and then broke his own record by fanning 382 in 1965. Two teenage records were set in 1964: Wally Bunker won 19 games for the Orioles, and Tony Conigliaro rapped out 24 home runs for the Red Sox. Steve Carlton set a major league record in 1969 by striking out 19 Mets, and Willie Mays tied the major league record by collecting four home runs in one game. Rod Carew of the Twins tied the major league record by stealing home seven times in 1969. Triple Crowns were won by Frank Robinson and Carl Yastrzemski, and Sandy Koufax won pitching's trifecta. Significant pitching records were set in 1968, which I will discuss further.

Team records were set or tied as well during the decade. The Yankees set a major league record with 240 home runs in 1961, with six players having 20 or more. They also tied their own record by winning five consecutive pennants from 1960-64. Incredibly, they finished in sixth place in 1965 and even more incredibly, they finished last the following year. One of the reasons for their rapid decline was the institution of the amateur draft, thus giving all teams an equal shot at the talent pool. I will discuss the other reason later.

Ted Williams, Mickey Mantle, Eddie Mathews, and Hank Aaron all joined the 500 home run club, and Warren Spahn and Early Wynn won their 300th games. Ty Cobb died and Casey Stengel was fired as manager of the Yankees. Musial, Williams, Berra, Spahn, and Koufax retired. Whitey Ford retired with a .690 winning percentage, the best in the modern era for a pitcher with at least 200 victories.

Anomalies and strange events were plentiful. Sixty-five-year old Satchel Paige pitched three scoreless innings for the A's against the Red Sox, making him the oldest player to play in a major league game. Both Bert Campaneris of the A's and Cesar Tovar of the Twins each played all nine positions in a game (not at the same time). Brothers Matty and Felipe Alou finished first and second in the National League batting race in 1966. The Astros beat the Mets 1-0 in 24 innings, in one of the longest games in baseball history.

The Washington Senators became the Minnesota Twins in 1961, the Milwaukee Braves moved to Atlanta in 1965, and the Kansas City A's moved to Oakland. The California Angels and a second iteration of the Washington Senators were added to the American League in 1961; the New York Mets and Houston Colt 45s joined the National League in 1962. The Kansas City Royals, Seattle Pilots, San Diego Padres, and Montreal Expos were added in 1969, bringing the total number of teams to 24 and necessitating two divisions in each league with an additional playoff round to determine the pennant winner

In a decade chock full of incredible years, 1968 may have been the most remarkable. It was the "year of the pitcher." After the barrage of home runs in 1961 and '62, baseball expanded the top of the strike zone in 1963 to give the pitchers an edge. By 1968, however, they didn't need the edge. Thirteen teams had an ERA of less than 3.00. Five pitchers had an ERA under 2.00, and 339 shutouts were thrown. Bob Gibson of the Cardinals had an amazing 1.12 ERA, Detroit's Denny McClain won 31 games, and big Don Drysdale of the Dodgers pitched 58 consecutive scoreless innings! Only six players batted over .300 in both leagues, and Carl Yastrzemski won the American League batting title with a .301 average. The following year the old strike zone was restored and the mound was lowered from 15 inches to 10.

When Jackie Robinson broke baseball's color line, he opened the floodgates for a rush of fresh new talent into the game. The 1950s witnessed the arrival of veteran pioneers like Jackie, Roy Campanella, Don Newcombe, and Larry Doby, as well as the Negro Leagues best young stars, including Willie Mays, Hank Aaron, and Ernie Banks. The National League led the charge in signing the black players, specifically the Dodgers, Giants, Braves, Cubs, and

Pirates.

From 1949-1959, eight black players won the Rookie of the Year award in the National League; black players won every NL MVP award from 1953-59. Roy Campanella won the award three times and Ernie Banks won it twice.

But it was the 1960s that saw the multitude of great black players reach their prime and outshine their white counterparts in the National League. The style of play changed dramatically with the introduction of so many of these new players. Speed became paramount. Stealing bases, bunting for base hits, stretching singles into doubles, and going from first to third on a single epitomized play in the National League during the decade of the 1960s. In the 24 years from 1947-70, black players led one league or the other in hitting 17 times, and in home runs 15 times. Black pitchers won 20 or more games 22 times. Black players won seven more National League MVP awards during the 1960s and three American League MVP awards.

The National League dominated the All-Star games throughout the 1960s, due primarily to the number of black players. When the Yankees dropped into the cellar immediately after their 1964 pennant winning year, a major reason, probably *the* major reason, was their refusal to sign the young black and Hispanic players. The American League, noticing the enormous talent streaming into their rival league, finally started to sign these players themselves. By 1957, only the Tigers and Red Sox did not have a black player on their roster. The Tigers signed Ozzie Virgil in 1958, and the Red Sox, who at one time had a chance to sign both Jackie Robinson and Willie Mays, became the last team to sign a black player, Pumpsie Green, in 1959.

Frank Robinson

87. The Cincinnati Reds executed one of the worst trades in history after the 1965 season. They traded Frank Robinson to the Baltimore Orioles for whom?

1B	Willie Stargell	P	Steve Carlton
2B	Joe Morgan	P	Tom Seaver
3B	Mike Schmidt	P	Jim Palmer
SS	Dave Concepcion	P	Jim Hunter
OF	Lou Brock	RP	Rollie Fingers
OF	Pete Rose		
OF	Reggie Jackson		
C	Johnny Bench		
DH	Rod Carew		

Designated Hitter

*"Most pitchers ought to have
'For Display Purposes Only' on their bat."*
Joe Garagiola on the Designated Hitter

During the 1970s, several teams moved to new, boringly symmetrical stadiums with artificial turf. The fake grass changed the strategy of the game, making speed paramount. Infielders had to play back, and outfielders had to be more cautious when charging a ground ball, lest it bounce over their heads and go for a triple or an inside the park home run. Charlie Finley, the flamboyant owner of the Oakland A's, even signed world class sprinter Herb Washington as a designated runner. By 1980, only five original stadiums were left standing: Boston's Fenway Park, Chicago's Wrigley Field and Comiskey Park, Detroit's Tiger Stadium, and Yankee Stadium.

Salaries skyrocketed and attendance increased by 64%. In the last year of the decade Major League Baseball set a new attendance record, as more than 43 million fans flocked to the ballparks. Games took on a rock concert/carnival atmosphere to attract more fans. Mascots like the San Diego Chicken and Phillie Fanatic started dancing atop dugouts and teasing the umpires, delighting children and casual fans. Ear-piercing music and exploding scoreboards echoed (or even overwhelmed) the action on the field.

The Washington Senators became the Texas Rangers and the Seattle Pilots became the Milwaukee Brewers. The Seattle Mariners and Toronto Blue Jays were born. The American League instituted the designated hitter rule in 1973, whereby a batter who did not play in the field would hit for the pitcher each time his turn came up in the order. I will discuss this change later.

But the most significant change to the old ballgame during the 1970s was the ascendance of the players union. Marvin Miller, its executive director, led the victorious assault on the reserve clause, freeing the players and launching the era of free agency.

Major League Baseball experienced its first strike in 1972. It only lasted 13 days, but it set the groundwork for future seismic shifts. Salary arbitration was instituted whereby a player could contest his salary and have his case decided by a judge rather than the owner. The "5 and 10" rule was also adopted. It specified that a player with at least 10 years in the majors and five years with his present club could veto a trade. It came too late to help Curt Flood, but Ron Santo used it successfully to block a trade from the Chicago Cubs. When pitchers Andy Messersmith and Dave McNally refused to sign their contracts after the 1974 season, a judge ruled that they were free agents for the 1975 season. The floodgates were finally opened for all players to become free agents at the end of their existing contracts. Baseball would never be the same again.

The Oakland A's dominated the first half of the decade. They set a major league record by winning six consecutive postseason series (three league championships series and three World Series). Earl Weaver's Baltimore Orioles, Cincinnati's "Big Red Machine," George Steinbrenner's Yankees, and the Pittsburgh Pirates of Clemente and Stargell also enjoyed a successful decade. In 1972, the Orioles boasted four 20-game winners: Jim Palmer, Dave McNally, Pat Dobson, and Mike Cuellar.

Relief pitchers continued to play an ever more important role, frequently surpassing save records set during the 1960s. Cincinnati's Wayne Granger set a major league record in 1970 by collecting 35 saves, only to be bested in 1973 by Detroit's John Hiller who managed to save 38 games. Relief specialist Mike Marshall of the Dodgers set a major league record by pitching in an incredible 106 games in 1974. He became the first reliever to win the Cy Young Award that year.

Flamethrower Nolan Ryan set a major league record in 1972 by allowing a miserly 5.26 hits per game, then set another modern era record by tallying 383 strikeouts in 1973. At the end of the 1979 season he signed the first $1 million contract as a free agent with the Astros. The hapless Phillies won only 59 games in 1972, but Steve Carlton won 27 of them! Catfish Hunter threw 30 complete games in 1975. With today's five man rotations and strict adherence to pitch counts, he will probably be the last pitcher to accomplish that. Yankee Ron Guidry had a year for the ages in 1978 when he went 25-3 and set a record for the best winning percentage for a 25-game winner at .893. The Niekro brothers tied for most wins in the National League with 21.

Ron Hunt set a modern day record by getting plunked 50 times in 1971. Padre Nate Colbert hit five home runs in a doubleheader. Fred Lynn was the first player to win both Rookie of the Year and Most Valuable Player in the same year, Reggie Jackson hit three home runs in a World Series game, and Willie Stargell became the oldest player to win a Most Valuable Player Award (tied with Keith Hernandez). Then there was Pete Rose. He set major league records by making 770 plate appearances in 1974, and collecting 200 or more hits in 10 different seasons. He set a modern National League record in 1978 by hitting safely in 44 consecutive games. He was named Player of the Decade by The Sporting News.

The 3,000 hit club nearly doubled, with the addition of Hank Aaron, Willie Mays, Roberto Clemente, Al Kaline, Pete Rose, Lou Brock, and Carl Yastrzemski. Brock broke Cobb's career stolen base record, finishing his career with 938.

Hank Aaron broke the most sacred record of all, surpassing Babe Ruth's career home run total of 714, which long seemed unbreakable. Hammerin' Hank retired as the all-time home run leader in home runs(755), RBI's (2,297), and total bases(6,856). Barry Bonds has since surpassed Aaron's home run record (with the help of steroids, some might argue), but Aaron's RBI and total bases record still stand 40 years later. Frank Robinson followed in Jackie's footsteps when he became the first black manager, taking the helm of the Cleveland Indians in 1975. The careers of Roberto Clemente and Thurman Munson were tragically cut short when they died in separate plane crashes.

* * *

Recently I watched the Hall of Fame induction ceremony for the class of 2014. I thought Frank Thomas' appearance was special for two reasons, first, it was the most tearful induction speech I have ever heard. Second, it was the first induction speech given by a player who spent most of his career as a designated hitter (DH). Today, I watched the Red Sox beat the Yankees, thanks in large part to the hitting prowess of David Ortiz, who up to this point, is arguably the best designated hitter of all-time.

The DH rule was adopted by the American League in 1973, but it was first suggested by Connie Mack in 1906. It is said that he grew weary of watching his two Hall-of-Fame pitchers Eddie Plank and Chief Bender flailing away at fastballs for sure strikeouts. Ever since 1968, the "year of the pitcher," Major League Baseball, and particularly the American League, tried to change the game to promote more offense. Their real concern was that fans were losing interest in pitchers' duels.

In 1972 the American League attendance was a mere 74% of the National League's. The casual fans, who were the majority of those attending games, wanted to see home runs and high scores. The designated hitter role accomplished both more run production and greater attendance for the American League. At least one pitcher would have liked to see the rule delayed by a year. Nolan Ryan set a major league record by striking out 383 in 1973, the first year of the DH. If he were able to pitch to pitchers instead of designated hitters, he surely would have had in excess of 420 strikeouts

Jo Craven McGinty of the Wall Street Journal has suggested that the designated hitter rule has given the American League a distinct home field advantage over the National League in interleague play over the years. The reason is that American League teams actively look for and sign sluggers specifically for the DH role. These hitters are usually so one-dimensional, the dimension being hitting for power, that National League teams would be loathe to waste a roster spot on them. So when National League teams play in American League parks, and thus have to play by American League rules, they have to employ a bench player to hit in the DH spot. These players are no match for the likes of David Ortiz and the other good-hit no-field sluggers that most American League teams use.

The DH rule has been the subject of many a heated argument since its inception. Opponents of it argue that it goes against the tried and true fundamentals of the game. Baseball, after all is a game for traditionalists, who maintain that there should be no specialization in baseball and that everyone should play the "whole game." They say that American League managers play a "dumbed down" version of the game and don't have to employ the strategies of sacrifice bunting and pinch-hitting that National League managers must use. They claim that pitchers stay in the game longer because they don't have to come out for a pinch-hitter. They also say that American League pitchers can throw at opposing batters with impunity because they won't be hit themselves in retaliation since they don't come to the plate.

Proponents of the rule argue that the DH makes the game more exciting because it eliminates the "automatic out" whenever the pitcher steps up to the plate. It extends the careers of aging sluggers like Orlando Cepeda, Carl Yastrzemski, Jim Rice, Frank Thomas, Tony Oliva, and Paul Molitor. They also argue ironically, that strategy is enhanced with the DH rule because managers now have to decide when to remove a pitcher without the ready-made excuse of using a pinch-hitter.

The DH rule is in effect at every level of baseball except the National League. Since 2010, all All-Star games have been played with a DH, regardless of whether it's played in a National or American League park.

David Ortiz
88. Who was the first designated hitter?

1B	Eddie Murray	P	Nolan Ryan
2B	Ryne Sandberg	P	Bert Blyleven
3B	Mike Schmidt	P	Jack Morris
SS	Ozzie Smith	P	Fernando Valenzuela
OF	Ricky Henderson	RP	Dennis Eckersley
OF	Robin Yount		
OF	Dale Murphy		
C	Gary Carter		
DH	Wade Boggs		

Relievers

*"If you don't have outstanding relief pitching,
you might as well piss on the fire and call in the dogs."*
Whitey Herzog

The 1980s witnessed parity in both leagues and across all divisions. The Dodgers were the only team to win more than one championship during the decade. Players moved from team to team in unprecedented numbers as free agency became commonplace. But attendance continued to set records and television contracts skyrocketed, enabling player salaries to soar from an average of $45,000 in 1975 to $371,000 in 1985.[25]

The word "strike" took on a new meaning as three seasons experienced work stoppages, including a 50-day strike in 1981 that necessitated first-half and second-half division winners. It was a decade that saw Mike Schmidt win three MVP Awards and Davey Johnson of the Mets become the first manager to win 90 or more games in each of his first five seasons.

Dr. Frank Jobe's revolutionary "Tommy John" surgery (named for the player who first tried it) prolonged the careers of many pitchers. Chicago's Wrigley Field became the last stadium to install lights, and Commissioner Bart Giamatti banned Pete Rose from baseball for life, then died of a heart attack 10 days later. Speed remained a significant weapon, especially with the proliferation of artificial turf. But nothing had more of an impact on the game than the expanded role of the relief pitcher.

From the early days through the 1960s, starting pitchers were expected to finish the games they started unless lifted for a pinch hitter. At the beginning of the 20th century, teams would have 120 to 140 complete games! Joe Page of the 1940s Yankees and Firpo Marberry of the 1920s and 30s Washington Senators were among the first pitchers who toiled strictly in relief. Soon, relief specialists like Jim Konstanty, Roy Face, Ted Abernathy, and the great Hoyt Wilhelm began to demonstrate the value of the "closer."

In the 1970s, Sparky Anderson of the Cincinnati Reds took relief pitching to another level. "Captain Hook" pulled his starting pitchers so frequently that in his five championship years they only completed a total of 151 games. By the beginning of the 1980s pitchers were no longer expected to pitch a complete game. One result of this practice was that starting pitchers were now urged to go "all out," rather than try to preserve their strength for the whole game.

This change in the use of relief pitchers has made life decidedly more difficult for hitters. Hitters say that it takes them two or three at bats to fully take the measure of a pitcher. Now, in a typical game, the batter will face the starting pitcher for two at bats, then a middle reliever who may have one or two good pitches, then a set-up man with one "out" pitch, and finally a closer who possesses one or two great "out" pitches, and is meaner than a junk yard dog. Closers are now so integral to a team's success that Hall-of-Fame manager Tony LaRussa has said that if he were putting together a pitching staff from scratch, his first selection would be a flame-throwing closer.

At the close of the decade there was only one relief pitcher in the Hall of Fame: the ageless Hoyt Wilhelm. As of 2015, there are four, with Rollie Fingers, Dennis Eckersley, "Goose" Gossage, and Bruce Sutter having been elected. Sutter, by the way, is the first pitcher to be elected to the Hall who never started a game. Mariano Rivera and Trevor Hoffman are sure to get in when they become eligible, and several more on today's teams are strong candidates. The age of the closer is upon us.

Records and milestones for the decade were:

1980 • Ricky Henderson became the first American Leaguer to steal 100 bases.

1981 • Pete Rose became the oldest player (40) to lead the league in hits(140). He broke Stan Musial's National League record of 3,630 hits.

• Steve Carlton recorded his 3,000th strikeout.

• Nolan Ryan recorded his 5th no-hitter.

1982 • Steve Carlton won his fourth Cy Young Award.

• Henderson stole 130 bases, shattering Lou Brock's modern-day single season record.

• Carl Yastrzemski retired after 23 years, tying Brooks Robinson for most years with a single team.

• Rollie Fingers recorded his 300th save.

• Gaylord Perry won his 300th game.

1983 • Steve Garvey's consecutive game streak ended at 1,207 after he broke his thumb.

• Dan Quisenberry saved a record 45 games.

• Both Nolan Ryan and Steve Carlton passed Walter Johnson's career strikeout record.

• Carlton won his 300th game.

1984 • Rookie Dwight Gooden recorded 276 strikeouts as a 19-year old.

• Pete Rose notched his 4,000th hit, and collected 100 or more hits for the 22nd consecutive year.

• Reggie Jackson hit his 500th home run.

• Bruce Sutter tied Quisenberry's record with 45 saves.

• Sparky Anderson became the first manager to win a World Series in both leagues.

1985 • Pete Rose collected his 4,192nd hit to pass Ty Cobb for the all-time career hit record.

- Rookie Vince Coleman stole 100 bases.

- Don Sutton became the first pitcher to strikeout 100 or more batters in 20 consecutive seasons.

- Nolan Ryan recorded his 4,000th strikeout.

- Rod Carew collected his 3,000th hit.

- Phil Niekro and Tom Seaver each won their 300th game.

1986 • Roger Clemens struck out 20 Mariners on April 29.

- Mike Schmidt led the league in home runs (37), for the eighth time. He also won his 10th Gold Glove

- Pete Rose retired as the major league leader in hits (4,256), games (3,562), and at bats (14,053).

- Dave Righetti broke the save record with 46.

- Steve Carlton collected his 4,000th strikeout.

- Don Sutton won his 300th game.

1987 • Andre Dawson of the Cubs became the first player to win the MVP Award for a last place team.

- Rookie Mark McGwire hit 49 home runs.

- Don Mattingly tied the major league record by hitting a home run in eight consecutive games.

1988 • Orel Hershiser pitched 59 consecutive scoreless innings, breaking the record held by fellow Dodger Don Drysdale.

- Jose Canseco became the first player to hit 40 home runs and steal 40 bases in the same season.

1989 • Robin Yount became the first player to win an MVP Award at two positions.

- Nolan Ryan recorded his 5,000th strikeout.

Bruce Sutter

89. What teams did Rollie Fingers play for?

1B	Frank Thomas	P	Roger Clemens
2B	Roberto Alomar	P	Randy Johnson
3B	Cal Ripken	P	Greg Maddux
SS	Barry Larkin	P	Tom Glavine
OF	Barry Bonds	RP	John Franco
OF	Ken Griffey Jr.		
OF	Tony Gwynn		
C	Mike Piazza		
DH	Ricky Henderson		

Iron Man

"What Cal has done is incomprehensible to me.
I don't think another player will come along and do what he has done. We are
seeing the last of a dinosaur."
Lou Piniella

Baseball has several records that will probably never be broken. Some are unbreakable because the nature of the game has changed so dramatically in more than 100 years. Cy Young's 511 victories immediately comes to mind. But, Young also lost 316 games. Pitchers simply pitched more games back then, and when they did start a game, they stayed to the bitter end, recording either a win or a loss. Pitchers today simply don't pitch as many games as they did a century ago. Other records are unbreakable because of a fluke. Johnny Vander Meer threw two consecutive no-hitters. No one will ever throw three.

In the 1990s, however, two of the game's greatest stars retired with records that were neither unique to an era, nor, were they flukes; they were a testament to the superiority of these players over their peers in the particular categories in which the records were set. Nolan Ryan retired in 1993 with 5,714 strikeouts. His closest rivals are Randy Johnson (4,874), Roger Clemens (4,672), and Steve Carlton (4,136). It's not out of the question for a flamethrower to come along some day and pass him, but it's highly unlikely. He also threw seven no-hitters. I'd like to see someone top that.

The other unbreakable record set in the 1990s is truly as remarkable as it is unbreakable. In fact, I think it's the most significant record in all of sports. I'm talking about Cal Ripken playing in 2,632 consecutive games. That's more than 16 years without missing a single game! It would be extremely rare for a player today to go three years without missing a game. And by the way, he did it by playing one of the most punishing positions on the field, shortstop. That's the guy who has to complete the double play with the likes of Frank Thomas, Albert Belle, and Kirk Gibson barreling down the line so they can slide into you hard enough to disrupt your throw to first. Cal did not escape injuries from plays like this, he simply played through them.

When people think of Cal Ripken, they naturally think of the streak, but his contribution to Major League Baseball was more than that. He was the prototypical big, tall, beefy shortstop. Virtually all of the so-called experts said that he was too big to play shortstop when he made his major league debut. At 6'4", 220 pounds, he should be a third or first baseman. Shortstops need not be fast, but they must be quick.

The prototypical shortstop before Ripken's debut were the likes of Luis Aparicio, Pee Wee Reese, and Phil Rizzuto. None were over 5'10" or 180 pounds. Even tall shortstops in the past were not big, they were skinny guys like Mark Belanger or Marty Marion. Earl Weaver was Ripken's manager when he broke into the major leagues with the Baltimore Orioles, and Earl needed a shortstop, as he already had a third baseman in Doug DeCinces. Being somewhat unconventional himself, and noticing Ripken's quickness, Weaver "threw away the book," and penciled him in at the shortstop position.

It was a fortuitous move. Cal went on to become one of the greatest fielding shortstops ever. He led the American League in assists for shortstops seven times, a record. From 1989-94, he only committed 58 errors, the best percentage ever for an American League shortstop. In 1990, he played 95 games without an error, another American League record. One secret to Ripken's success as a fielder was his superior intellect and cunning. He was truly a student of the game. He studied opposing batter's tendencies to hit a certain way in particular situations. He was intimately familiar with his pitcher's abilities and patterns, thus allowing him to "cheat" in one direction or the other in order to get a step ahead as the ball is being released from the pitcher's hand. Asked about his prowess in the field, he once quipped, "I'm not blessed with the kind of range that a lot of shortstops have. The way I have success is, I guess, by thinking." The Orioles one time general manager, Roland Hemond, said of Ripken, "He plays the infield like a manager."[26]

Despite his outstanding defensive abilities, Cal Ripken is better known for his offense and of course, his endurance. He retired with a .276 average, 3,184 hits, 431 home runs, and 1,695 RBIs. He is the only player to win the Rookie of the Year and Most Valuable Player Awards in consecutive years, and was the first shortstop in history to hit over .300 with 30 home runs, and 100 RBIs in a season. That combination won him his second Most Valuable Player Award in 1991.

Ripken played in 19 All-Star games, won two Gold Gloves, and was a significant member of the World Series champion Orioles in 1983. He not only broke Lou Gehrig's consecutive game streak, he shattered it! Gehrig's record of 2,130 consecutive games stood for 56 years and was considered unbreakable. During one stretch in the 2,632 game streak, Ripken played in 8,243 consecutive innings over 904 games! The Orioles rewarded him with a five-year contract for $30.5 million in 1992. In 2007, he was elected on the first ballot to the Hall of Fame with 98.53% of the vote.

* * *

Major League Baseball added four new teams during the 1990s: the Colorado Rockies and Florida Marlins in 1993, and the Tampa Bay Devil Rays (they later changed their name to just the Rays) and Arizona Diamondbacks in 1998. That brought the number of teams to 30, necessitating a six-division format and the inclusion of a "wild card" team to qualify for the playoffs. The winner of the wild card spot was the team with the best record of the second place teams in each division.

In 1968 the Detroit Tigers and the St. Louis Cardinals were the only two teams playing in the postseason. Thirty years later, eight teams competed in postseason play. John McGraw must surely have been spinning in his grave. A devastating strike took place in 1994-95, cancelling the World Series and causing millions of fans to turn away from the game. The 1997 season saw the introduction of interleague play.

Baseball was "saved" in 1998 when sluggers Mark McGwire and Sammy Sosa battled to see who could break Roger Maris' home run record of 61. Fans were glued to their television sets and filled the National League stadiums to witness the contest. In the end, both men eclipsed Maris's record, with Big Mac hitting 70 round trippers and Slammin' Sammy hitting 66.

It's unusual for a team to go from worst to first, but in 1991, both World Series participants did just that. Both the Minnesota Twins and the Atlanta Braves finished last in their respective divisions in 1990, yet made it all the way to the Series the following year. The Twins won in what many regard as the finest fall classic of them all.

The decade also witnessed numerous individual achievements: Barry Bonds became the only player to amass 400 home runs and 400 stolen bases. Nolan Ryan won his 300th game. Eddie Murray and Mark McGwire joined the 500-home-run club. Murray also joined the 3,000-hit club, along with George Brett, Robin Yount, Paul Molitor, Dave Winfield, Tony Gwynn, and Wade Boggs. Rickey Henderson stole his 1,000th base on his way to the all-time stolen base record; he also set a record with 11 single-season stolen base titles. Brett became the only player to win a batting title in three different decades.

The Toronto Blue Jays and the Colorado Rockies drew over four million fans in a single season. The Minnesota Twins turned two triple plays in a single game, the Mariners hit 264 home runs in 1997, and the 1998 Yankees won 114 games.

Greg Maddux and Roger Clemens each won four Cy Young Awards in the decade, and Clemens set a record by winning 19 straight games in 1999. The Cubs' Kerry Wood tied Clemens' record of 20 strikeouts in nine innings. It was a good decade for catchers, as Carleton Fisk set a record with 328 home runs, most by a backstop. Mike Piazza enjoyed the best offensive year ever for a catcher in 1997 when he hit .362 with 201 hits, 40 home runs, and 124 RBIs. Ozzie Smith won his 13th consecutive Gold Glove in 1992.

Ken Griffey Sr. and Jr. became the first father/son pair to play in the same game; Bret Boone joined his father Bob and grandfather Ray in the first three-generation family to play in the major leagues.

On the sad side, Pete Rose went to jail for cheating on his taxes, and Joe DiMaggio died.

Cal Ripken

90. Cal Ripken and Lou Gehrig have the first and second longest consecutive games played streak. Who is number three?

1B	Albert Pujols	P	John Smoltz
2B	Chase Utley	P	Pedro Martinez
3B	Chipper Jones	P	Randy Johnson
SS	Derek Jeter	P	Roy Halladay
OF	Barry Bonds	RP	Mariano Rivera
OF	Ichiro Suzuki		
OF	Vladimir Guerrero		
C	Ivan Rodriguez		
DH	Alex Rodriguez		

Juicers

"Do you realize that if Babe Ruth had used steroids, he would have far surpassed his own record--or died before he reached it."
Don Addis, St. Petersburg Times

In the entire history of baseball, a player has hit 60 or more home runs in a season on eight different occasions. It happened first in 1927, when Babe Ruth hit 60, and then again in 1961, when Roger Maris hit 61. So, the law of averages says one could expect to see another 60-plus home run season about every 30 years right?

But, in the four years from 1998-2001, three players crossed the 60 threshold a total of six times! Sammy Sosa did it three times, hitting 66, 63, and 64. Mark McGwire did it twice, hitting 70 and 65, and Barry Bonds outdid them all by walloping 73 home runs in 2001. What happened? How did three sluggers break this seemingly unbreakable record repeatedly in just four years?

An argument can be made that today's sluggers are simply bigger and stronger than those of years past. When I first started following baseball in the mid 1950s, there were a handful of big, strong sluggers. Ted Kluszewski comes to mind. So, do Hank Sauer, Gil Hodges, Eddie Mathews and later on Boog Powell and big Frank Howard. Today, every team has two or three players of Hodge's size. Yes, the increase in the number of bigger, stronger players is certainly a factor in the dramatic increase of home runs starting in the 1990s and continuing into the 2000s. Better training and conditioning is also a factor.

However, the pervasive use of anabolic steroids and human growth hormone are probably the most significant factors in the power surge of those two decades. Anabolic steroids are synthetic substances that are similar to testosterone. They make muscles bigger and bones stronger. They can be taken orally, as injections directly into the muscle, or even as a cream rubbed into the skin.

In 2005 Jose Canseco published his controversial book "Juiced," which alleged that up to 80% of all major league ballplayers were taking some form of steroids in order to enhance their performance on the field. David Wells, the colorful pitcher, stated that 25 to 40% were "dopers." Indeed, "doping" is nothing new in baseball or other sports, but the pervasiveness of its use among so many ballplayers as well as the amount taken by many, is a new phenomenon.

Hall of Fame pitcher Pud Galvin supposedly used a supplement from the testicles of live animals to boost his performance, and even Babe Ruth, on at least one occasion, gave himself an injection of an extract from sheep testicles. It did not help his performance, but it did make him sick and he missed a game because of it.

Major League Baseball turned a blind eye toward the rampant use of steroids for a long time, in large part because McGwire and Sosa's 1998 assault on the home run record revived a sport that was still reeling from the work stoppage that canceled the World Series in 1995.

Canseco's tell-all book and a March 17, 2005 Congressional hearing finally forced the league to address what legions of fans could see with their own eyes. Stars past and present, including McGwire, Sosa, Alex Rodriguez, and Rafael Palmeiro, were called to testify. None admitted wrongdoing, and Palmeiro went so far as to wag his finger and assert "I have never used steroids, period."

But, when Palmeiro failed a drug test just five months later, baseball increased the penalties for using performance-enhancing drugs from a 10-game suspension to 50 for the first violation, a 100-game suspension for a second offense, and a lifetime ban for a third strike. Owners and players also agreed to a thorough investigation of the sport, headed by former Senator George Mitchell. The Mitchell Report, released in 2007, found that nearly 100 players had used steroids at one time or another during their careers. The list included such stars as Chuck Knoblach, David Justice, Mo Vaughn, Kevin Brown, and Eric Gagne. Eventually, over a dozen of the biggest stars in the game admitted taking steroids, and over two dozen more were implicated by others to have taken steroids as well.

Since Major League Baseball toughened its steroid policy in 2005, it has suspended more than 25 players for violating it, including All-Stars like Ryan Braun, Melky Cabrera, Bartolo Colon, and Manny Ramirez. Before the beginning of spring training in 2009, Alex Rodriguez admitted taking steroids during the 2001-03 seasons; he was not disciplined as that was before baseball's tougher drug policy. But, when he was found guilty of using them again in 2013, Major League Baseball suspended him for the entire 2014 season.

Are these suspensions justified? What's the big deal of players enhancing their skills to be more competitive? To me, it is a big deal, and yes, the suspensions are justified. I believe that records are made to be broken, but I also support a level playing field. When players use performance-enhancing drugs to distinguish themselves from their peers, that's not on the level.

Doctoring a ball on the mound or corking a bat can help to varying degrees. Stimulants such as amphetamines can provide an enormous short term boost of energy that can provide a physical advantage. However, no substance can materially change a human being more than anabolic steroids. They are not simply a short lived "fix." They represent a pharmacological means to radically modify skeletal musculature. Their side effects are significant and often irreversible and potentially life-threatening. They represent a "game changer" for those who partake and are an unfair advantage over those who do not partake. There has never been a more egregious example of cheating in sports than the use of steroids in baseball. While they have their place in treating disease and rehabilitation, they had no place in breaking baseball's most hallowed records.

We'll never know the degree to which steroids played a part in some other records that were broken during the first decade of the 21st century, or even in the following personal milestones. Palmeiro, Cal Ripken, Rickey Henderson, and Craig Biggio collected their 3,000th hit during the decade. A-Rod, Palmeiro, Frank Thomas, Manny Ramirez, Gary Sheffield, and Jim Thome joined the 500-homer club, and Sammy Sosa and Ken Griffey joined the 600-homer club. Randy Johnson, Curt Schilling, Pedro Martinez, and John Smoltz recorded their 3,000th strikeouts. Roger Clemens, Greg Maddux, Tom Glavine, and Randy Johnson won their 300th game, and Trevor Hoffman and Mariano Rivera saved their 500th game.

Rickey Henderson, already the all-time leader in stolen bases for more than a decade, added two more all-time records to his ledger: runs scored (2,295), and unintentional walks (2,129). Barry Bonds won an unprecedented four straight MVP awards (to go with the three he won in Pittsburgh in the 1990s), and broke both the single-season home run record (with 73) and Hank Aaron's all-time career record (finishing with 762 round-trippers). Roger Clemens added two Cy Young Awards, bringing his total to seven, and set the all-time American League strikeout record of 4,672. Eric Gagne set a major league record with 84 consecutive saves.

Longevity and endurance records were set by Jesse Orosco (1,252 games pitched), Omar Vizquel (2,584 games at shortstop), and Ivan Rodriguez (2,227 games at catcher). Greg Maddux set records by winning 15 or more games for 16 consecutive years, and by winning 10 or more games in 20 consecutive seasons. He also tied a major league record for pitchers by winning 16 Gold Gloves. Mark Buehrle pitched a perfect game, amid a streak in which he retired a record 45 consecutive batters. Finally, Ichiro Suzuki set a record by collecting 200 or more hits in eight consecutive seasons.

The Tampa Bay Rays appeared in a World Series for the first time. The Seattle Mariners won 116 games in 2001, as Suzuki won both Rookie of the Year and Most Valuable Player. The Atlanta Braves won their 11th consecutive division title that same year. The 2002 World Series was an anomaly in that it did not feature a division champion. The contestants were two wild card teams, the Angels and Giants. The 2004 playoffs were among the most dramatic ever. The Boston Red Sox overcame a 3-0 deficit in the American League Championship Series against the Yankees to win the next four games. They then swept the St. Louis Cardinals in the World Series for Boston's first championship in 86 years.

The Red Sox added seats atop the legendary green monster in Fenway Park's left field, and began a streak of sellouts that topped 500 by 2009. (It ended in April, 2013, at 794 regular season games). In 2005 the Montreal Expos became the Washington Nationals. In 2006, Minnesota's Joe Mauer became the first catcher to ever win an American League batting title, then he did it again in 2008 and 2009.

Barry Bonds

91. Mariano Rivera retired as the all-time saves leader.
How many did he have?

1B	Paul Goldschmidt	P	David Price
2B	Dustin Pedroia	P	Justin Verlander
3B	Josh Donaldson	P	Clayton Kershaw
SS	Troy Tulowitzki	P	Stephen Strasburg
OF	Bryce Harper	RP	Craig Kimbrel
OF	Mike Trout		
OF	Andrew McCutchen		
C	Buster Posey		
DH	Miguel Cabrera		

The Next Generation

"Ohhh, what a curveball! Holy mackerel!
He just broke off Public Enemy No. 1!"
Vin Scully describing Clayton Kershaw's devastating hook

The list of players above, compiled in 2015, contains what I consider the best of the current young stars playing today. Some of them are already bound for Cooperstown, barring unforeseen problems. Buster Posey, Troy Tulowitzki, Miguel Cabrera, David Price, Justin Verlander, and Stephen Strasburg already have Hall-of-Fame potential. Clayton Kershaw of the Los Angeles Dodges and Mike Trout of the Los Angeles Angels are as good as any players in history at their age.

The Claw

It's eerie how much Clayton Kershaw looks like the young Lefty Grove. It's even more uncanny how dominant each man was at this point in his career. At 6'3" Kershaw is Grove incarnate. Born in Dallas, Texas on March 19, 1988, Kershaw was a high school standout. He once struck out every batter in a playoff game, getting the attention of major league scouts across the country. He made his major league debut with the Dodgers on May 24, 2008.

Possessing a 98-mph fastball and a knee-buckling 12-6 curve ball, Kershaw won pitching's triple crown and Cy Young Award in 2011 by winning 21 games, striking out 248 batters, and posting a 2.28 ERA. He won the Cy Young Award again in 2013 when he went 16-9, posted a 1.83 ERA, and struck out a league-leading 232 batters. His performance earned him the highest salary ever awarded: $215 million over seven years (David Price has since eclipsed that figure by signing a $217 million over seven years contract with the Boston Red Sox). Kershaw hit the trifecta by winning the Cy Young Award yet again in 2014, posting a 21-3 record with 239 strikeouts and a stingy 1.77 ERA. His numbers were so dominant that he also took the Most Valuable Player Award to boot.

The Millville Meteor

If Clayton Kershaw is the re-incarnation of Lefty Grove, then Mike Trout is the re-incarnation of Mickey Mantle. From the moment he arrived in the big leagues at age 19, he was a complete five-tool player. At 6'2", 230 pounds, he looks more like an NFL linebacker than a center fielder, but he is deceptively fast in tracking down fly balls and rounding the base paths. He hits for both power and average, has a powerful throwing arm, and will soon be winning Gold Gloves.

He became the Angels' starting center fielder in 2012, and not only won the Rookie of the Year Award, but almost won the Most Valuable Player Award; only a Triple Crown year by Detroit's Miguel Cabrera prevented him from doing so. And some argue that Trout's season was even better than the defensively mediocre Cabrera's. Trout was the only player to hit 30 home runs, steal 45 bases, and knock in 125 runs in a season. He finished second in the Most Valuable Player Award voting again in 2013, but finally won the coveted award for the 2014 season with a .287 batting average, 36 home runs, and 111 RBIs.

The Post-Steroid Era

The elimination of steroids, plus the expansion of the strike zone, helped to usher in another "year of the pitcher" in 2010. That same year Major League Baseball instituted video monitoring of umpires' calls, resulting in an expansion of the lower part of the plate. Those umps who consistently called balls and strikes incorrectly were fired. Those who called them correctly kept their jobs.

Pitchers made the most of this new opportunity, and started striking out batters at an accelerated rate. Both batting and slugging averages dropped. In 2010 there were six no-hitters, including two perfect games, and one by Roy Halladay to open the National League Division Series. Stephen Strasburg of the Washington Nationals, struck out 41 batters in his first four starts, a major league record. Another pitching anomaly occurred in 2010, when Jamie Moyer, age 47, became the oldest pitcher to ever pitch a complete game shutout. In so doing, he became the only man to ever pitch a complete game in four separate decades.

There was still plenty of hitting, however. In 2010, Ichiro Suzuki tied Pete Rose's record of 200 or more base hits in 10 consecutive seasons, and Albert Pujols became the first player to begin a career with 10 straight 30+ home run seasons. In 2011, in one of the most exciting pennant races of all time, four playoff berths were decided on the last day! Mariano Rivera, the legendary closer for the Yankees, became the first player to pitch 1,000 games for the same team. He also set a major league record by achieving nine consecutive seasons of 30 or more saves. Tony LaRussa joined Connie Mack as the only two men to manage 5,000 games.

In 2012, Major League Baseball added two additional wild card teams, bringing the number of teams involved in postseason play to five in each league. The two wild card teams faced each other in a one-game playoff to join the three division winners in the Division Series.

The second major shake-up of the decade was the move of the Houston Astros to the American League Western Division at the beginning of the 2013 season. The odd number of teams (15) now in each league necessitated interleague play on a daily basis, instead of in a few series during midsummer. The change also increased each team's total number of interleague games to 20.

Personal milestones in 2012 included Miguel Cabrera becoming the first player to win the Triple Crown since 1967, and Derek Jeter tying Hank Aaron with 150 or more hits in 17 consecutive seasons. Felix Hernandez and Matt Cain threw perfect games, so did the unheralded White Sox journeyman Phillip Humber. Johan Santana threw the first no-hitter in Mets history (they traded away Nolan Ryan before he blossomed); six Seattle Mariners combined on a no-hitter against the Dodgers. Jamie Moyer kept piling up his "old man" records by becoming the oldest pitcher ever to win a game. He was 49 years and 151 days old.

Reflecting the increase in foreign players in the big leagues, baseball introduced a rule allowing coaches to bring an interpreter to the mound to talk to foreign-born pitchers, many of whom were Japanese. Speaking of Japanese, the great Ichiro Suzuki collected his 4,000th hit in professional baseball (including the 1,278 he hit in Japan from 1992-2000). Alex Rodriguez broke Lou Gehrig's long-standing record of 23 grand slam home runs. In 2014, Alex's teammate Derek Jeter set a major league record by starting 2,610 games at shortstop. A fascinating milestone was reached on July 27; Cleveland's Danny Salazar struck out Kansas City's Norichika Aoki for baseball's 2,000,000th strikeout.

In the first half of the decade, Alex Rodriquez hit his 600th home run, Derek Jeter collected his 3,000th hit, and Trevor Hoffman and

Mariano Rivera notched their 600th saves.

David Ortiz walloped his 500th home run, and Alex Rodriquez passed Willie Mays for fourth place on the career home run list in 2015. That same year the aforementioned Mike Trout became the youngest player in history to reach 100 home runs and 100 stolen bases at the tender age of 23 years 253 days, breaking the record held by Alex Rodriquez, and Adoldis Chapman of the Cincinnati Reds became the fastest pitcher to collect 500 strike-outs, doing so in 292 innings, breaking the record held by Craig Kimbrel. Seven no-hitters were thrown in 2015, including two by Max Scherzer of the Washington Nationals.

Mike Trout

92. Craig Kimbrel set a record for saves by a rookie.
How many did he save?

317

Eighth Inning

All-Time Teams

Originally, I had just three teams in this section; the all-time American League and National League teams, and the all-time major league team. However, I thought players who stayed with one team for their entire careers deserved recognition, so I put together an all-time loyalty team from each league as well. Christy Mathewson and Honus Wagner are on the National League Loyalty team because Mathewson played just one game for the Cincinnati Reds, and that was a publicity stunt pitting him against "Three Finger" Brown in a re-enactment of their old rivalry. Wagner played for the Louisville Colonels which became the Pittsburgh Pirates.

That brought my total of teams to 97, so I decided to make it an even 100, plus one for fun. If Walt Disney can have "101 Dalmatians," then I can have 101 all-time teams. Accordingly, I added the all-time left handed, right handed, switch-hitting, and defensive teams. It's going to be very difficult for that switch-hitting team to win any games without a pitching staff. To date, no ambidextrous pitcher has made a career of it in the big leagues.

American League Loyalty Team

1B	Lou Gehrig	P	Walter Johnson
2B	Charlie Gehringer	P	Bob Feller
3B	George Brett	P	Whitey Ford
SS	Cal Ripken	P	Jim Palmer
OF	Carl Yastrzemski	RP	Mariano Rivera
OF	Joe DiMaggio		
OF	Mickey Mantle		
C	Yogi Berra		
DH	Ted Williams		

National League Loyalty Team

1B	Bill Terry	P	Christy Mathewson
2B	Jackie Robinson	P	Sandy Koufax
3B	Mike Schmidt	P	Bob Gibson
SS	Honus Wagner	P	Don Drysdale
OF	Mel Ott	RP	Carl Hubbell
OF	Tony Gwynn		
OF	Roberto Clemente		
C	Johnny Bench		
DH	Stan Musial		

Righties

1B	Jimmie Foxx	P	Walter Johnson
2B	Rogers Hornsby	P	Nolan Ryan
3B	Mike Schmidt	P	Greg Maddux
SS	Honus Wagner	P	Roger Clemens
OF	Joe DiMaggio	RP	Mariano Rivera
OF	Willie Mays		
OF	Hank Aaron		
C	Johnny Bench		
DH	Frank Thomas		

Lefties

1B	Lou Gehrig		P	Randy Johnson
2B	Joe Morgan		P	Steve Carlton
3B	George Brett		P	Sandy Koufax
SS	Arky Vaughn		P	Lefty Grove
OF	Stan Musial		RP	Warren Spahn
OF	Ty Cobb			
OF	Babe Ruth			
C	Yogi Berra			
DH	Ted Williams			

Switch Hitters

1B	Eddie Murray		OF	Pete Rose
2B	Roberto Alomar		OF	Mickey Mantle
3B	Chipper Jones		OF	Carlos Beltran
SS	Ozzie Smith		C	Ted Simmons
DH	Lance Berkman			

Defense

1B	Keith Hernandez		P	Greg Maddux
2B	Bill Mazeroski		P	Jim Kaat
3B	Brooks Robinson		P	Bob Gibson
SS	Ozzie Smith		P	Mike Mussina
OF	Al Kaline		RP	Bobby Shantz
OF	Willie Mays			
OF	Roberto Clemente			
C	Ivan Rodriguez			

American League

1B	Lou Gehrig	P	Walter Johnson
2B	Eddie Collins	P	Roger Clemens
3B	George Brett	P	Randy Johnson
SS	Cal Ripken	P	Bob Feller
OF	Ty Cobb	RP	Mariano Rivera
OF	Joe DiMaggio		
OF	Babe Ruth		
C	Yogi Berra		
DH	Ted Williams		

National League

1B	Stan Musial	P	Greg Maddux
2B	Rogers Hornsby	P	Warren Spahn
3B	Mike Schmidt	P	Tom Seaver
SS	Honus Wagner	P	Steve Carlton
OF	Barry Bonds	RP	Trevor Hoffman
OF	Willie Mays		
OF	Hank Aaron		
C	Johnny Bench		
DH	Pete Rose		

All-Time Team

1B	Lou Gehrig	P	Walter Johnson
2B	Rogers Hornsby	P	Greg Maddux
3B	Mike Schmidt	P	Roger Clemens
SS	Honus Wagner	P	Randy Johnson
OF	Hank Aaron	RP	Mariano Rivera
OF	Willie Mays		
OF	Babe Ruth		
C	Johnny Bench		
DH	Ted Williams		

Ninth Inning

Answers

1. Pablo Sandoval
2. Tony Conigliaro
3. 341
4. Hank Greenberg
5. To represent the colors of the departed Dodgers and Giants
6. Nolan Ryan
7. He pitched under a pseudonym for the San Francisco Seals
8. He would ask for a piece of pie whenever he frequented his neighborhood grocery store
9. Tennessee
10. Puerto Rico
11. The Gashouse Gang
12. Carl Hubbell
13. 9
14. The Grey Eagle
15. Dick Allen
16. William McKinley
17. Eddie Cicotte
18. Willie McCovey
19. New York Giants
20. 43
21. Tris Speaker
22. Toronto Blue Jays
23. The wind blew him off the mound
24. Bill Buckner
25. Pitcher Johnny Murphy
26. 16
27. 478
28. Dave Kingman
29. St. Louis Cardinals
30. Carl Yastrzemski and Jim Rice
31. His beard
32. Phil Cavaretta
33. 1958-59
34. Rob Dibble and Randy Myers
35. 61 games, San Francisco Seals, 1933

36. Hoyt Wilhelm
37. Kerry Wood
38. Stan Musial
39. 4
40. .356
41. Giants and Pirates
42. 3
43. He hit a home run in every inning 1-16
44. 35
45. Bill Terry
46. Dave McNally, Mike Cuellar, and Pat Dobson
47. Carl Hubbell
48. Don Money
49. Chick Hafey
50. St. Louis Cardinals
51. Boston Americans (later became Red Sox)
52. Jim Rice
53. 1,406
54. Dodgers, Braves, and Cardinals
55. 1,815 at home. 1,815 on the road
56. 1908
57. Johnny Roseboro
58. Willie Mays
59. 111
60. 8
61. Greg Luzinski
62. Honus Wagner
63. Johnny Bench and Dave Concepcion
64. Doug Mientkiewicz
65. Norm Cash
66. Mark Fidrych
67. Eddie Collins, Ray Schalk, and Red Faber
68. Ralph Houk
69. Ken Griffey Jr. and Tom Seaver
70. Willie Davis
71. Clint Hurdle

72. Larry Doby
73. Jimmie Foxx, Manny Ramirez, and Rafael Palmiero
74. 84
75. Hoyt Wilhelm
76. .388 in 1977
77. Bill Melton
78. Mike Epstein
79. Tony Gwynn
80. Mike "King" Kelly
81. Ichiro Suzuki
82. Joe Jackson, Eddie Collins, and Ray Schalk
83. Tony Lazzeri
84. Paul and Lloyd Waner
85. "I want a player with guts enough not to fight back."
86. Jim Hickman of the New York Mets
87. Milt Pappas
88. Ron Blomberg
89. Oakland A's, San Diego Padres, and Milwaukee Brewers
90. Everett Scott (1,307 games)
91. 652
92. 46

References

1. Epstein, Dan, *Stars and Strikes: Baseball and Americas in the Bicentennial Summer of '76* (Thomas Dunne Books, St. Martin's Press New York, NY April 2014), pg. 276.

2. Baseball Almanac (Yogi Berra quotes)

3. Okrent, Daniel & Steve Wulf, *Baseball Anecdotes* (Harper & Row, New York, NY 1989), pg. 294.

4. Thorn, John and David Reuther, Eds., *The Complete Armchair Book of Baseball,* (Simon & Schuster, New York, NY 2004), pg. 378.

5. Aaron, Hank & Lonnie Wheeler, *I had a Hammer: The Hank Aaron Story* (Harper Collins Publishers, New York, NY 2007), pg. 47.

6. Ritter Lawrence, *The Glory of Their Times* (Harper Collins Publishers, New York, NY 2002), pg. 322

7. Hirsch, James, *Willie Mays* (Scribner, New York 2010), pg. 318.

8. Okrent, Daniel & Steve Wulf, *Baseball Anecdotes*, Harper & Row, New York, NY 1089 pg. 285

9. Astor, Gerald, *The Baseball Hall of Fame 50th Anniversary Book* (Prentice Hall Press, New York, NY November 1988), p. 165

10. Okrent, Daniel & Steve Wulf, *Baseball Anecdotes* (Harper & Row, New York, NY 1989), pg. 287

11. Okrent, Daniel & Steve Wulf, *Baseball Anecdotes* (Harper & Row, New York, NY 1989), pg. 237

12. Okrent, Daniel & Steve Wulf, *Baseball Anecdotes* (Harper & Row, New York, NY 1989), pg. 285

13. Astor, Gerald, *The Baseball Hall of Fame 50th Anniversary Book* (Prentice Hall Press, New York, NY November 1988), p. 278

14. Astor, Gerald, *The Baseball Hall of Fame 50th Anniversary Book* (Prentice Hall Press, New York, NY November 1988), p. 115

15. NY Times (March 18, 2005)

16. SABR Baseball Biography Project Jim Kaplan

17. Rader, Benjamin, *Baseball, A History of America's Game* (University of Illinois Press, Chicago, IL 1992), p. 125.

18. Okrent, Daniel & Steve Wulf, *Baseball Anecdotes* (Harper & Row, New York, NY 1989), pp.279-280.

19. Rader, Benjamin, *Baseball, A History of America's Game* (University of Illinois Press, Chicago, IL 1992), pg. 75.

20. Rader, Benjamin, *Baseball, A History of America's Game* (University of Illinois Press, Chicago, IL 1992), pg. 5.

21. *Cooperstown*, The Sporting News, (St, Louis, Missouri), pg. 25.

22. *Cooperstown*, The Sporting News, (St, Louis, Missouri), pg. 64

23. *Cooperstown*, The Sporting News, (St, Louis, Missouri), pg. 196

24. Burns, Ken PBS Special, "Baseball," Florentine Films Production

25. Rader, Benjamin, *Baseball, A History of America's Game* (University of Illinois Press, Chicago, IL 1992), pg. 194.

26. Will, George, *Men at Work* (Simon & Schuster New York, NY 1998), pg. 253.

Bibliography

Aaron, Hank & Lonnie Wheeler, *I had a Hammer: The Hank Aaron Story* (Harper Collins Publishers, New York, NY 2007)

Alexander, Charles C., *Rogers Hornsby* (Henry Holt & Co. New York, NY 1995)

Astor, Gerald, *The Baseball Hall of Fame 50th Anniversary Book* (Prentice Hall Press, New York, NY November 1988)

Baseball Almanac (2014)

Baseball World Chart of Foreign Major Leaguers, NBC Sports

Bronson, Eric, *Baseball and Philosophy* (Carus Publishing Company Peru, IL 2004)

Burns, Ken PBS Special, "Baseball" Florentine Films Production

Clavin, Tom and Danny Peary, *Gil Hodges* (New American Library New York 2012)

The Complete and Definitive Record of Major League Baseball, The Baseball Encyclopedia *(Simon & Schuster 1996)*

Cooperstown, The Sporting News, (North Lindbergh Boulevard St, Louis, Missouri 63132)

Costas, Bob, *Fair Ball* (Broadway Books New York, NY 2000)

Cramer, Richard Ben, *Joe DiMaggio* (Touchstone New York, NY 2000)

Dawidoff, Nicholas, *The Catcher Was a Spy: The Mysterious Life of Moe Berg* (Vintage Books, New York 1994)

Epstein, Dan, *Stars and Strikes: Baseball and Americas in the Bicentennial Summer of '76* (Thomas Dunne Books, St. Martin's Press New York, NY April 2014)

Gay, Timothy M., *Tris Speaker* (The Lyons Press, Guilford, Conn. 2007)

Hirsch, James, *Willie Mays* (Scribner, New York 2010)

Haupert, Michael J., "The Economic History of Major League Baseball", University of Wisconsin

Kahn, Roger, *The Era* (Houghton Mifflin Co. New York, NY 1993)

Leavy, Jane, *Sandy Koufax* (Harper Collins, New York 2012)

The Major League Baseball Book of Ultimate Records, Major League Baseball (October, 2013)

Maransis, David, *Clemente* (Simon & Schuster, New York, NY 2006)

Montville, Leigh, *The Big Bam* (Knopf Doubleday Publishing Group New York, NY 2006)

NY Times (March 18, 2005)

Okrent, Daniel & Steve Wulf, *Baseball Anecdotes* (Harper & Row, New York, NY 1989)

Rader, Benjamin, *Baseball, A History of America's Game* (University of Illinois Press, Chicago, IL 1992)

Reichler, Joseph L., Ed., *The Baseball Encyclopedia* (Macmillan Publishing Co., Inc. New York, NY 1982)

Ritter Lawrence, *The Glory of Their Times* (Harper Collins Publishers, New York, NY 2002)

Sabr Baseball Biography Project (Phoenix, AZ 2014)

Stewart, Wayne, *Stan the Man* (Triumph Books Chicago, IL 2010)

Stump, Al, *Cobb* (Algonquin Books of Chapel Hill, Chapel Hill, N.C. 1994)

Thorn, John and David Reuther, Eds., *The Complete Armchair Book of Baseball,* (Simon & Schuster, New York, NY 2004)

Will, George, *Men at Work* (Simon & Schuster New York, NY 1998)

Williams, Ted & John Underwood, *My Turn at Bat* (Simon & Schuster New York, NY 1969)

Index

Boyer, Ken 154, 155, 156, 157

Branca, Ralph 59, 95, 166

Braves 49, 50, 51, 52, 62, 81, 83, 104, 115, 119, 150, 151, 152, 162, 168, 169, 183, 194, 195, 196, 219, 232, 233, 234, 256, 263, 273, 284, 285, 289, 306, 312, 324

Brett, George 1, 84, 129, 175, 212, 213, 214, 229, 306, 319, 320, 321

Brewers 131, 212, 218, 293, 325

Bridges, Rocky 4

Brock, Lou 84, 154, 155, 156, 157, 292, 294, 300

Browns 97, 104, 144, 171, 271, 278, 279, 280, 284

Burns, Ken 44, 56, 93, 326, 329

Cabrera, Miguel 6, 11, 87, 191, 218, 237, 313, 314, 316

Campanella, Roy 64, 87, 115, 130, 161, 162, 163, 165, 221, 222, 283, 285, 289, 290

Cardinals 18, 28, 43, 60, 68, 75, 102, 103, 141, 142, 154, 155, 156, 157, 175, 176, 189, 213, 227, 235, 248, 250, 271, 273, 274, 275, 278, 280, 284, 286, 287, 289, 306, 312, 323, 324

Carew, Rod 87, 194, 215, 221, 237, 288, 239, 292, 301

Carlton, Steve 157, 175, 177, 211, 287, 292, 294, 300, 301, 303, 320, 321

Cartwright, Alexander 254, 255, 279

Chadwick, Henry 255

Chapman, Ray 7, 267

Charlton, Norm 87, 90, 183

Cicotte, Eddie 198, 199, 200, 201, 323

Clemens, Roger 29, 54, 87, 187, 301, 303, 307, 311, 319, 321

Clemente, Roberto 43, 67, 87, 115, 125, 159, 174, 178, 181, 182, 237, 286, 294, 295, 319, 320

Cobb, Ty 5, 22, 29, 31, 41, 69, 74, 81, 87, 88, 90, 91, 102, 103, 106, 116, 117, 129, 138, 139, 140, 191, 215, 222, 248, 250, 259, 262, 263, 265, 267, 268, 275, 286, 288, 300, 320, 321

Collins, Eddie 5, 70, 87, 146, 198, 262, 268, 321, 324, 325

Made in the USA
Middletown, DE
25 January 2017